D0031457

Making Sense of the Children Act

THIRD EDITION

Making Sense of the Children Act

A Guide for the Social and Welfare Services

THIRD EDITION

Nick Allen

JOHN WILEY & SONS

Chichester • New York • Weinheim • Brisbane • Singapore • Toronto

Copyright © 1998 by John Wiley & Sons Ltd,
Baffins Lane, Chichester,
West Sussex PO19 1UD, England

National   01243 779777
International (+44) 1243 779777
e-mail (for orders and customer service enquiries):
cs-books@wiley.co.uk
Visit our Home Page on http://www.wiley.co.uk
or http://www.wiley.com

First edition 1990 published by Longman Group (UK) Ltd
Second edition 1992

Other Wiley Editorial Offices

John Wiley & Sons, Inc., 65 Third Avenue,
New York, NY 10158-0012, USA

WILEY-VCH Verlag GmbH, Pappelallee 3,
D-69469 Weinheim, Germany

Jacaranda Wiley Ltd, 33 Park Road, Milton,
Queensland 4046, Australia

John Wiley & Sons (Asia) Pte Ltd, 2 Clementi Loop #02-01,
Jin Xing Distripark, Singapore 129809

John Wiley & Sons (Canada) Ltd, 22 Worcester Road,
Rexdale, Ontario M9W 1L1, Canada

Library of Congress Cataloging-in-Publication Data

Allen, Nick.
    Making sense of the Children Act: a guide for the social and welfare services / Nick Allen. – 3rd ed.
        p.   cm.
    Includes index.
    ISBN 0-471-97831-0 (pbk.)
    1. Child welfare – Great Britain.   2. Children – Legal status, laws, etc. – Great Britain.
3. Social work with children – Law and legislation – Great Britain.   4. Foster home care – Law and legislation – Great Britain.   5. Child abuse – Law and legislation – Great Britain.
6. Great Britain. Children Act 1989.   I. Title.
HV751.A6A475   1998
362.7'0941 – dc21   97-38899
                                                                     CIP

British Library Cataloguing in Publication Data

A catalogue record for this book is available from the British Library

ISBN 0-471-97831-0

Typeset in 10/12pt Times by Best-set Typesetter Ltd., Hong Kong
Printed and bound in Great Britain by Biddles Ltd, Guildford and King's Lynn
This book is printed on acid-free paper responsibly manufactured from sustainable forestry, in which at least two trees are planted for each one used for paper production.

Contents

About the author

Nick Allen, BA, M.Phil, lectures in Family Law and Public Law at The Nottingham Trent University, which he joined after working for the Official Solicitor and a London local authority. He was closely involved in the consultation exercise conducted by the Law Commission prior to the Children Act and has lectured and trained extensively on the new legislation. From 1990 to 1992 he was editor of the *Practitioners' Child Law Bulletin* published by Longman.

Preface

When this book was first published in 1990 the Children Act had just been passed by Parliament. Those of us who had followed the long and painstaking examination of child law which got under way in 1984 were aware of how much was set to change. By the time the Act came into force, in October 1991, its contents and implications were much more widely known. There had been a massive training programme for child care professionals and steps had been taken to alert the general public to some of the Act's effects. A large number of rules and regulations had been made to supplement the Act and the Government had produced a considerable volume of official guidance. In the second edition of this book I endeavoured to take account of this formidable additional material. Now the Children Act has been in force for over six years and it is possible, not simply to speculate about what the future might hold, but to make judgments about the actual operation of the new legislation.

The Children Act has affected different people, both children and adults, in different ways and I hope that this third edition shows how and why this is so. In an age when people are quick to point out the defects of legislation it is pleasing to note that after six years the Children Act remains a much admired statute. In the course of a submission to the House of Commons Health Committee in 1997, the Children's Society expressed the opinion that 'the current legislative and regulatory framework for providing for the needs of children in care is probably as good as it has ever been'. For my part, I would extend this assessment to most of the other topics regulated by the Act. This is not to deny the enormous problems, seen every day across the country, affecting children caught up in private law and public law arrangements. The statistics on the profile of teenagers leaving local authority care, for example, continue to reveal a deeply depressing picture. So do the statistics on delays in the court system. Shortfalls in resources and political will are, sadly, beyond the scope of legislation and it is a great pity that the enactment and implementation of the Children Act coincided with a decline at central government level in support for the notion of the public service. The Children Act is in many important respects a public service statute and it needs a positive political and financial climate in order to thrive.

In preparing this new edition I have sought to incorporate all relevant developments occurring since 1992, and this has led to a substantial reorganization and rewriting of the text. One sizeable development with which I have had to deal is the case law on the Act emanating from the superior courts. This has, I think, exceeded everybody's expectations and has produced both problems and benefits. The problems arise largely out of the sheer volume of cases (over 250 at the time of writing); the benefits arise out of what we can learn from the scenarios involved, the way the families and the professionals responded to them, and the rulings delivered by the judges. These cases form a real treasure house of 'child law situations' and I make no apology for including substantial extracts where this serves a useful illustrative purpose. Inevitably, the emphasis in them tends to be on mistakes and misjudgments rather than successes but they are no less important for that. For readers unfamiliar with reports of decided cases I have included an explanatory note (see page xiv).

In order to keep this edition within reasonable bounds, I have omitted the chapters on young offenders and education supervision orders. On both topics the provisions in the Children Act had the effect of amending only part of the relevant law and they have in some respects been overtaken by subsequent legislation. Since legal aid is about to undergo radical change at the hands of the Blair government, I have excised this topic as well. I have, however, added a new chapter on financial provision, partly because of the introduction of the Child Support Act. That disastrous piece of legislation, so different from the Children Act, shows only too clearly how much damage can be caused by the legislative process when there is insufficient planning.

As with previous editions, it is right that I record the enormous support I have received during the preparation of the text from my family, especially my wife Anne. I have been given insights, both personal and professional, which I could not have obtained anywhere else.

NFA
March 1998

Acknowledgements

The publishers are indebted to the Controller of Her Majesty's Stationery Office for permission to reproduce extracts from:

DHSS *Review of Child Care Law* (1985); Butler-Sloss *Report of the Inquiry into Child Abuse in Cleveland 1987* (1988); House of Commons Social Services Committee *Children in Care* (1984); DHSS *The Law on Child Care and Family Services* (1987); *Law Commission Working Paper No 96* (1986); *Law Commission Supplement to Working Paper No 96* (1986); *Law Commission Working Paper No 100* (1987); *Law Commission Report No 172: Guardianship and Custody* (1988); DHSS *Protecting Children* (1988); Department of Health *Introduction to the Children Act 1989* (1989); Department of Health *The Care of Children: Principles and Practice in Regulations and Guidance* (1989); *Law Commission Working Paper No 113* (1989); Department of Health *The Children Act 1989 Guidance and Regulations Volumes 1–9* (1991); Department of Health *Working Together* (1991); Department of Health *Patterns and Outcomes in Child Placement* (1991); Department of Health *Contact Orders Study* (1994); Department of Health *Child Protection – Messages from Research* (1995); Department of Health *The Challenge of Partnership in Child Protection: Practice Guide* (1995); Department of Health *The Guardian ad Litem and Reporting Officer Service Annual Reports 1994–1995: An Overview* (1995); Booth *Avoiding Delay in Children Act Cases* (1996); NSPCC *Report of the National Commission of Inquiry into the Prevention of Child Abuse* (1996); Lord Chancellor's Department *Children Act Advisory Committee Annual Reports 1992/93* (1994) *1993/94* (1995) and *1994/95* (1996).

Crown copyright is reproduced with the permission of the Controller of Her Majesty's Stationery Office.

The publishers are also indebted to the London Borough of Greenwich for their permission to reproduce extracts from Blom-Cooper *et al. A Child in Mind* (1987).

A note on the Children Act case law

In this book there are cited numerous reported cases arising under various parts of the Children Act. These cases, which have been heard by one or more of the superior courts (the Family Division of the High Court, the Court of Appeal and the House of Lords), will usually have been reported in the law reports because of their legal significance. They may be significant for a number of reasons. They might, for example, provide an authoritative interpretation of a word or phrase appearing in the Act (e.g. 'parental responsibility') which will be applied in subsequent cases; or they might reveal a particular approach to a particular type of situation or problem (e.g. contact between children and parents or expert evidence). I have cited each case by its law report title and by the year in which it was decided (which may well be different from the year in which the report of the case was actually published). Since most children's cases are reported in anonymous terms to respect the privacy of the parties, there are quite a few cases in this book called *Re A* and *Re B* etc. After much thought, I decided not to include detailed law report references for the cases. Those readers who wish to look up the judgment of a case in full should be able to track it down by using the indexes to the specialist law reports in this field (these are the *Family Court Reporter* (FCR) and the *Family Law Reports* (FLR)).

1

Introduction

Why the Children Act is different

About 50 Acts of Parliament are passed in this country each year. There are, in total, several thousand Acts currently in force. The majority of these measures make at most only a transient impact on the public consciousness, either because of their extreme technicality or because of the mundane nature of their subject matter. The Children Act 1989 stands out from this generally unmemorable mass of legislation. After it was passed, a government minister responsible for its implementation stated (at one of the many launches of training materials) that 'the Act creates a whole code of law about the upbringing of children which aims to bring about the very best we can achieve within the bounds of legislation for children whether they are living within their families, or in need of local authority services or in want of protection from abuse'.

The statement just mentioned contains two important messages. First, it emphasizes the *codifying function* of the Act, that is to say, it was designed to recast the existing law – with appropriate amendments – in a single coherent instrument. The previous law relating to children, scattered across numerous Acts and judicial rulings, was notoriously complex and inconsistent. Second, the statement acknowledges *the limits of the law* in the field of family relations. The Children Act is without doubt a landmark development in English law but it contains no magic cure for family problems. Rather, it aims to create an enlightened and practical framework for decision-making, whether the decision is taken in the family home, in a local authority office, in a health centre or in a courtroom. The object of the Act is to provide the necessary legal tools to parents, relatives, foster carers, child minders, child care professionals and judges, so as to further the best interests of children in their care. Which tools are selected, and how exactly they are used, tends to be left to the discretion of the parties using their judgment. No cast-iron guarantees of children's welfare or safety are given in the Children Act and none could reasonably be demanded. No law can force an absent parent to see their child regularly, nor can separated parents be made to co-operate over their child's upbringing. No law can ensure that a child at risk is removed (or is not removed) from the family home at exactly the right time for exactly the right period. What we *can* reasonably demand of the law in this field is that it is clear, consistent and fair, and that it properly reflects the values to which our society subscribes. Judged by these criteria, the Children Act has scored highly since it was introduced in October 1991. It has succeeded in making its mark on the public consciousness, partly through its exceptional clarity – enabling people actually to understand what the law is trying to do – and partly through its sheer timeliness, arriving as it has during a period in which public and political interest in 'the family' has been intense.

In this book I intend to look at the provisions of the 1989 Act, together with the accompanying rules, regulations and guidance, and consider their effects and implications, especially for those working in the social and welfare services. I shall also be looking at the way in which the courts have reacted to the new legislation. The Children Act presented a major challenge to the judiciary and to court staff, and with the experience of five years of its operation we can reflect on what has been achieved and what remains to be done.

Public and private child law

During the reform phase leading up to the Children Act, it became fashionable to discuss children's legislation by reference to two organizing labels: public law and private law. These labels have remained quite important – indeed, they feature prominently in the Department of Health's guidance on the Act and are widely used in the courts – and so they deserve a mention here, but it is worth bearing in mind that they have no legal force. They do not appear in any legislation, for example, not even the Children Act itself. Nor have any official definitions been supplied. They are simply loose shorthand expressions which are used to describe different sets of statutory provisions. The names of the labels provide clues to their meaning.

'The public law relating to children' essentially means all the legislation concerning intervention in children's cases by public authorities. The work done by social services departments of local authorities obviously falls within this, but so does the work of voluntary organizations, even though these bodies are not statutory ones. The other label – 'the private law relating to children' – is really a residual one. It is taken to refer to the legislation which is primarily designed to deal with children's cases which, initially at any rate, do *not* involve public authorities. These two categories of public and private law are not completely self-contained (there are, for example, provisions in the Children Act which apply to both areas) but as a means of breaking up the legislation into reasonably distinct blocks for the purposes of discussion and debate, they have a useful role to play. Remember, however, that they have no legal force.

Background to the Act

One of the many problematic aspects of the law as it stood before the Children Act was its chaotic nature. The main features of child law were not deliberately planned, rather they emerged over a period of years. Successive governments got into the habit of producing an Act here and an Act there, each one designed to tackle a particularly pressing problem but seemingly without any real connection to what had gone before. This piece-meal development – which is by no means unknown in other branches of English law – caused immense frustration for practitioners in the field, who found it difficult to acquire a command of statutory provisions which were supposed to be guiding their professional work. The general public, needless to say, were left far behind in this process.

In 1984 the decision was taken to attempt a comprehensive restatement of the law. Prompted by a highly critical report from a House of Commons select committee, the Department of Health established an interdepartmental working party with the job of examining the so-called public law relating to children. The recommendations of this working party were contained in a report published in 1985 under the title *Review of Child Care Law*. This formed the basis of a government White Paper, *The Law on Child Care and Family Services*, published in 1987. The White Paper stated that the Government's proposals would involve 'a major overhaul of child care law intended to provide a clearer and fairer framework for the provision of child care services to families and for the protection of children at risk'.

Alongside the examination of the public aspects of child law, there took place an in-depth review of the private law. This was undertaken by the Law Commission (the standing law reform agency in this country) over the period 1984–88 and involved the publication of four discussion papers followed by the issue of a report (*Review of Child Law: Guardianship and Custody*). Annexed to the report was a draft Bill designed to encapsulate both the Commission's own proposals and many of those contained in the government White Paper. The Children Act is based on this draft.

The process described above shows that the Children Act was a very carefully constructed measure, which is more than can be said for much of the legislation that it replaced. The particular method of reform which was employed, though time-consuming, is by far the most satisfactory for this

branch of the law and is undoubtedly one of the main factors behind the
very favourable reception which the Act has had.

Cleveland, Staffordshire and other local reports

Looking back at some of the statements which were made during and after
the passage of the Children Act, one would be forgiven for thinking that it
represented a swift response by the Government to the 1987 child abuse
crisis in Cleveland. This was not the case, as the chronology described
above demonstrates. By the time the Butler-Sloss Report was published in
1988, the intention to reform child law, and many of the features of the
reform, had been clearly signalled. In any case, the Report, though detailed
and powerfully written, covered only one small part (sexual abuse) of the
proposed field of reform. The Report has not been without influence,
however. In the field of sexual abuse – and, in particular, in relation to
investigatory work – its recommendations have been adopted by the courts,
so that practitioners are now expected to know them and to follow them
(see further, Chapter 7).

Since 1989, other official reports into local episodes of abuse have been
published. These include the Levy/Kahan report on the Staffordshire 'pin-
down' controversy (1991) and the Kirkwood report on the management of
children's homes in Leicestershire (1993). Care needs to be taken with such
documents, since many of the critical events described in them took place
before the Children Act was passed. The Staffordshire and Leicestershire
reports, for example, are important insofar as they expose the harm that can
befall children as a result of bad practice and weak management, but they
cannot by their very nature be used to measure the success or otherwise of
the new legislation.

The scheme and style of the Children Act

Sections and schedules

The Children Act consists of over 100 sections, which makes it a relatively
large piece of legislation. This should not occasion surprise, however, in
view of its objectives: to restate both the public and private law relating to
children. In addition to the sections there are a number of schedules at the
back of the Act. Schedules of statutes can cause confusion among non-
lawyers, there sometimes being a feeling that they do not have quite the
same legal significance as the sections. This is a misconception: sections and
schedules have an identical effect in law. Whether a provision goes into a
section or a schedule is very much a matter of judgment and there can often
be disagreement as to which is appropriate. There is a good example of this

within the Children Act, in the collection of provisions concerning children in need (discussed in Chapter 5).

The 12 Parts of the Act

In large statutes, it is usual for the sections to be arranged into Parts, each Part dealing with a particular subject. This obviously facilitates a better understanding. The sections of the Children Act are arranged into 12 Parts. These Parts are not completely self-contained, but arranged in this way they do give a fairly good idea of the overall effect of the Act. Part II of the Act is the one which is devoted to the reform of the private law, while Parts III to XI are concerned with the public law. Part I and Part XII contain provisions affecting both areas. As indicated earlier, the schedules at the back of the Act supplement some of the sections.

The style of drafting

Mention was made earlier of the convoluted style of drafting which tended to infect the pre-1989 children's legislation. The steady stream of complaints about this obviously hit home because the framers of the Children Act went out of their way to make their product intelligible to a wide range of individuals. The Department of Health (DH), in its own *Introduction to the Children Act* (HMSO, 1989), is fully entitled to state that the Act 'has been drafted in a clear style which should make it accessible to non-lawyers'.

This has been very welcome news to child care practitioners. It has enabled them to refer directly to the text of the Act when considering their position and advising (or challenging) others. Nor should parents, relatives and other carers be left out of the discussion of this aspect of the new law. They are, after all, principal consumers in this context and for too long their interests were undervalued by those who put statutes together. It is good to see that a conscious effort has been made to make the law relating to children more accessible to them.

All this is not to suggest, of course, that the Children Act is plain sailing. It would be unreasonable to expect a statute of such breadth and importance not to contain any points of difficulty or complexity and the cases decided in the superior courts continue to bring out unforeseen consequences flowing from the use of a particular word or phrase (see, for example, the difficult case law surrounding the meaning of the threshold criteria in section 31 of the Act, discussed in Chapter 10). And it has to be said that during its journey through Parliament numerous amendments were made which had the effect of spoiling the initial veneer of simplicity, a process which has indeed continued over the years since 1989 (see below).

What should be acknowledged, however, is that the Act, taken as a whole, does reflect a departure from the traditional approach to drafting and has accordingly made it much easier for those lacking legal training to understand the rules. In this respect, it can only be described as an unqualified success.

Amendments to the Act since 1989

Many Acts of Parliament are the subject of later amendment. This can occur for a number of reasons. In some cases, the legislation is found to be simply unworkable; in others, gaps or ambiguities are discovered (often through the litigation process in the courts). Many amendments are purely technical and come about because other statutes referred to in the legislation are themselves changed, thereby necessitating a substitution of references.

In the case of the Children Act, numerous amendments have indeed been made but they have tended to be minor ones. Quite a few gaps and ambiguities were spotted shortly after the Act was passed and these were quickly rectified (by the Courts and Legal Services Act 1990) in time for implementation. Many other technical amendments have been effected since 1989. For example, the wording of the Act has had to be changed to take account of the creation of NHS trusts, the new health authorities, the new local government system in Wales and the new jobseeker's allowance.

Two rather more weighty rafts of amendments, however, need to be noted, each arising out of the Family Law Act 1996. This Act is destined to have a substantial impact on the lives of many children in the future. It deals with two quite separate matters: divorce and domestic violence. The divorce provisions (due to be implemented in 1999) will replace those devised in 1969 and reflect a new emphasis on resorting to mediation in order to resolve the disputes of divorcing couples (including disputes concerning their children). The relationship between the divorce provisions of the 1996 Act and the provisions of the Children Act will obviously be crucial and is an issue addressed in Chapter 3 of this book (page 42). The domestic violence provisions of the Act (implemented in October 1997) replace a complex and confusing mass of legislation. As part of this reform, Parliament has taken the opportunity of inserting into the Children Act several new sections which enable a suspected abuser to be excluded from the family home. These important, and in some ways difficult, provisions are considered in Chapters 8 and 10 (pages 138 and 205).

Rules, regulations and orders made under the Act

A striking feature of the Children Act is its frequent reference to rules or regulations to be made by central government. There is nothing particularly objectionable in this sort of practice, provided always that the really funda-mental matters are covered by the statute. In other words, the proper object of subordinate legislation is to deal with detailed, supplementary issues, mention of which in the Act itself would only serve to confuse the reader. As with the sections/schedules division, it is ultimately a matter of judgment as to whether a particular subject should be dealt with in the statute or in regulations, and reasonable people can differ over the appropriateness of the end result.

By 14 October 1991, when the Children Act came fully into operation, 48 sets of subordinate legislation (or 'statutory instruments' to use the techni-cal legal term) had been made. All of this has the full force of law and should be regarded in much the same way as the provisions of the Act themselves. Nothing turns on an instrument being entitled 'rules' as op-posed to 'regulations' or 'order'. Although it covers a wide range of matters, this legislation can be conveniently classified according to two distinct cat-egories. The first category consists of predominantly court-oriented mate-rial. The biggest items here are the rules of court, which seek to regulate legal procedures under the Act, including the use of appropriate application forms. The second category is a residual one, consisting of everything else, and it is here that one will find the regulations imposing detailed obligations on social services departments.

The effect of the numerous provisions in these two categories will be discussed in appropriate sections of this book. It should be remembered, however, that subordinate legislation, like primary legislation, undergoes amendment from time to time and so the position set out in the text will not necessarily endure. Indeed, various amending rules, regulations and orders have already accumulated in the years since 1991.

The guidance documents

In addition to completing the legislative framework by making rules, regu-lations and orders, the Government has issued a series of guidance docu-ments covering various topics. One purpose of these is to explain (in official, uncritical terms, of course) relevant provisions of the Act and any accompa-nying rules or regulations. Another purpose, however, is to give an indica-tion of what central government expects from local authorities in terms of practical implementation of the law. The preface to the first volume of guidance, issued in March 1991, set the pattern for the others. It states that:

> this guidance is issued under section 7 of the Local Authority Social Services Act 1970. It is the first in a series designed to bring to managers and practitioners an understanding of the principles of the Children Act and associated regulations, to identify areas of change and to discuss the implications for policies, procedures and practice.

The significance of the reference to the 1970 Act, which is perhaps not obvious, has been explained by the DH in *The Care of Children* (HMSO, 1989) in the following way:

> Guidance documents are usually issued as general guidance of the Secretary of State as described in section 7(1) of the Local Authority Social Services Act 1970. Local authorities are required to act in accordance with such guidance which is intended to be a statement of what is held to be good practice. Though they are not in themselves law in the way that regulations are law, guidance documents are likely to be quoted or used in court proceedings as well as in local authority policy and practice papers. They could provide the basis for a legal challenge of an authority's action or inaction, including (in extreme cases) default action by the Secretary of State.

In spite of these words, the precise legal standing of such government guidance remains unclear. In the highly publicized case of *Davis v London Borough of Sutton* (1994) the High Court seemed reluctant to lay down a comprehensive ruling and was able to dispose of the case – which concerned the issue of smacking by child minders – by concentrating on the 1989 Act itself. What is clear, however, is that the guidance documents are capable of being influential in the courts. In 1992, for example, in the case of *Manchester City Council v F*, it was stated that care plans submitted to the courts by local authorities in child protection cases should accord with the recommendations contained in Volume 3 of the Guidance (see further, page 173 below); and in *JR v Oxfordshire County Council* (1992) the guidance in Volume 1 concerning secure accommodation orders was described by a judge as 'authoritative' and 'valuable'.

Those documents of guidance issued as a set in 1991 are described as appropriate throughout this book. A complete list of them will be found in Appendix A (page 277). Further guidance drawn up after 1991 has tended to be published by the DH in the form of circulars addressed to Directors of Social Services (a good example is Circular LAC (94) 23, issued in December 1994 with the object of clarifying the guidance contained in Volume 2 on the use of physical punishment by child minders). These too are referred to as appropriate.

The Care of Children

Shortly after the Children Act was passed, the DH published *The Care of Children: Principles and Practice in Regulations and Guidance*. This is an unusual document. Compiled by an advisory group led by Jane Rowe, it seeks to set out in 17 pages 'a guide to the principles of good child care'. It is aimed primarily at social services departments of local authorities. Although the group was established before the Act was passed and although the document would have been perfectly valid and appropriate under the old legislation, the timing of publication was no accident: *The Care of Children* was very definitely geared towards the implementation of the 1989 Act.

Forty-two principles are set out in the guide. They are reproduced in summary form in Appendix B of this book (page 278). The principles are intended to 'apply to all social work with children and their families' but they are certainly not intended to remove discretion and professional judgment from practitioners. Indeed, this could not be achieved by the principles as they stand because of the potential for conflicts between them. For example, principle 3 states that 'children are entitled to protection from neglect, abuse and exploitation'. Nobody would disagree with this, but can it always be reconciled with principle 11: 'when out-of-home care is necessary, active steps should be taken to ensure speedy return home'?

The advisory group were well aware of this potential. As they clearly state, where conflict occurs it is for the professionals involved in the case to decide on a 'hierarchy of importance', basing their decision on the particular circumstances and needs of the child. 'It may be helpful', they suggest, 'to think of principles as the colours on the social work painter's palette to be used in the combinations and patterns required for each picture painted/ child care case handled. Social workers need to be as familiar with the principles of good child care as painters are with the colours in their paint box.'

Patterns and Outcomes in Child Placement

This valuable document, published in 1991, bears the sub-title 'messages from current research and their implications'. It was not designed as a guide to the Children Act, rather it aims 'to make recent research findings accessible to social workers and demonstrate their relevance to day to day practice'. Proceeding from the assumption that the 1989 Act, to achieve its objectives, requires shifts in thinking and consequent alterations in practice, it focuses on three central themes and offers suggestions based on recent research projects. It is a sequel to the influential *Social Work Decisions in Child Care* (HMSO, 1985). The three themes addressed are 'promotion of the child's welfare', 'partnership with parents and carers' and 'policies, planning and decision making'. A lengthy supplement, entitled 'What is your Evidence?', contains a set of tools, checklists and exercises for managers and practitioners.

The Children Act Advisory Committee

The Children Act Advisory Committee was established in March 1991 with the following terms of reference:

> To advise the Lord Chancellor, the Home Secretary, the Secretary of State for Health and the President of the Family Division on whether the guiding principles of the Children Act are being achieved and whether the court procedures and the guardian ad litem system are operating satisfactorily.

It is unusual for a single Act of Parliament to have its own monitoring committee and this is yet further evidence of the radical nature of the Children Act reforms and the importance which was attached to them by the various public agencies involved. Fourteen individuals were initially appointed to serve on this Committee, which was chaired by Mrs Justice Booth. Membership of the Committee fluctuated over subsequent years until it was wound up in June 1997, the Government having come to the conclusion that its primary tasks had been accomplished.

The most obvious manifestation of the Committee's work consists of the Annual Reports it produced. These are valuable documents, for two reasons. First, they reveal problems which emerged across the country in the course of the implementation process, particularly in the court system. The Committee was clearly regarded (and regarded itself) as a channel through which practical difficulties could be aired and in this way matters which might not otherwise have come to light were exposed. Secondly, the Committee devised a number of best practice statements for use by child care professionals and the courts (the most important of these were brought together in the Committee's *Handbook of Best Practice in Children Act Cases* (1997)). Since the Committee's work was carried out on a wholly non-statutory basis, these statements do not have the force of law but the strength of the Committee's membership and its quasi-governmental supporting apparatus have given the statements considerable weight. For these reasons, extracts from the Committee's reports are included in this book as appropriate.

Scotland and Northern Ireland

There are some provisions in the Children Act which apply to Scotland and Northern Ireland, but not many. Child law in those territories has recently been revised by separate measures (the Children (Scotland) Act 1995 and the Children (Northern Ireland) Order 1995) and therefore this book is concerned only with the law of England and Wales.

2

Parental responsibility

Parental rights and duties

When the review of children's law began in earnest in 1984, it was realized that extended consideration would have to be given to the vexed question of parental rights and duties. It is indeed an obvious place to start, for what could be more fundamental in this particular context than the legal relationship between parent and child? In addition, how can the legal effects of court orders, and State intervention generally, be properly stated without some prior understanding of the nature of this relationship? Surely the one is founded on the other?

These are powerful arguments, and they would no doubt lead many people to anticipate a comprehensive statement (or re-statement) of the parental rights and duties in the Children Act. But no such statement is there.

The old law

Under the old law, there was no doubt that parents (by which I mean birth parents) had certain legal rights and duties in relation to their children. Indeed, some Acts of Parliament actually used the expression 'parental rights and duties'. These rights and duties, however, were not set out in a single statutory document. Nor did the courts produce an authoritative catalogue – in fact, they positively retreated from such an exercise. All that happened was that legal commentators scrutinized the various pieces of legislation concerning children, studied the different rulings of the courts over the years, and came up with suggested lists of probable 'rights' and 'duties' which parents possessed. They included the following:

Parental rights

1 The right to determine where the child should live
2 The right to determine education
3 The right to determine religion
4 The right to discipline the child
5 The right to consent to the child's marriage
6 The right to authorize medical treatment
7 The right to administer the child's property
8 The right to appoint a guardian
9 The right to agree to adoption
10 The right to change the child's name.

Parental duties

1 The duty to protect the child
2 The duty to maintain the child
3 The duty to secure the child's education
4 The duty to control the child.

Several things need to be emphasized about this list. First, it is unofficial in the sense that it is not directly derived from any single piece of legislation or court ruling. As previously stated, it is simply a list which could be said to be supported by a large number of different statutes and judicial decisions (e.g. the Marriage Act 1949 for the fifth right, the Adoption Act 1976 for the ninth right and the Education Acts for the third duty).

Secondly, the expression 'parental rights and duties' was liable to mislead, because by no means all of the rights and duties in the list are exclusive to birth parents: some of them will in fact attach to anybody who happens to be caring for a child, irrespective of the existence of a biological tie. For example, although the Education Acts have over the years created a range of rights and duties for parents (including the duty to cause a child of compulsory school age to receive efficient full-time education), the term 'parent' has always been defined for the purposes of the Acts so as to cover any individual who has care of a child.

Thirdly, the use of the word 'rights' in the context of the parent/child relationship has become controversial. As has been demonstrated on numerous occasions, the decisions of parents are capable of being overruled by the courts, which invariably operate in what they see as the best interests of the child. This being the case (so it is argued), to talk of parents having rights is misleading: whatever 'rights' they possess are heavily qualified by the ability of the courts to intervene on the application of an interested person or public authority. On this view, it is perhaps more accurate to refer to children's rights than parental rights (a notion undoubtedly strengthened by the adoption of the United Nations Convention on the Rights of the Child in 1989).

To summarize, then, the old legislation certainly made reference to the concept of parental rights and duties, as did the judicial case law, but nowhere were these rights and duties clearly and authoritatively spelt out.

The effect of the Children Act

The Children Act continues this tradition, although in an attempt to improve the legal framework it introduces an important new concept: 'parental responsibility'. One of the reasons why this is important is simply the frequency of its appearance in the Act, the regulations and the guidance. We will see, for example, that when a residence order is made by a court under section 10 of the Act, the holder of the order is given parental responsibility. Similarly, when a care order is made under section 31, the local authority acquires parental responsibility. The Act also provides that birth parents will share parental responsibility in respect of their children, unless, that is, the parents are not married to each other, in which case the mother alone has it (although there are ways in which the father can acquire it).

What does this new concept mean? Section 3(1) of the Act defines it as follows:

> 'Parental responsibility' means all the rights, duties, powers, responsibilities and authority which by law a parent of a child has in relation to the child and his property.

As can be seen, the concept is simply a shorthand term designed to cover the whole panoply of parental rights and duties. In this respect, it is similar – though not identical – to the old statutory concept of 'legal custody'. The 1989 Act is also similar to the previous legislation in that it makes no attempt to define what the parental rights, duties, powers, etc. actually are. In the reform phase, the Law Commission took charge of this aspect of child law and it came to the view that to attempt to produce an exhaustive and detailed list of the legal rights and duties of parents would be an unprofitable exercise. It felt that it would be a practical impossibility, as the list 'must change from time to time to meet differing needs and circumstances'. It might also be said that such an exercise would, without any doubt, prove to be exceedingly contentious, with no guarantee of public consensus at the end of the day. If evidence for this is needed, it is amply supplied by the sustained controversy over recent years concerning parents' rights to inflict corporal punishment on their children.

Recent developments in Scotland show the wisdom of not attempting to define the parental rights and duties in law. In contrast to its English counterpart, the Scottish Law Commission had no hesitation in recommending (in 1992) a statutory list of rights and responsibilities, and these now appear in the opening sections of the Children (Scotland) Act 1995. Under that Act, parents in Scotland have (amongst other things) the responsibility to 'safeguard and promote the child's health, development and welfare', to 'provide, in a manner appropriate to the stage of development of the child, direction and guidance', and to 'maintain personal relations and direct contact with the child on a regular basis' if living away. They also have the right to 'have the child living with [them] or otherwise to regulate the child's residence'. These provisions, though undoubtedly well-intentioned, are seriously defective for a number of reasons. They do not, for example, pretend to be comprehensive (since they are stated to be supplementary to any other rights and duties found in other legislation), they are hedged with substantial qualifications, they are drafted in imprecise terms and they are in some respects virtually unenforceable. The overall result is deeply unsatisfactory.

'Parental rights and duties', therefore, have continued under the Children Act, but they are now subsumed under the all-embracing notion of parental responsibility. The introduction of the word 'responsibility' was essentially symbolic: it was felt by the Law Commission to reflect more closely 'the everyday reality of being a parent' and to be more in keeping with modern ideas relating to child care. The word 'rights', on the other hand, conjures up the idea of absolute power, which, as far as parent/child relationships are concerned, is not only outdated but also legally inaccurate. The shift in emphasis from rights to responsibilities is therefore to be welcomed.

A price has been paid, however, for the creation of this new, enlightened, concept. 'Parental responsibility' is one of those expressions which are capable of being adopted as a slogan and used as the centre-piece of an ideological crusade. So it has turned out. In the fierce debates which have recently taken place over child maintenance and juvenile crime, protagonists have been eager to point out that the law – in the shape of the Children Act – already supports the view that parents are 'responsible' for their children's upbringing (thus legitimizing punitive action against absent fathers who do not pay maintenance) just as it supports the view that parents are 'responsible' for their children's actions (thus facilitating punitive action against the parents of young offenders). The parental responsibility provisions of the Children Act were, of course, never designed with these issues in mind but this fact has been conveniently overlooked in the heat of the argument. The whole episode affords an excellent illustration of the power of language, especially language which appears prominently in a piece of legislation.

The initial allocation of parental responsibility

According to section 2 of the Act, where a child's father and mother were married to each other at the time of his birth, they shall each have parental responsibility for the child and each of them may act alone and without the other in meeting that responsibility. Whilst the statutory wording differs from the old legislation, the substance is the same: married parents have had in law equal parental rights and duties for many years.

The Act enables either parent to take action in pursuance of their responsibility, without reference to the other. Joint decision-making by parents concerning their children's upbringing has obviously got a lot to recommend it, but Parliament wisely followed the Law Commission's proposal in not making it mandatory: it would be totally impractical. However, the Act is careful to make clear that this independence rule does not affect any statutory provision requiring both parents' consent (e.g. consent to adoption). Nor will a parent be able to act unilaterally if to do so would be incompatible with any court order which has been made (e.g. an order made following a divorce which requires one parent to consult the other before arranging holidays for the child). This last rule concerning court orders is one of the key provisions in the Children Act, as will be seen in later chapters of this book.

Unmarried fathers

For unmarried parents, the rules are different. Here, parental responsibility starts off with the mother exclusively. Again, however, there is no real change in the law because unmarried fathers have always been denied automatic and full recognition of their parenthood. It would have been unrealistic to expect the Children Act to do anything to alter the status quo because the traditional rule excluding fathers had been reaffirmed by Parliament as recently as 1987 when it passed the Family Law Reform Act. That Act brought in many changes concerning children born outside marriage (notably the abolition of affiliation proceedings) but it left intact the basic rule under discussion. The Law Commission proposed no change and no change was made.

Whatever may have been the received wisdom in the 1980s, the blatant discrimination against unmarried fathers embodied in the Children Act is rapidly becoming untenable. This is not simply due to the dramatic increase in the proportion of children born outside marriage (up from 9.1 per cent in 1975 to 33.9 per cent in 1995). More crucial has been the way in which the arguments traditionally adduced in favour of discrimination have come to be exposed as flawed. Reference was made earlier to the Scottish Law Commission's 1992 report on child law north of the border. While that report's recommendations on the content of parental responsibility are vulnerable to criticism, it is suggested that the analysis of the position of unmarried fathers completely demolishes the case for maintaining the current law. The Commission's argument runs as follows:

1 The existing rule encourages irresponsibility in some men. This cannot be in the interests of their children.
2 The rule ignores the fact that an unmarried father may be just as motivated to look after his child as a married father.
3 Giving parental responsibility automatically to unmarried fathers would not prevent mothers from making decisions since the Children Act contains the rule of independence (described above).
4 It is argued that some children of unmarried fathers are born as a result of a casual liaison. However, in such cases the mother is automatically given parental responsibility for the child and there is no self-evident reason why the father should be denied it.
5 It is argued that many unmarried fathers are not committed to their children. Some married fathers, however, show no interest in their children whatsoever and yet the law still gives them parental responsibility automatically.
6 It is argued that changing the law would result in more interference by unmarried fathers in the lives of their children. However, what is regarded as interference by a mother might in fact be seen by others as beneficial involvement. No doubt many divorced mothers dislike interference by their former husbands and yet the law encourages divorced fathers to play an active role in their children's upbringing.
7 It is argued that some unmarried fathers are so obviously unmeritorious (e.g. rapists) that it would be absurd to give them automatic parental responsibility. However, some married fathers are unmeritorious. Furthermore, court orders are available where it is felt necessary to ensure the exclusion of a man from his child's life.

As the Commission pointed out, a man who abandons his wife as soon as she becomes pregnant and who never sees his child nevertheless has full parental responsibility, whereas a man who is cohabiting with his child's mother and who is playing a full paternal role has none. It is not easy to see why this should be the case. Until the law is changed, however, unmarried fathers who seek parental responsibility will have to rely on the two procedures – one involving a written agreement made with the child's mother, the other involving a court order – established by section 4 of the 1989 Act. These procedures are explained below.

In the absence of a court order or an agreement, it might be thought that the unmarried father would be completely bereft of any aspect of parental responsibility. This is not the case, however. In the first place, he will always be liable to maintain his child in the sense that the mother (and, given the right circumstances, others) can apply to the Child Support Agency for an assessment against him. Secondly, if he is actually caring for the child – and of course very large numbers of fathers do this – from a legal point of view he will be in a position to exercise the powers which any carer has. These include powers in relation to education, religion, discipline, medical treatment and change of name. At the same time he will have the duties to protect, educate and control the child. All of this flows quite naturally from the characteristics of the 'rights' and 'duties' mentioned, which depend for their existence not on any blood tie or legal status but simply on the fact that the child is being looked after by the person concerned. If the mother of the child is opposed to the idea of the father possessing these powers, her remedy is to remove the child from his care: this she can do by virtue of her parental responsibility.

In this connection, however, it is suggested that account should be taken of a provision introduced by section 3(5) of the Children Act. This states that a person who is caring for a child but who lacks parental responsibility 'may do what is reasonable in all the circumstances of the case for the purpose of safeguarding or promoting the child's welfare'. This intriguing new rule – new in the sense that it did not appear in the previous legislation – has generated a considerable number of questions which have yet to be addressed by the courts. In the present context, it is likely that it could be relied upon by an unmarried father who is looking after his child to justify his refusal to allow the child's mother to resume caring for the child. The argument would be that the father reasonably believes that the child would be at risk if he was released into the mother's care. Whether or not the Law Commission, which recommended the rule in section 3(5), intended it to have this effect is unclear (the only example of its significance which it gave concerned the making of arrangements by the child's carer for urgent medical treatment while his parents are on holiday) but the wording of the Act certainly seems to permit it. Moreover, as is explained in Chapter 6 of this book, the provision has been interpreted in this fashion by the Government itself in relation to the legal position of foster carers.

Acquiring and losing parental responsibility

Married parents

As explained earlier, birth parents who are married to each other acquire parental responsibility automatically. They will not lose it until the child reaches the age of majority, unless the child is adopted or freed for adoption. If a court order other than adoption is made in respect of the child – an order following a divorce, for example, or a care order in favour of the local authority – others may well acquire parental responsibility but the

parents will not lose theirs. This arrangement, whereby parental responsibility is enjoyed by several persons at the same time, reflects the Law
Commission's view that the law should encourage parents 'to feel concerned and responsible for the welfare of their children' and that 'parents
should not be deprived of their very parenthood unless and until the child
is adopted'. However, it should be noted that there is applicable here the
rule referred to earlier, that a parent may not act in any way which would be
incompatible with a court order; so although parents will not lose parental
responsibility when an order is made, their ability to exercise it will be
restricted in accordance with the terms of the order.

Unmarried fathers

Unmarried fathers are, of course, in a special position, since automatic
parental responsibility is denied them. One obvious way in which it can be
acquired is through marriage to the child's mother. If marriage is not
possible or not desired, section 4 of the Children Act makes available two
mechanisms whereby parental responsibility can be obtained. Both have
been designed exclusively for unmarried fathers.

Section 4(1)(b) states that unmarried parents may by agreement provide
for the father to have parental responsibility. Such an agreement must be
made 'in the form prescribed' and recorded 'in the prescribed manner'.
These prescriptions are not dealt with in the Act; they are covered by the
Parental Responsibility Agreement Regulations 1991 (as amended in
1994). Under the regulations, an agreement is to be made in the form set
out, witnessed by an authorized court official or magistrate and then filed in
the Principal Registry of the Family Division in London. This aspect of the
procedure is designed to emphasize its importance but neither the authorized official nor the Principal Registry undertakes any welfare scrutiny
of the case. The prescribed form reminds the parents that the agreement
will not take effect until it has been properly filed. It also informs them
that making it will seriously affect their legal position and suggests that
they both seek legal advice before the form is completed. The effect, of
course, will be that the father, by acquiring parental responsibility, will gain
access to a wider range of rights and powers. Careful counselling of the
parties will therefore be needed in some cases. Identifying those persons
who have parental responsibility for a child has assumed considerable importance under the Children Act and the 1991 regulations facilitate this
process by providing that the record of an agreement shall be available for
inspection by any person upon written request to the Registry (a fee may be
payable).

In the first four years of the Children Act's operation, over 16000 parental responsibility agreements were registered. An alternative mechanism

for the unmarried father – and one which in practice would only be used if the child's mother was unwilling or unable to make an agreement – is the parental responsibility order, obtainable from a court under section 4(1)(a) of the Act. The ability of a court to grant parental responsibility to an unmarried father was first provided for in the Family Law Reform Act 1987 (although in that Act the relevant expression was 'the parental rights and duties') and since that time there has accumulated a substantial body of case law on the subject. This is not really surprising because the legislation has failed to give the courts any specific guidance on the correct approach. One of the most important cases is *Re S*, decided by the Court of Appeal in 1995. In the course of a detailed review of earlier decisions, the following propositions were set out:

1 Applications under section 4(1)(a) are governed by the principle contained in section 1(1) of the Children Act, namely that the welfare of the child is the paramount consideration.
2 In considering whether to make an order the court will have to take into account a number of factors of which the following will be particularly significant: (a) the degree of commitment which the father has shown towards the child; (b) the degree of attachment which exists between the father and the child; and (c) the father's reasons for applying for the order.
3 If the factors noted in proposition 2 above are favourable to the father, the court may presume, in the absence of evidence to the contrary, that it will be for the welfare of the child that an order is made.
4 The fact that the father may not currently be in a position to exercise parental responsibility is not in itself a reason to refuse an order. Parental responsibility carries 'rights in waiting' which may become beneficial to the child if circumstances change ('though existing circumstances may demand that his children see or hear nothing of him, and that he should have no influence upon the course of their lives for the time being, their welfare may require that if circumstances change he should be reintroduced as a presence, or at least as an influence, in their lives').
5 Where the child is being looked after by the mother, a parental responsibility order will not give the father the right to interfere in matters within the day-to-day management of the child's life. If the father misuses the 'rights' given to him under an order, he can be restrained by appropriately worded section 8 orders (on which see Chapter 3 of this book). In extreme cases the court may decide to revoke the order (see below).

These propositions reveal a generally benevolent attitude towards parental responsibility order applications and the later case of *Re H* (1996) confirms how far the judiciary have travelled on the issue. There, a father of two children aged 4 and 7 had been denied a section 4 order by a county court judge principally because of his obstinate refusal to pay maintenance for them. The Court of Appeal ruled that such an approach was wrong: 'the court ought not to use the weapon of withholding a parental responsibility order for the purpose of exacting from the father what may be regarded as his financial dues'. In most other respects the father had shown commitment to his children and his shortcomings on the financial front were not enough to displace the positive factors which pointed towards an order. The underlying thinking of the judiciary is nicely encapsulated in the following extract from the leading judgment in Re S (above):

> I have heard, up and down the land, psychiatrists tell me how important it is that children grow up with good self-esteem and how much they need to have a favourable positive image of the absent parent. It seems to me important, therefore, wherever possible, to ensure that the law confers upon a committed father that stamp of approval, lest the child grow up with some belief that he is in some way disqualified from fulfilling his role and that the reason for the disqualification is something inherent which will be inherited by the child, making her struggle to find her own identity all the more fraught.

If the unmarried father does acquire parental responsibility, through either an agreement or a court order, it may be brought to an end by a later court order. This is laid down by section 4(3) of the Act. The decision of the High Court in Re P (1994) suggests that this power will only be exercised in extreme circumstances. 'The ability of a mother to make such an application,' it was said, 'should not be allowed to become a weapon in the hands of the dissatisfied mother of the non-marital child: it should be used by the court as an appropriate step in the regulation of the child's life where the circumstances really do warrant it and not otherwise.' In that case, a parental responsibility agreement was in fact discharged, the court taking the view that the father, having gravely injured the child, had in effect forfeited his responsibility.

Third parties

Parental responsibility may be acquired by persons other than birth parents. This can happen through the making of a residence order under section 10 of the Children Act, a care order under section 31 and an emergency protection order under section 44. An adoption order and a parental order (made in a surrogacy case) will also confer parental responsibility. These matters are covered in later chapters of this book. Another way, however, which will be dealt with here, is through the appointment of a guardian.

Under the previous legislation, parents were able to appoint persons to act as guardians of their children after their death, but this had to be done by deed or by will. Alternatively, the court was able to appoint a person to act as guardian where one or both parents had died. As the Law Commission observed, very little was known about the practical operation of this legislation. The available statistics did not disclose the number of guardians, nor did they indicate the number of children who were potentially subject to guardianship. Furthermore, there was only limited knowledge of the sorts of circumstances in which guardians were appointed, the types of people who were actually appointed and the expectations of appointers and appointees. What research there was on the subject suggested considerable variation. In addition to this, the precise legal position of guardians, and the differences in law between guardians and parents, remained in many respects obscure.

Clearly, therefore, this was a subject ripe for revision, and sections 5 and 6 of the Children Act were designed to restate the law so as to remove the former uncertainties. They also introduced a number of changes in the substance of the rules. The main features of the new law are as follows:

- Guardians have parental responsibility for the child. In other words, they have access to the full range of the rights and powers described earlier, including the right to determine where the child is to live. They are also, of course, subject to the usual parental duties.
- Parental appointments of guardians no longer have to be made by deed or will. The new minimum requirement is that the appointment is in writing, is dated and is signed by the appointer or signed at his direction.
- A parental appointment only takes effect when the surviving parent dies. This represents a change to the old law and it has been introduced in an attempt to minimize the room for damaging conflict between the appointee and the surviving parent. The Law Commission put it this way:

> Those, comparatively few, children who experience the death of a parent while they are under 18 will usually have been living with both parents at the time. There can be little doubt that those children's interests will generally lie in preserving the stability of their existing home and thus in confirming the continued responsibility of the survivor. There seems little reason why the survivor should share that responsibility with a guardian who almost invariably will not be sharing the household.

As was pointed out, this rule does not prevent the surviving parent seeking guidance from the guardian, nor does it prevent the guardian taking action through legal proceedings (described in Chapter 4) if the situation requires it.

- The rule just described does not apply if the appointing parent held a residence order in respect of the child. In such a case, the appointment takes immediate effect on the death of the appointer. Residence orders, described in the next chapter, have replaced custody orders under the old legislation, and the situation envisaged here is that where the parents are living apart, perhaps divorced, with the caring parent having obtained this type of court order. The view which has prevailed is that if the caring parent dies having appointed a guardian for the child, the guardian should step into the picture immediately. This means that parental responsibility is shared between the guardian and the surviving parent. Conflicts are obviously possible here, depending on the degree of involvement of the surviving parent, and if necessary court proceedings can be instituted in order to resolve them.

• The court may appoint a guardian either if the child has no parent or if one parent has died and that parent held a residence order in respect of the child. It can be seen that these conditions are very similar to those which apply to parental appointments.

• Parental appointments can be subsequently revoked.

• An appointment is automatically revoked if the person appointed was married to the appointer but the marriage was later terminated in divorce or nullity proceedings. This rule has been added by the Law Reform (Succession) Act 1995 and is aimed primarily at cases in which a step-parent has been appointed guardian.

• Persons appointed guardians by parents may disclaim their appointment within a reasonable time (regulations may lay down a procedure for doing this).

• A guardian may be removed at any time by court order.

These rules have done much to improve the law of guardianship. Their impact in practice, though, is difficult to measure. Certain kinds of case involving the death of a birth parent will continue to be better dealt with under the adoption law; others will require the intervention of the local authority or a voluntary organization. Obviously many cases will continue to occur where no legal mechanism of any kind is necessary.

3

Court orders in favour of parents

Obscurity of the previous legislation

During the 12 months preceding the implementation of the Children Act the courts of England and Wales made more than 80 000 custody orders in respect of children following divorce proceedings between parents. What were the exact legal consequences of these court orders? Amazingly, we do not know the answer to this question, and the fact that we do not know is one of the reasons why the Children Act was such a badly needed piece of legislation. One of the most fundamental objects of any 'private' children's law is to make clear the effect of orders of the court. During the 1980s it was increasingly recognized that the legal framework then existing was woefully deficient in this respect. The legislation was obscure on many vital issues and this obscurity led to considerable speculation and, indeed, differences of opinion and practice among practitioners and judges.

This extraordinary state of affairs can be illustrated by reference to the situation referred to above, concerning orders for custody granted on or after a divorce. The statute in question (the Matrimonial Causes Act 1973) did not explain the meaning of the expression 'custody' – this, of course, was part of the problem – but the conventional view for many years was that a person granted custody in this way acquired a number of exclusive 'rights' over the child, covering not just his place of residence but also such matters as his education, religious upbringing and medical treatment. In 1980, however, this general understanding was obliterated by a court ruling to the effect that a parent granted custody, far from being in a position of dominance, had a duty to consult the other about the future education of the child 'and any other major matters'. People working in the matrimonial law field were completely unprepared for this ruling and, not surprisingly, the result was utter confusion.

Complexity and inconsistency of the previous legislation

Prior to the Children Act, there were more than 12 separate statutory procedures authorizing the courts to make orders for custody and access. In the words of the Law Commission, the provisions:

> are neither clear nor consistent on such important matters as the meaning of custody, who may apply, which children are concerned, how their own point of view may be put before the court, what kinds of order may be made and what test the court should apply. The different powers are classic examples of ad hoc legislation designed for particular situations without full regard to how they fit into the wider picture.

Nobody could disagree with the Commission's conclusion that there was an unanswerable case for reform. The fact that each year some 170 000 children fell to be dealt with under the legislation obviously served to reinforce this.

The new legal framework: Part II of the Children Act

Part II of the Children Act, consisting of sections 8–16, represented a new beginning as far as the private law is concerned. Its provisions replaced the following:

- The provisions concerning custody and access orders in divorce and other matrimonial proceedings
- The provisions concerning custody and access disputes between parents (where no other issues were at stake)
- The custodianship law
- The various provisions concerning access orders in favour of grandparents.

The principal objective was to set out in a clear and coherent manner a range of court orders and associated procedures which are necessary for the effective and sensitive disposal of private disputes and applications concerning the upbringing of children, whether such cases involve parents, relatives or 'strangers'. For reasons of convenience it is proposed to deal separately with orders in favour of parents and orders in favour of non-parents. The present chapter is devoted to parents' cases.

Section 8 orders

The most obvious feature of the private law provisions of the Children Act is the appearance of four new types of court order. These have come to be known collectively as 'section 8 orders' – indeed, the Act itself uses this terminology. These four orders, which were designed to supersede the various species of custody and access order to be found in the old legislation, are:

1 The residence order
2 The contact order
3 The prohibited steps order
4 The specific issue order.

These are the orders which the courts now use to settle issues between parents concerning children. The court is able to make any, or all, of them, and it can do this either in proceedings brought specifically for that purpose or in the course of other family proceedings where the central issue does not directly relate to children – a divorce case, for example, or an application for maintenance. The nature of the four orders is such that there is an infinite number of packages which the court can sanction at the end of the day. Given the enormous variety of situations which can arise in practice, this is greatly advantageous.

Residence orders

According to section 8(1) of the Act, a residence order 'means an order settling the arrangements to be made as to the person with whom a child is to live'. Such an order will obviously be appropriate in a case where separating or divorcing parents are unable to reach agreement on the child's future home. It might also be suitable where an agreement has been reached by the parties but the circumstances suggest that a confirmatory order from the court would be beneficial.

Like the other section 8 orders, the residence order is designed to be flexible. The court can, if it wishes, order that the child should live with one parent. On the other hand, it may order that the child's home is to be divided between the two parents, with a precise timetable of moves being built in (section 11(4)). The order can contain directions about how it is to be carried into effect and it can impose conditions which must be complied with by the parties (section 11(7)). It can also be expressed to have effect only for a specified period or contain particular provisions which will have only a limited life. By using these supplementary powers imaginatively, the court should be in a position to tailor the residence order to the special requirements of the family concerned.

The power of the court to make a shared residence order under section 11(4) represents a departure from the previous law and predictably has generated different views. In *A v A* (1994) the Court of Appeal took the opportunity to make some general observations on the correct approach. It stated that the conventional arrangement in a parents' case where orders were needed was that there would be a residence order to one parent with contact granted to the other. Normally a child should have one home, since competing homes are liable to produce confusion and stress. Consequently, it would be unusual for a court to make a shared residence order. However, if it could be demonstrated that on the particular facts of a case a shared order would benefit the child, such an option could be selected. The court acknowledged the force of the Department of Health's Guidance (Volume 1, paragraph 2.28) which states:

> a shared residence order has the advantage of being more realistic in those cases where the child is to spend considerable amounts of time with both parents, brings with it other benefits (including the right to remove the children from accommodation provided by a local authority under section 20), and removes any impression that one parent is good and responsible whereas the other parent is not.

Lady Justice Butler-Sloss said that it was not likely that a shared order would be made if there were concrete issues still arising between the parties which had not been resolved, such as the amount of contact, whether it should be staying or visiting contact or another issue such as education, which were 'muddying the waters' and which were creating difficulties between the parties which reflected the way in which the children were moving from one parent to the other in the contact period. 'If a child, on the other hand, has a settled home with one parent and substantial staying contact with the other parent, which has been settled, long-standing and working well, or if there are future plans for sharing the time of the children between two parents where all the parties agree and where there is no possibility of confusion in the mind of the child as to where the child will be and the circumstances of the child at any time, this may be, bearing in mind all the other circumstances, a possible basis for a shared residence order, if it can be demonstrated that there is a positive benefit to the child.' In *A v A* itself, the arrangements agreed between the parents meant that the children would be staying with their father in total for one-third of the year (including half of school holidays and half of school half-term breaks). This, in conjunction with the other circumstances, was said to justify the making of a shared residence order. Other judges, however, might simply have granted a residence order to the mother and a contact order to the father: there is a fine line between the two outcomes.

   In the later case of *Re H* (1995) Lord Justice Ward said that orders for shared residence 'may gradually win more grudging approval from the courts as the judges begin to acknowledge that such orders can reflect practical arrangements made by parents and their children which work well in putting into satisfactory practice that purpose promoted by the Act which emphasizes that parenting is a continuing and shared responsibility even after a separation'. He referred to the distinct psychological impact of a shared order as opposed to the conventional residence/contact package: 'here it was necessary for the boys to know they lived with the respondent and that they did not just visit him'.

The position of the non-caring parent

The Law Commission, in framing its recommendations on the private law, was very anxious to do what it could to lower the stakes in matrimonial cases – to get away from the 'winner takes all' approach which the existing custody legislation tended to generate. It wanted the law to emphasize instead the fact that parenthood continues even when marriage does not. The residence order is seen as playing a significant role here, because the Children Act is careful to make clear that the making of such an order will not destroy the parental responsibility which *both* parents possess. In principle, therefore, each party's rights and duties in relation to the child will be preserved.

A note of caution needs to be entered here, however. The Act also makes it clear (in section 2(8)) that the fact that a person has parental responsibility 'shall not entitle him to act in any way which would be incompatible with any order made with respect to the child'. So if a residence order is made in favour of, say, a wife, her husband will certainly retain his parental responsibility for the child, but he will have to make sure that in exercising it he does not interfere with the arrangements set out in the order, otherwise he will be in contempt of court. His power to remove the child will consequently be curtailed (unless, that is, the wife agrees to the removal, for a person who holds a residence order is quite free to arrange for someone else to care for the child). This does obviously mean that the scope for actually making use of parental responsibility in a case where the other parent has been granted a residence order may in practice be rather limited. Choice of school, for example, is a matter which largely goes hand in hand with residence.

Having said this, the legal position is not entirely one-sided. In the first place, one of the other section 8 orders (see below) may be made along with the residence order, which may well have the effect of enhancing the position of the non-caring parent. A similar result will often be achieved by attaching special conditions to the residence order under section 11(7). Secondly, the Children Act itself contains provisions (in section 13) designed to prevent unilateral action in relation to two specific matters: the changing of the child's surname and the removal of the child from the UK. Where a residence order is in force, nobody may take such action without either the written consent of every person who has parental responsibility or the leave of the court (which will aim to act in the child's best interests). These rules, which are modelled on parts of the previous legislation, have been deemed necessary in view of the particularly serious nature of the acts in question. There is an exception to the prohibition on removal from the UK, and that arises where the holder of the residence order takes the child abroad for less than one month, but this is subject to any special conditions (e.g. regarding notice to the other parent or the maximum number of journeys abroad that can be made) that the court may choose to impose.

Significant case law on the questions of change of name and emigration has emerged since implementation of the Act. The case of *Re B* (1995) must now be regarded as the leading authority on change of name. There, the parents had been living apart for nearly 10 years and the mother had remarried. Their three children, aged 16, 14 and 12, had had no direct contact with the father for five years because of their implacable opposition to it (fuelled, so it was alleged, by the mother's attitude towards him). All attempts by the father to resurrect his relationship with the children had ended in failure. The mother applied to the court for leave to change the children's surname to that of her second husband, arguing that the children themselves wished this to happen so that embarrassment at school and other places would no longer occur. The children told a court welfare officer that their father was 'of the past and not of the present'. The judge refused permission. He said:

> I do not think that to allow this change of name is in the children's best interests. Mr [B] is their father. He has maintained them since the separation, albeit with some breaks and some arrears. It seems to me that what would be in the children's interests would be if access were to be re-established with their father, and to allow this change of name would hamper that process, if not indeed make it totally impossible. And while it may be true that the children will in fact insist on being called [H], for me to allow this application would be to give the court's approval to a process which I do not believe is in their best interests.

The Court of Appeal agreed with the judge's approach. 'Save following adoption,' it stated, 'a father, while he lives, is always of the present.' It pointed out that refusing permission to the mother would not prevent the children asking other people to call them by their preferred surname: it merely prevented the mother from altering their names on official documents (e.g. school records). As for the argument concerning embarrassment, the court played down its significance: 'in these days of such frequent divorce and remarriage, of such frequent cohabitation outside marriage, and indeed increasingly of preservation of different surnames even within marriage, there is no opprobrium nowadays upon a child who carries a surname different from that of the adults in his home'. Not all judges have taken this view. In 1977, for example, a leading family law judge said that too much significance was being attached to surnames: 'it should not be beyond our capacity as adults to cope with the problem of dealing with children who naturally do not want to be picked out and distinguished by their friends and known by a surname other than their mother's . . . We are in danger of losing our sense of proportion'. In the 1990s the courts seem particularly keen to emphasize the importance of maintaining links between children and their absent fathers and the name of a child is seen as playing a part in this process. One can see the same sort of approach in the case law on parental responsibility orders in favour of unmarried fathers (see page 19 above).

As far as emigration is concerned, the Court of Appeal has confirmed (in *H v H* (1994)) that the Children Act has not altered the underlying factors which need to be taken into account by a court when deciding whether a parent should be given permission to remove a child from the country. The onus is on the residential parent to show that it is in the best interests of the child that leave is given, and in reaching its decision the court will be concerned particularly with the clarity and reasonableness of that parent's plans for the future and also the likely effect on the child of a refusal of permission. The reasonableness of the emigration plan is not the overriding factor, however. In the later case of *Harris v Pinnington* (1994), the High Court refused permission to the mother of a four-year-old boy who wished to emigrate to New Zealand. Although her plans were well thought out and not unreasonable, the judge took the view that they were outweighed by the child's need to maintain and develop a relationship with his (unmarried) father. The evidence suggested that the mother would make the necessary adjustment and sacrifice following the rejection of her application.

Contact orders

According to section 8(1) of the Children Act, a contact order means 'an order requiring the person with whom a child lives, or is to live, to allow the child to visit or stay with the person named in the order, or for that person and the child otherwise to have contact with each other'. It can be seen that this definition is framed in positive terms: the court is imposing on the child's carer (who may or may not hold a residence order) a positive duty to facilitate whatever contact is specified. The contact may involve face-to-face contact or less direct forms of contact such as the sending or exchange of letters and birthday cards. It may also involve overnight stays. The carer's obligation under the order is to *allow* the contact to take place. This means that the carer must not erect any obstacles. This is not the same thing as saying that the contact which is specified must occur. The Act does not permit the courts to force an absent parent to take advantage of a contact order; nor does it prevent the child from effectively thwarting contact arrangements by running away on each occasion or making a scene. Such problems are not really amenable to legal regulation.

Because the definition of a contact order was framed positively, it was at first widely (and reasonably) believed that the court could not use such an order to prohibit contact. This has, however, proved not to be the case. In the case of *Nottinghamshire County Council v P* (1993), the Court of Appeal stated that:

> the sensible and appropriate construction of the term 'contact order' includes a situation where a court is required to consider whether any contact should be provided for. An order that there shall be 'no contact' falls within the general concept of contact and common sense requires that it should be considered to fall within the definition of 'contact order' in section 8(1).

It is difficult to see how the court's decision in this case can be squared with the clear statutory language, but it has been consistently followed since 1993. An important rider was added, however, in the later case of *Re H* (1995). There, the Court of Appeal observed (surely correctly) that a contact order can only be directed at 'the person with whom a child lives, or is to live'. It follows that a 'no contact' order will prohibit the child's carer from allowing contact with another person. Should the court wish to impose a prohibition directly upon the other person (e.g. an absent parent) some other type of order will be needed. The prohibited steps order – considered below – is seen as the appropriate vehicle for this, although it is interesting to note that the head of the Law Commission's Children Act team has written that such an order was not originally designed for the purpose.

Supplementary conditions

Reference has already been made to the power of the court to attach specially crafted conditions to a residence order under section 11(7). This important power applies to all four section 8 orders and is consequently of relevance to contact disputes. The case of *Re O* (1995) provides an excellent example of its value. There, an unmarried father wished to maintain contact with his two-year-old son but the mother was implacably opposed to any form of contact (the courts' general approach to such opposition is considered below). Following unsuccessful attempts at establishing face-to-face contact, the county court judge made an order for indirect contact which contained the following conditions:

1 The mother to send the father photographs of the child every three months.

2 If and when the child commences nursery or playgroup the mother shall inform the father and send copies of all reports pertaining to the child's progress.
3 Should the child suffer any significant illness, the mother shall inform the father and supply copies of all medical reports.
4 The mother shall accept delivery of cards and presents for the child from the father via the public postal service or the court welfare service and upon acceptance of the same should read and show the child any such communication and deliver any such present to the child.
5 These arrangements were to last for six months, after which time they would be reviewed by the court.

On appeal, the Court of Appeal ruled that all of these conditions were within the powers of the court and were rightly imposed in the particular circumstances of this case. It stated that if the father proceeded to abuse his right of contact by, for example, deluging the child with presents or writing long and obsessive screeds, that right would be curtailed. Section 11(7), it was said, confers on the courts a wide and comprehensive power to make orders which will be effective to ensure contact between a child and an absent parent where this is felt to be in the child's interests.

Conduct during contact

If a contact order is made in favour of a parent, he will be able to exercise parental powers during the period of contact. Care will have to be taken, however, not to go too far because he will be subject to the rule that a person with parental responsibility may not act in any way which would be incompatible with any court order. So if special conditions have been attached to the order, or if a residence order has been made in favour of the other parent, he will have to ensure that he conducts himself consistently with them. The Law Commission illustrated the point in this way:

> If the child has to live with one parent and go to a school near home, it would be incompatible with that order for the other parent to arrange for him to have his hair done in a way which will exclude him from the school. It would not, however, be incompatible for that parent to take him to a particular sporting occasion over the weekend, no matter how much the parent with whom the child lived might disapprove.

The general approach to contact

The attitude of the superior courts to contact order applications made by parents has been consistently positive over the last 30 years and it is there-

fore surprising that they have felt it necessary to reiterate the principles on
so many occasions. The case of *Re O* (1995), cited earlier, is one of the most
recent examples. The Court of Appeal described the following as 'fundamental principles':

1 The welfare of the child is the court's paramount consideration (section
   1(1) of the Children Act). The court is concerned with the interests of the
   mother and the father only insofar as they bear on the child's welfare.
2 Where parents of a child are separated and the child is in the day-to-day
   care of one of them, it is almost always in the interests of the child that he
   should have contact with the other parent. ('The reason for this scarcely
   needs spelling out. It is, of course, that the separation of parents involves
   a loss to the child, and it is desirable that that loss should so far as possible
   be made good by contact with the [absent] parent.')
3 The court has power to enforce orders for contact, which it should not
   hesitate to exercise where it judges that it will overall promote the welfare of the child to do so.
4 Cases do occasionally arise in which a court is compelled to conclude that
   in existing circumstances an order for immediate direct contact should
   not be ordered because so to order would injure the welfare of the child.
   (However, 'the courts should not at all readily accept that the child's
   welfare will be injured by direct contact. Judging that question the court
   should take a medium-term and long-term view of the child's development and not accord excessive weight to what appear likely to be short-
   term or transient problems. Neither parent should be encouraged or
   permitted to think that the more intransigent, the more unreasonable, the
   more obdurate and the more uncooperative they are, the more likely they
   are to get their own way'.)
5 In cases in which, for whatever reason, direct contact cannot for the time
   being be ordered, it is ordinarily highly desirable that there should be
   indirect contact so that the child grows up knowing of the love and
   interest of the absent parent with whom, in due course, direct contact
   should be established.

The issue of enforcement of contact orders, with which the third principle is
concerned, continues to be problematic. As the Court of Appeal noted in
Re O, it is possible for a court to seek obedience to a contact order by
removing the child from the residential parent altogether. It is also possible
to send that parent to prison for contempt, and some judges have done this.
The utility of such sanctions, however, is highly questionable. In its Annual
Report 1994/1995, the Children Act Advisory Committee expressed the
view that 'penal enforcement of contact orders is unlikely to be in the
interests of the child and should not be encouraged as a punitive approach
to non-compliance'.

Supervision of contact

Should the court consider that direct contact with the absent parent ought to be supervised, it can devise a direction to this effect under section 11(7). The exception is where the supervisor is to be a local authority worker. Here, the courts have stated that the wording and structure of the Act require a family assistance order to be used (these orders are considered below at page 40). The case of *Re DH* (1994) shows that if a contact order is made in proceedings brought by a local authority for a care order or supervision order, supervision of contact by the authority can also be achieved by the making of a supervision order. Such an arrangement would be highly unusual, however (in *Re DH*, the parent to whom contact was granted was suffering from Munchausen Syndrome by Proxy and had already tried to suffocate the child).

Prohibited steps orders

According to section 8(1) of the Act, a prohibited steps order (PSO) means 'an order that no step which could be taken by a parent in meeting his parental responsibility for a child, and which is of a kind specified in the order, shall be taken by any person without the consent of the court'. Whereas residence orders and contact orders, by their very titles, indicate which aspect of a child's upbringing is being regulated, the title 'prohibited steps order' serves only to indicate that something is being forbidden. The order was designed by the Law Commission to enable the court to assume a measure of control over a specified element of parental responsibility, the control to be exercised through the imposition of a qualified ban ('you may only do this type of act with our agreement'). This idea of continuing court control was borrowed from the law of wardship: under that jurisdiction, where a child is made a ward of court, no important step in the child's life may be taken without the agreement of the High Court (see Chapter 14 below). With a PSO, the 'step' in question is specified by the court at the outset – in contrast to wardship – and the court making the order can be the magistrates' court or the county court, as well as the High Court.

In its report, the Law Commission expressed the view that PSOs would be 'few and far between'. In fact, the courts have been making some 6000 such orders every year. The reason for this remarkable development almost certainly lies in the interpretation which was commonly given to the wording of section 8(1) when the Act was passed. According to the statutory definition, a PSO has the effect of imposing a ban on 'any person'. Given the Law Commission's desire to base the order on the important steps rule in wardship, it is almost certain that the draftsman of the Act intended the ban, if imposed, to extend to the whole world. Instead, and crucially, the words have been construed so as to enable the court to target the ban at a named individual (including a parent). Such an interpretation opens up at a stroke a much wider range of possibilities and has been seized upon with alacrity by judges and practitioners alike, with the result that the PSO has been transformed into a very useful and commonly used device for regulating the behaviour of a single person.

The prohibition imposed by a PSO must be spelt out by the court and it must relate to some aspect of parental responsibility. It cannot, however, be used to achieve a result which could be achieved by a residence order or contact order (section 9(5)). Reported cases reveal the following examples of use:

- prohibiting the removal of the child from the UK
- prohibiting the absent parent from contacting the child, either at home or at school
- prohibiting the residential parent from arranging for the child to feature in a TV programme.

One thing which *cannot* be done by way of a PSO is excluding a parent from the family home (*D v D* (1996)). This has to be done through the Family Law Act 1996.

Specific issue orders

Section 8(1) of the Act states that a specific issue order (SIO) means 'an order giving directions for the purpose of determining a specific question which has arisen, or which may arise, in connection with any aspect of parental responsibility for a child'. This order is similar to the PSO in so far as it may be used in relation to a wide range of matters falling within the concept of parental responsibility. The difference is that a PSO will always be framed in negative terms whereas under an SIO the court will give 'directions', which may be either positive or negative. In addition, an SIO will not necessarily require a referral back of the disputed issue to the court. As with PSOs, an SIO cannot be used so as to achieve a result which could be achieved by a residence order or a contact order (section 9(5)).

The number of SIOs made by the courts each year is about 2000. Two reported cases demonstrate the order's versatility. In *Re D* (1992) a father obtained an SIO directing his child's mother to bring the child back from Turkey forthwith. The court accepted the argument that such an order would prove useful to the father in legal proceedings for child abduction in the Turkish courts. In *Re F* (1994) an unmarried father obtained an SIO authorizing his solicitor to interview his children. The father faced a charge of assault against the mother and the children were thought to have witnessed the incident in question. The mother, who held sole parental responsibility, had refused to consent to an interview and so the father felt obliged to seek a court order.

The criterion for section 8 orders

The welfare principle

Previous sections of this chapter have described the range of private orders which the Children Act enables the court to make. On what basis ought the court to act when the question of making an order arises? On this, the Act makes no great change in the law, for its opening provision (section 1(1)) reads:

> When a court determines any question with respect to the upbringing of a child, the child's welfare shall be the court's paramount consideration.

This welfare principle has been a feature of our private law legislation since 1925 and, in spite of the criticisms levelled at it – too vague, unpredictable and value-laden in its application, productive of inconsistencies – it has proved to be the best available criterion in the sorts of cases at which it is aimed. It has therefore been retained. In the old legislation the principle was to be found in section 1 of the Guardianship of Minors Act 1971, where the words 'first and paramount consideration' were used. As can be seen, the word 'first' has been dropped from the statutory formula. This has been done on the grounds that, first, it is superfluous, and second, it could lead the reader to believe that considerations other than the child's welfare (e.g. doing 'justice' to one parent) are of equal weight in the decision-making process.

The welfare checklist

The Children Act goes on to supplement the welfare principle with four further provisions. The first – section 1(3) – contains a checklist of factors for the court to bear in mind in any disputed case. These are as follows:

(a) the ascertainable wishes and feelings of the child concerned (considered in the light of his age and understanding)
(b) his physical, emotional and educational needs
(c) the likely effect on him of any change in his circumstances
(d) his age, sex, background and any characteristics of his which the court considers relevant
(e) any harm which he has suffered or is at risk of suffering

(f) how capable each of his parents, and any other person in relation to whom the court considers the question to be relevant, is of meeting his needs

(g) the range of powers available to the court under the Act in the proceedings in question.

The welfare checklist is not particularly novel in substance because its contents reflect long-standing good practice in the courts. Very experienced judges and practitioners are unlikely to need reminding of the significance of the factors which are mentioned. For others, however, it is a valuable tool for decision-making, report-writing and case-preparation, which is no doubt why it has been generally well received. In *B v B* (1994) it was said that the checklist 'is there to remind the judge of important pointers, and in a finely balanced case a judge may well be prudent to use it as a compass to steer him towards a conclusion', while in *H v H* (1994) the Court of Appeal noted that the Act does not have to be applied in a mechanical way:

> one should remember that when one calls it a checklist, that is not like the list of checks which an airline pilot has to make with his co-pilot, aloud one to the other before he takes off. The statute does not say that the judge has to read out the seven items in section 1(3) and pronounce his conclusion on each. Sometimes judges will do that, maybe more often than not; but it is not mandatory.

Case law on some of the items in the checklist has developed since 1991. As far as paragraph (a) is concerned – the wishes and feelings of the child – while its position at the beginning should not be taken as signifying greater importance than the other items, it is no accident that it has been placed first. It is a telling symbol of the law's increasing acknowledgment of the child's right to state a point of view. It also conveys a supremely practical point, namely that orders in respect of older children will often only 'work' if the children are prepared to co-operate. Thus in the case of *Re F* (1993) a transsexual father of two boys aged 9 and 12 was refused contact orders, not because of his unsuitability but because of the boys' firmly expressed view that they did not wish to see him. Having taken the unusual step of talking to the children directly in his office, the trial judge could find nothing as consistent and compelling as the children's own wishes and feelings. He felt unable to make orders which could only be implemented by coercion: 'if anything good is to come out of all this as between the father and the boys it must come naturally in the course of time as they get older and more knowledgeable'. Where issues of residence or contact are not at stake, the views of the older child may be more easily overridden. In *Re B* (1995) the Court of Appeal acknowledged that 'orders nowadays which run flatly counter to the wishes of normal children aged 16, 14 and 12 are virtually unknown to family law'. This, however, did not stop the court prohibiting a mother from changing the surname of her children of those ages who had requested such a change (see page 28 above). The wider interests of the children were said to require this link with their father to be preserved.

Paragraph (e) of the checklist refers to past and future harm. 'Harm' is an expression which is defined elsewhere in the Act, in section 31(9). It means ill-treatment or the impairment of health or development (these terms are also explained in section 31 – see page 156 below). Whether or not harm has occurred is a question of fact for the court to decide on the balance of probabilities. Future harm is quite different and in this context depends on an assessment of risk by the court. Whether rightly or wrongly, the Court of Appeal in the case of *Re M and R* (1996) has decided that the approach to the 'risk of suffering harm' element of the checklist should be the same as the approach to the 'likely to suffer significant harm' element of the threshold criteria for care and supervision orders. This approach is more fully considered in Chapter 10 of this book (see page 158) but for present purposes the consequence is that the risk of future harm may only be extracted from proven facts, not mere suspicions. So, for example, it may be argued by one parent that there is a risk of the child suffering sexual abuse at the hands of the other parent. If, however, the risk of future abuse is said to stem from past abuse and the court concludes that there is insufficient evidence to prove past abuse, then it is not permitted to conclude that there is a risk of future harm for the purposes of the checklist, even though it feels that the abuse may have occurred ('the fact that there might have been harm in the past does not establish the risk of harm in the future'). It will be different if there are other facts in existence which point towards a real possibility of harm in the future. While many important factors are contained in the checklist, no indication is given of how much weight should be attached to each one in the inevitable balancing exercise which the court is required to conduct. This gives the court maximum freedom to focus on the particular facts and circumstances of each case and consider how they bear on the child's welfare. In practice, however, it is quite clear that judges do approach parental disputes with certain preconceived notions of what is good and what is not good for children, and these can play a significant role in many cases. Mention has already been made, for example, of the very positive attitude towards ongoing parental contact. Other discernible trends and presumptions include the following:

- 'Continuity of care is one of the most important single factors in deciding what is in the best interests of young children.' (*S v S* (1977)) Judges are hesitant about disturbing the status quo.
- 'There is a rebuttable presumption of fact that the best interests of a baby are served by being with its mother.' (*Re W* (1992))
- 'Nature has endowed men and women with very different attributes and

it so happens that mothers are generally better fitted than fathers to provide for the needs of very young children . . . It is neither a presumption nor a principle but rather recognition of a widely-held belief based on practical experience and the workings of nature.' (*Brixley v Lynas* (1996))

The courts have been careful to emphasize that the overriding principle is the one contained in section 1(1) of the Act. The general statements set out above are not binding rules of law and whatever preference is indicated by them is liable to be outweighed by other factors in a case. It may be, however, that the 'other factors' will need to be particularly powerful for this to happen, especially in situations where several of the preferences coincide. Thus in *Brixley v Lynas* it was said that 'where a very young child has been with its mother since birth and there is no criticism of her ability to care for the child only the strongest competing advantages are likely to prevail'.

To comply with its duty to have regard to all the matters contained in the checklist and to any other circumstances relevant to the child's welfare, the court will obviously require a considerable amount of information. Much of this will come via social workers' reports, a matter discussed in Chapter 13 of this book.

The presumption of no order

The second supplementary welfare provision – section 1(5) – is also important. It reads:

> Where a court is considering whether or not to make one or more orders under this Act with respect to a child, it shall not make the order or any of the orders unless it considers that doing so would be better for the child than making no order at all.

The wording of this subsection makes it clear that it covers all orders under the Act, i.e. public law ones as well as private; consequently, it will become relevant in the discussion of care orders etc. later on. For the moment, however, we need to consider its significance in the context of parents' cases.

Where estranged parents are in serious dispute about some aspect of their child's upbringing and an application to resolve the matter is made to the court, then an order of some sort will probably be needed. It will have a positive function. Where estranged parents are involved in legal proceedings for divorce or maintenance, but there is no dispute regarding their child's upbringing, should any children's order be made? This is the issue addressed by section 1(5). Research carried out for the Law Commission revealed that many lawyers representing wives in matrimonial proceedings would tag an application for custody onto the claim, even if there was no likelihood of a dispute over the children arising: 'a custody order is "part of the package" for the client and will be requested from the court as a matter of course'. It is clear that many judges and magistrates were sucked into this mechanical approach as well.

If no section 8 order is made on, say, a divorce, then quite obviously the existing legal position with regard to the parents' powers and duties will continue, so that they will each retain the independent power to act. In many cases, there is absolutely no reason why this should not be so. It goes without saying that children's orders can have beneficial effects even in the absence of a dispute – the reinforcement of a new family unit, for example – but they also contain a significant potential to be used as psychological weapons or viewed as the winner's prize, thereby reducing the prospects of co-operation between the parents in the future. The inclusion of section 1(5) is therefore an important reminder that court orders should not be regarded as in any way routine but should be made only where they are likely to bring about real benefits for the child concerned.

The other supplementary provisions, concerning delays, are discussed in the next section.

Countering delays in legal proceedings

The problems associated with delays in children's cases are too obvious to need rehearsing here. Since the implementation of the Children Act concern about this matter has become acute, especially on the public law front, with the result that delay emerged as the main focus of work for the Children Act Advisory Committee (see page 170 below). Section 1(2) of the Act contains a provision of general application. It requires the court to have regard to the principle that any delay in determining a question with respect to the upbringing of a child is likely to prejudice his welfare. This is a reminder both for the courts and for practitioners to give priority to children's cases wherever possible.

In private law cases section 1(2) is supplemented by section 11, which requires the court to draw up a timetable 'with a view to determining the question without delay'. Directions may be given to the parties so as to ensure that the timetable is adhered to. In *B v B* (1994) residence order applications had been allowed to drag on for several years during which time the parents lived 'at daggers drawn' in the matrimonial home. The Court of Appeal stated firmly that both practitioners and the courts have a duty to avoid delay in children's cases. The courts, it was said, should be proactive through the use of directions appointments in ensuring that applications once launched are not allowed to moulder.

Whilst delays in family litigation can be damaging to all the adults and children involved, it is a well known fact that the spinning-out of a case can be, and is, used as a weapon in itself, especially by a party who currently has care of the child and who is aware of the reluctance of the courts to disturb established arrangements. What can be done to prevent such manoeuvres? This is a difficult question. If the court has set a timetable which one party has for no good reason disregarded, sanctions by way of orders for costs can be imposed. It is also possible for the court to refuse to hear evidence which has been filed too late, but this may well result in the court having to reach a conclusion with an incomplete picture of the family's situation, an exercise hardly calculated to promote the child's welfare. As in other areas of family law, injustice suffered by a parent is liable to be outweighed by the best interests of the child.

Family assistance orders

Section 16 of the Children Act introduced another new type of order: the family assistance order (FAO). Such an order can be made in any family proceedings, whether or not any other type of order is made. A large proportion of them are made in divorce proceedings.

The former position was that in divorce, maintenance, custody and adoption cases the court could, in exceptional circumstances, make an order that the child 'be under the supervision' of a probation officer or a local authority. These matrimonial supervision orders, as they were often called, were quite distinct from supervision orders made by the juvenile court in care proceedings under the Children and Young Persons Act 1969, but of course they shared the same name, and experience showed that there were considerable confusion and variation regarding their making, implementation and general significance. The opportunity was therefore taken of revising both the wording and the substance of the rules.

The main features of section 16 are as follows:

• The family assistance order will impose a duty on the probation service or the local authority to make an officer available to advise, assist and (where appropriate) befriend any person named in the order.
• The persons who can be named in the order are the child, his parents or guardian and any other person who is caring for him or who holds a contact order with respect to him.
• The order may only be made in exceptional circumstances.
• The consent of every person named in the order (other than the child) must be obtained.
• Any person named in the order can be required to keep the assisting officer informed of relevant addresses so as to facilitate visits.
• The order is to last for no more than six months.

- The assisting officer may return to court at any time and ask it to consider varying or discharging any section 8 order it has made.

It will be apparent that the FAO provisions are aimed at situations where it is felt that short-term social work support will be welcomed by the parties and will be beneficial for the child concerned. It is a voluntary procedure and is certainly not to be looked upon as part of the machinery of compulsory State intervention – that is governed by the completely separate set of provisions in the Act relating to care orders, supervision orders, emergency protection orders, etc. If, in a divorce or other family case, it is thought that the child is at risk, then those other provisions may be activated, assuming of course that the relevant statutory grounds can be made out.

As with old-style matrimonial supervision orders, these assistance orders have a part to play in a wide variety of circumstances – for example, facilitating contact arrangements, enabling advice and support to be given to a new family unit, providing mediation between the parties – but of course the Act continues to require those circumstances to be 'exceptional'. This criterion is vulnerable to criticism on account of its vagueness, but its retention was advocated by the Law Commission on the grounds that it 'may be at least partially effective in concentrating resources where they are most needed'. The resources in question will be those of either the probation service or the local authority: which agency is selected will depend on the circumstances of the case and on any local arrangements which have been established. In many cases, the social worker providing the welfare report for the court will be appointed as advisor.

Two practice statements on FAOs have been issued by the Government since 1989. The first is contained in the Department of Health's *Children Act Guidance* of 1991 (Volume 1, paragraphs 2.50–2.53). This states that 'it will be particularly important for the court to make plain at the outset why family assistance is needed and what it is hoped to achieve by it'. The second statement is contained in Chapter 5 of the *National Standards for Probation Service Family Court Welfare Work*, published by the Home Office in 1995. These standards cover such matters as making initial contact with the family members, providing written information to them, fixing a timetable of meetings and reviewing the operation of the order. They state (paragraph 5.13) that if the family ceases to co-operate with the social worker further directions should be sought from the court, but since the entire FAO structure is built upon voluntariness, it is difficult to discern a meaningful role for the court in such a situation.

Family assistance orders have the effect of placing increased burdens on public agencies and these inevitably raise difficult issues of resource allocation. *Re C* (1995) is a case in point. There, a High Court judge made an FAO after a residence order dispute but the designated local authority returned to court with the response that it did not have the resources to put the order into effect. The judge conceded that there was nothing he could do to rectify the situation. In theory, penal sanctions could have been imposed on the authority but these were regarded as unrealistic. This is one of a number of reported cases in which the courts have struggled to maintain a balance between promoting the welfare of the child and preserving the financial autonomy of the local authority (for further examples, see the cases on assessments under interim care orders noted at page 204 below).

Section 8 orders and divorce

The fact that the parents of a child get divorced does not in itself indicate a need for the court to make orders in respect of the child and the presumption of no order contained in section 1(5) of the Children Act reflects this (see page 38 above). At the same time, however, it has been accepted by successive governments that a formal application by a parent for a divorce can be a critical event in the life of a child such as to require at least some degree of official scrutiny of the proposed arrangements for his future care. The Children Act maintained the role of the divorce court in relation to children but altered the procedure. Under a revised section 41 of the Matrimonial Causes Act 1973, the court is obliged to consider (a) whether there are any children of the family to whom the section applies (this refers mainly to children under 16) and (b) whether it should exercise any of its powers under the Children Act with respect to any of them. The Family Proceedings Rules 1991 provide for divorce petitions to be accompanied by a Statement of Arrangements for Children, in which the petitioning parent gives details of all relevant children, their circumstances and any proposals for change. This statement is served on the respondent spouse, who is given the opportunity to submit a written reply. The Statement of Arrangements, together with any response to it, is considered by the district judge before the granting of a divorce decree. If necessary, the judge can direct that further evidence be filed, that a welfare report be prepared or that the parties attend the court for an examination of the circumstances and issues. Section 8 orders can, of course, also be made. The granting of a decree absolute of divorce can be held up by the court pending the resolution of children's matters, but only where specified conditions (including one concerning 'exceptional circumstances') are satisfied.

All this will change when the new divorce provisions of the Family Law Act 1996 are brought into force (probably during 1999). Although the detailed procedural rules have yet to be made, the principal elements of the future regime are clear enough:

• New terminology will be introduced. Spouses will file a 'statement of marital breakdown' rather than a divorce petition. The court will make a 'divorce order' rather than a decree of divorce.

- A divorce order can normally be made by the court only when the statutory requirements about the parties' arrangements for the future are satisfied. These include the arrangements for the children (section 9 of the 1996 Act).
- When there is a child of the family under 16 at the time of the commencement of divorce proceedings, the general rule is that there is an extended period of 15 months which must elapse before an application for a divorce order can be made (section 7(11)). This so-called period for reflection and consideration is reduced to 9 months if there is an occupation order or a non-molestation order in force in favour of the applicant or a child of the family, or if the court is satisfied that delaying the divorce would be significantly detrimental to the welfare of any child of the family (section 7(12)).
- Mediation facilities will be more widely available to enable the parties to reach agreement about their children.
- The court must consider (a) whether there are any children of the family under 16 (or children over 16 whose position needs to be looked at) and (b) where there are any such children, whether it should exercise any of its powers under the Children Act with respect to any of them (section 11(1)).
- Where it appears to the court that (a) the circumstances of the case require it, or are likely to require it, to exercise Children Act powers and (b) it is not in a position to exercise those powers without giving further consideration to the case and (c) there are exceptional circumstances which make it desirable in the interests of the child, then the court may direct that the divorce order is not to be made until it orders otherwise (section 11(2)). In deciding whether condition (a) is met, the court must treat the welfare of the child as paramount (section 11(3)) and must have 'particular regard, on the evidence before it' to the following:
  1 The wishes and feelings of the child considered in the light of his age and understanding and the circumstances in which those wishes were expressed.
  2 The conduct of the parties in relation to the upbringing of the child.
  3 The general principle that, in the absence of evidence to the contrary, the welfare of the child will be best served by his having regular contact with those who have parental responsibility for him and with other members of his family, and by the maintenance of as good a continuing relationship with his parents as is possible.
  4 Any risk to the child attributable to the proposed arrangements for his care and upbringing (including risks attributable to the home of the proposed carer and his or her partner).
  It is important to note that while the provisions of section 11 of the 1996 Act seek to guide the divorce court in part of its decision-making in relation to children, they do not displace the provisions of section 1 of the

Children Act, including the welfare checklist. It remains to be seen how the judges react to having two sets of principles – which say different things – to apply during divorce proceedings but it is certainly a bizarre arrangement, reflecting as it does the chaos that engulfed much of the Parliamentary passage of the Family Law Bill.

- The court should have regard at all times to the following general principles:
  1 The institution of marriage is to be supported.
  2 The parties to a marriage which may have broken down are to be encouraged to take all practicable steps to save it.
  3 A marriage which has irretrievably broken down and is being brought to an end should be brought to an end with minimum distress to the parties and to the children affected, and with questions dealt with in a manner designed to promote as good a continuing relationship between the parties and the children as is possible in the circumstances.
  4 Any risk to one of the parties and to any children of violence from the other party should, so far as reasonably practicable, be removed or diminished.
- The children's arrangements presented to the court are not, of course, set in concrete. The parents will be at liberty to make further applications for section 8 orders as well as applications to vary or discharge existing orders. (There is a facility under section 91(14) of the Children Act whereby the courts can regulate further proceedings but this is used very sparingly – see page 47 below.)

Unmarried fathers and section 8 orders

It was seen in the last chapter how the Children Act preserves the old principle that the parental rights and duties in respect of a child born outside marriage vest initially in the mother alone. It was also seen how the Act enables the father to acquire parental responsibility through an application to the court or through an agreement made with the mother. Whether or not such acquisition has taken place, the four types of section 8 order described in this chapter can all be sought by the unmarried father against the mother. If any such order is made, her powers will be restricted accordingly, for she will be unable to act in any way which is incompatible with it. In this connection, it is worth noting that should the father succeed in obtaining a residence order from the court, and he has not previously acquired parental responsibility, the Act (section 12) requires the court to make in addition an order giving that responsibility to him. This will enable him to exercise the full range of 'rights' recognized by law. The Law Commission felt that it would be wrong to deny these to a father who was going to have the child living with him. However, even if this does take place, the court may decide to attach conditions to the residence order and/or make another section 8 order in favour of the mother.

Applying for section 8 orders

The Children Act allows applications for section 8 orders to be made to the magistrates' court, the county court or the Family Division of the High Court (this 'concurrent jurisdiction' is discussed in Chapter 12). The choice of court essentially belongs to the applicant, although if he or she is depending on legal aid, the Legal Aid Board could well influence the decision. Furthermore, if an application is being made in the course of divorce proceedings it will be submitted to the divorce court. Whichever type of court is selected, however, the procedure to be followed will be regulated primarily not by the Act itself, but by the rules of court made under it in 1991. The two sets of rules which have been made (one for the magistrates' court, the other for the county court and High Court) are for the most part identical and lay down a procedure whose principal characteristics are as follows:

- The application is to be made using the officially prescribed form. The form is designed partly to elicit basic information about the child and his family and partly to enable the applicant to say what sort of section 8 order is desired and why it is desired.
- The form is filed with the court, together with sufficient copies for one to be served on each of the other parties. The range of parties is specified in a schedule to the rules (in the case of a dispute involving married parents alone, only they will be parties). In certain circumstances, e.g. where the child is currently being accommodated by a local authority, others will need to be told about the application. They can then apply to become full parties if they think this is appropriate.
- On receipt of the application form, the court will fix a date either for the hearing of the application or for a preliminary hearing (referred to in the rules as a 'directions appointment') at which preparations for the full hearing can be made. As indicated previously, the court should be aiming to curb unnecessary delay at all times and the directions appointment plays a critical role in this strategy. The Children Act Advisory Committee took a special interest in this matter and in its Annual Report 1993/4 it published a Best Practice Form of Directions which it recommended to all levels of court (Annex 2 to Chapter 2). As the Committee stated, however, 'the suggestions will not be employed to best advantage unless the person giving the directions, whether justices' clerk, magistrate, district judge, circuit or High Court judge, is prepared to adopt an interventionist role'.
- The rules permit the application to be made on an '*ex parte*' basis, i.e.

without notice to anybody else. Such a course is regarded as exceptional (especially where the order sought is a residence order) and where it is followed the rules require the applicant to serve a copy of both the application and the order on the other parties within 48 hours of the order being made. In most cases the court will arrange for a full '*inter partes*' hearing at an early date.

• Within 14 days of being served with the application, the respondents are required to file an answer to the application. This enables them to inform the court (and the applicant) whether or not they consent to the application.

Interim section 8 orders

Strictly speaking, there is no such thing as an interim section 8 order. Whereas the Children Act specifically provides for interim care orders and interim supervision orders, there is no mention of an interim residence order or an interim contact order. The reason for this is simple: since section 8 orders can be varied or discharged at the court's discretion, they are all 'interim' in the sense that they are effective until the court says otherwise. If the court wishes to place a time limit on an order (e.g. so as to protect the child's interests pending a full hearing) it can do this by attaching a suitably worded condition under section 11(7) of the Act. It can also arrange for the case to be reviewed upon the expiration of a stipulated time. In this way, the court can seek to monitor particular aspects of the child's upbringing (e.g. contact) at whatever intervals are deemed appropriate. As with so many private law situations, however, the court's ability to impose control will be partly dependent on the willingness of the family to co-operate.

Other aspects of section 8 orders

There are a number of other provisions in the Children Act which are relevant to the theme of this chapter and which deserve a mention. They are listed below.

• A section 8 order cannot be made with respect to a child who has reached the age of 16 unless the circumstances are exceptional (section 9(7)). This rule is a further illustration of the increasing recognition being given to the autonomy of the older child.

• A section 8 order will cease to have effect when the child reaches the age of 16 unless the court orders otherwise (section 91(10)).

• All section 8 orders may be varied or discharged by the court (section 8(2)).

• Residence orders and contact orders made in favour of one parent will automatically come to an end if the parents live together for more than six months (section 11(5) and (6)). For the orders to continue in these circumstances would be unrealistic.

- Section 8 orders are automatically discharged if a care order is made in respect of the child (section 91(2)).
- On disposing of a section 8 order application, the court may order that no further applications are to be made except with its permission (section 91(14)). The thinking behind this provision is revealed in the Law Commission's 1988 Report: 'we have in mind the sort of case where, after a fully argued hearing, a parent is denied contact, or granted only carefully defined contact, with the child but seeks a further order shortly afterwards. Vindictive or obsessive harassment of this kind is regrettably not unknown and it can seriously undermine the security and happiness of the child's home'. In *Re T* (1992) the Court of Appeal had an early opportunity to consider this mechanism. It emphasized that the power under section 91(14) should be used sparingly but it proceeded to uphold an order that there should be no application by the father for a section 8 order for three years. There had been 21, mostly unsuccessful, previous applications concerning parental responsibility, contact and change of name and the court was of the opinion that the father, with a history of violence and intimidation, would have nothing to offer the child in the immediate foreseeable future. The welfare of the child (who was two) required that her mother should have a period free from anxiety so that she could bring her up without the constant fear that there would be another application by the father. In the later case of *Re F* (1995) a direction under section 91(14) was described as 'a Draconian sanction of last resort, principally appropriate when there is a real fear that children may become distressed or have their stability disturbed through the vexatious, ill-judged or obsessive pursuit by a party of the litigious process'.
- No section 8 order, other than a residence order, may be made in respect of a child who is the subject of a care order (section 9(1)). This matter is discussed in Chapter 10, but it may be noted here that parents who wish to obtain a court order concerning contact with their child in care can use the procedure laid down in Part IV of the Act.
- Although the legislation concerning custody orders was repealed by the Children Act, the provisions of the Child Abduction Act 1984 and the Family Law Act 1986 were retained. The 1984 Act imposes criminal liability for certain abductions, while the 1986 Act contains provisions relating to the enforcement of orders (for example, it gives the court power to order a person to disclose the child's whereabouts). The 1989 Act amended these two earlier Acts so that they now refer to the new types of court order.

4

Court orders in favour of non-parents

The scope of the present chapter

The last chapter was concerned with children's cases brought by, and only involving, birth parents. This chapter aims to cover other private law applications. In view of their diversity, it may be useful to summarize at the outset the main types of situation falling under this heading and the way in which the old law made provision for them.

1. Applications by step-parents

A step-parent was able to apply for custody or access if he or she was involved in divorce proceedings (under the Matrimonial Causes Act 1973) or in maintenance proceedings (under the Domestic Proceedings and Magistrates' Courts Act 1978), provided the child concerned was a 'child of the family', i.e. had been treated by husband and wife as a child of their family. Step-parents could also, in some circumstances, apply for custodianship under the Children Act 1975, or for custody under the Matrimonial Causes Act where they had married a divorced birth parent. Obtaining a custodianship or custody order provided legal recognition of their position as carer of the child.

2. Applications by relatives

The only relatives singled out by the old private law legislation were grandparents. Provisions dating from 1978 enabled the court to make an access order in favour of a grandparent in a number of family proceedings. Apart from this, relatives generally were able to apply (subject to certain conditions) for a custodianship order. It was also possible for relatives to apply for custody in the context of a divorce case.

3. Applications by foster carers

In certain circumstances, foster carers were able to apply for custodianship.

In addition to these statutory procedures, it was open to a step-parent, relative or foster carer (or, for that matter, any interested person) to institute wardship proceedings in the High Court with a view to obtaining an order relating to the upbringing of the child. Nor should it be forgotten that in appropriate cases the adoption jurisdiction was available for use as well, and that the legislation enabled the court to refuse an adoption order but grant custodianship instead.

The creation of this network of provisions was undoubtedly well intentioned. As with the law relating to parental applications, however, it was not simple or clear nor consistent. This was true even of the custodianship rules, which only came into operation in 1985 and were supposedly tailor-made for non-parents. The Children Act enabled a fresh start to be made.

Section 8 orders in favour of non-parents

We saw in the last chapter how Part II of the Children Act was designed to improve the private law by introducing four new types of court order: residence orders, contact orders, prohibited steps orders and specific issue orders. The important point for the purposes of this chapter is that these orders are generally speaking available to non-parents as well as parents, and available in cases specially brought for the purpose or in cases where some other family issue is at stake (e.g. divorce). They have superseded the old orders for access, custody and custodianship. Wardship and adoption remain available but the need to resort to wardship has diminished after the creation of the new orders (this matter is explored in Chapter 14).

The nature of these four orders has already been described and it is not proposed to repeat the descriptions here. Suffice it to say that their availability, coupled with the fact that specially crafted conditions can be attached to them by the court, means that a position of great flexibility is achieved. The effect of the court's order is also clearer than it was under the old arrangements. Here are some examples of what can be done under the 1989 Act:

- The court makes a residence order in favour of a foster carer. This will enable the foster carer to keep the child, even if the birth parents and the local authority object.
- The court makes a contact order in favour of the child's aunt and uncle. The person caring for the child will have to permit the child to visit, and perhaps stay with, these relatives.

- The court makes a prohibited steps order in favour of the child's grand-parent: the order prohibits the child's parents from removing the child from his present school without the court's consent.
- The child's parents have arranged for him to undergo an operation: relatives obtain a specific issue order preventing the operation going ahead.

Needless to say, all applications for a section 8 order are subject to the principle that the child's welfare is the paramount consideration (section 1(1) of the Act). The wishes and feelings of the child, and all the other matters referred to in the statutory checklist (in section 1(3)) have to be taken into account, at any rate if the case is contested. Also applicable is the rule under which the court is not to make an order unless it considers that doing so would be better for the child than making no order at all (section 1(5)).

Special rules for non-parents' applications

Court applications by non-parents, especially relatives and 'strangers', tend to contain special features and consequently throw up special problems. The risk of the application being an unwarranted intrusion into the child's life is one which obviously springs to mind. The Children Act contains provisions designed to impose a proper balance between the various interests which can exist in these cases.

The need to obtain leave

First of all, non-parents as a rule have to obtain leave from the court to make an application for a section 8 order (section 10(2)(b)). This, clearly, is directed at the intrusion point. The argument is that without some sort of preliminary procedural hurdle, the way would be open for the bringing of all sorts of unnecessary and unmeritorious legal proceedings, the effect of which could be extremely damaging for the child concerned. This is, in fact, brought out fairly explicitly in the Children Act, for it states (in section 10(9)) that in deciding whether or not to grant leave, the court shall have particular regard to the following:

(a) the nature of the proposed application
(b) the applicant's connection with the child
(c) any risk there might be of the application disrupting the child's life to such an extent that he would be harmed by it
(d) where the child is being looked after by a local authority, the authority's plans for the child's future and the wishes and feelings of the child's parents.

This provision was first judicially considered in the case of *JR v Merton London Borough Council* (1992). The Court of Appeal decided that section 1(1) of the 1989 Act – containing the welfare principle – does not apply when an application for leave is being heard; it only becomes applicable at the hearing of the substantive application. The reason given for this decision was that at the leave stage the court is not determining a question with respect to the upbringing of a child. The Court of Appeal went on to refuse a former local authority foster carer leave to apply for residence orders in respect of four children who had been removed from her care by social workers. The factors which militated against the granting of leave included the children's firm opposition to the application and the likelihood of their being emotionally damaged by involvement in lengthy and acrimonious litigation. It is clear from this that while the child's welfare is not paramount at the leave stage, it is certainly relevant. The outcome in the case may be contrasted with that in *Re P* (1994). Here, foster carers of a young child did obtain leave to apply for a residence order in spite of fierce opposition from the birth parents. They had looked after the child for over two years and a close bond had developed between them, and whereas the local authority's attitude to the foster carer in the *Merton* case was negative, here it was neutral.

Difficulty has been experienced in formulating the correct test to be applied in weighing up these various factors. How strong a case has to be presented for leave to be granted? In *Re M* (1995) the Court of Appeal attempted to settle the issue by laying down the following rules:

1 If the application is frivolous or vexatious or otherwise an abuse of the process of the court, it will fail.
2 If the application for leave fails to disclose that there is any eventual real prospect of success, if those prospects of success are remote so that the application is obviously unsustainable, then it must also be dismissed.
3 The applicant must satisfy the court that there is a serious issue to try and must present a good arguable case.

The court emphasized the need to avoid over-analysis of these tests: 'one should approach the matter in the loosest way possible, looking at the matter in the round because only by such imprecision can one reinforce the importance of leaving the exercise of discretion unfettered'.

The special position of children being looked after

Section 10(9)(d) of the Act, referred to above, is directed at applications concerning children who are with local authorities, whether they are there as a result of a care order or as a result of voluntary arrangements made with the family. It is one of a number of provisions in the Act which are designed to deal with the difficult problem of providing easy access to the courts for foster carers and relatives where an order in their favour would benefit the child, while at the same time promoting confidence in the public child care system among birth parents and allowing local authorities the necessary measure of freedom to plan ahead. The response of the Act, as far as section 8 order applications by foster carers and other non-parents are concerned, is essentially twofold.

First, foster carers (and persons who have been foster carers within the last six months) who have had the child for less than three years need the consent, not only of the court, but also of the local authority, if they are to make an application for a section 8 order (and we are really talking about residence orders here). The only exception to this rule covers foster carers who are relatives. The rule, contained in section 9(3), quite clearly puts the local authority firmly in the driving seat in the situation described. The statutory dividing line of three years is fairly arbitrary, of course, but it appeared in the former custodianship law and was defended by the Government on the grounds that a shorter period would carry with it too many dangers. As will be seen shortly, foster carers who have cared for the child for *more* than three years are not subject to any leave requirement at all as far as residence and contact orders are concerned.

The second response of the Act is section 10(9)(d). This requires the court to have regard to the local authority's plans and the views of the birth parents when deciding whether or not to grant leave to apply for a section 8 order. A relative wishing to apply for a residence order in respect of a child in care will be caught by this provision. It is not, however, as onerous as the rule governing the foster carer with less than three years' care, since it does not give the local authority a power of veto; it simply directs the court to consider the authority's intentions.

Non-parents who do not need leave

Not every non-parent is subject to the leave requirement. In certain circumstances, the requirement is felt to be unnecessary:

- A person who has already been granted a residence order has the right to apply for any section 8 order in the future (section 10(4)(b)). So, for example, a foster carer holding a residence order could apply, without leave, for a specific issue order if a dispute arose with the birth parents over the child's schooling. As a residence order confers parental responsibility on the holder, access to the court should be unfettered.
- A husband or wife has the right to apply for a residence order or a contact order in respect of any child of the family (section 10(5)(a)). 'Child of the family' means (a) a child of both parties or (b) any other child, not being a child who is placed with those parties as foster carers by a local author-

ity or voluntary organization, who has been treated by both of those parties as a child of their family (section 105(1)). Many step-parents, therefore, are able to seek such orders without leave.

- Any person with whom the child has lived for at least three years has the right to apply for a residence order or a contact order (section 10(5)(b)). The three-year period need not be continuous but it must not have begun more than five years before the application and must not have ended more than three months before. This, like the exceptions which follow, is drawn from the old law of custodianship, which allowed 'three-year carers' to apply for custody. It will be recalled that those who have cared for the child for less than three years will need the consent of the local authority, as well as the leave of the court, if they are local authority foster carers.
- Any person who has the consent of those holding an existing residence order in respect of the child is entitled to apply for a residence order or a contact order (section 10(5)(c)).
- Any person who has the consent of the local authority, in a case where a care order has been made, is entitled to apply for a residence order (section 10(5)(c)).
- Any person who has the consent of each of those who have parental responsibility for the child (on which see Chapter 2) is entitled to apply for a residence order or a contact order (section 10(5)(c)).

In each of the above cases, there are thought to be good reasons why the procedural barrier of having to obtain leave should be lifted. It goes without saying, of course, that merely because a person is exempt from the requirement of leave does not mean that they are certain to obtain the order they want. The merits of their claim will remain to be tested in accordance with the welfare principle contained in section 1 of the Act.

The effect of a section 8 order

Let us assume that a section 8 order has been made in favour of a non-parent. What are the consequences? The answer to this question will obviously depend on a number of factors. These include the type of order made, the conditions, if any, which were built into the order by the court, the type of applicant involved (step-parent, relative, foster carer, etc.) and, of course, the general circumstances of the case (e.g. whether the child was already the subject of a court order of some sort).

Contact orders will require the child's carer to permit visits to be made to the person(s) named in the order. Prohibited steps orders and specific issue orders will be directed to particular areas of contention and to that extent will be one-off measures. Residence orders are more drastic and call for separate and extended treatment.

Residence orders

A residence order is an order 'settling the arrangements to be made as to the person with whom a child is to live'. If such an order is made in favour of a non-parent, that person will clearly be entitled to care for the child: indeed, that is what will have been envisaged by the court. It is only right that people in this position are given the 'tools' to get on with the job and therefore the Act (section 12(2)) provides that they will have parental responsibility for the child as long as the order remains in force. Accordingly, they will have access to all the rights, powers, etc. which birth parents acquire automatically.

There are exceptions to this rule, however. Non-parents do not acquire rights in relation to the adoption of the child (i.e. the right to consent or refuse to consent); nor are they able to appoint a guardian for the child. These matters remain within the parents' domain (section 12(3)). Nor are they in a position to effect a change of name or remove the child from the UK for longer than one month unless they obtain either the written consent of every other person who has parental responsibility for the child or else the leave of the court (section 13(1)). Those 'other persons' will include the birth parents (or, in the case of a child born outside marriage, the mother), because, as was mentioned in Chapter 2, the whole thrust of the Children Act is that parents remain parents in the eyes of the law, and so retain their responsibility, until such time as the child is adopted.

Whilst the birth parents retain parental responsibility – and in fact share it with the holder of the residence order – their ability to exercise it may well be diminished by the rule that they must not do any act which would be incompatible with the court's order (section 2(8)). So if the court grants a residence order to foster carers, or to a relative, the birth parents must take care not to interfere with this arrangement (unless there is agreement all round). They may, of course, be entitled to have the child visit or stay with them in accordance with a contact order.

The automatic conferment of parental responsibility as a concomitant of a residence order was always liable to propel a range of people into launching an application for an order simply to obtain this elevated legal status. So it has proved. Cases reported since implementation of the Act have revealed instances of the residence order being used by both grandparents and step-parents, not in order to resolve a dispute about the child's home, but simply to bring about the acquisition of parental responsibility. This has been done, of course, with the support of the courts. Perhaps the most extreme example of this strategy is the case of *Re AB* (1995). On one level, this was a relatively straightforward case of local authority foster carers wishing to adopt their foster child. The problem was that they were not married ('Mr E and Miss G are not people for whom formalities, dockets and titles are very significant'). The Adoption Act 1976 does not permit unmarried couples to adopt and so the foster carers decided that the male partner should apply to adopt on his own but that at the same time both of them should seek a joint residence order so that parental responsibility would be conferred on the female partner. The High Court accepted these suggestions, the judge commenting that he was not seeking to circumvent the eligibility provisions of the Adoption Act.

The problem with this sort of approach to residence orders is that it is inconsistent with the structure of the legislation. As we have seen, Parliament did make express provision for parental responsibility orders in section 4 of the 1989 Act (see page 19 above) and one may reasonably argue that this is the order which is apposite to the situations described above. The difficulty, of course, is that as things stand only birth fathers can make use of section 4. The residence order is therefore simply being used to fill a gap in the Act. While de facto carers of children cannot be blamed for doing this, the better way out, it is suggested, lies in expanding the scope of those provisions of the Act (like section 4) which are directly – as opposed to indirectly – concerned with parental responsibility. This has already been recognized in part, as the draft Adoption Bill published by the Department of Health in 1996 included a clause amending section 4 of the Children Act so as to allow parental responsibility agreements and orders to be made in favour of step-parents.

Applications by children for section 8 orders

The wording of section 10(2) of the Children Act ('on the application of a person') permits children to apply for section 8 orders in respect of themselves. This was deliberate. The *Gillick* case of 1985 gave a much needed boost to the law's recognition of the older child's right to self-determination and the Children Act contains a number of provisions which reflect this movement. We have already seen how the welfare checklist in section 1(3) refers to the ascertainable wishes and feelings of the child. Section 10(2) maintains this theme.

Children do not fall within the categories of persons who are entitled as of right to apply for a section 8 order. Accordingly they need to obtain leave to apply from the court and the Act provides that the court may only grant leave to a child if it is satisfied that he or she has sufficient understanding to make the proposed application (section 10(8)). There is no fixed age laid down by the Act on this point .

When the 1989 Act was passed, nobody knew how frequently children would seek to invoke the section 8 order jurisdiction. In the event, this aspect of the new law rapidly became something of a *cause célèbre* which at one point threatened to get out of hand. The judges, having come under an intense media spotlight, were forced to respond and eventually, whether because of their measures or for other reasons, the issue appeared to die down.

The first reported case was *Re AD*, decided by the President of the Family Division of the High Court in December 1992. This involved a girl of 14 who, in the aftermath of her parents' divorce, went to stay with her boyfriend's family. The boyfriend's mother, aware that the girl was under great stress, consulted the local authority which declined to intervene but suggested that legal advice be obtained. There followed an application by the girl for leave to apply for a residence order, which was granted. At the hearing of the substantive application, the President said that 'although it is interesting to see that this provision of the Children Act has been used and has in fact enabled the matter to be brought to the attention of the court, it is not a course of action which one expects to be repeated very frequently'. He went on to say that all future children's applications for leave should be dealt with by the High Court. This was the first brake to be applied by the judiciary in response to uninformed comments in the media to the effect that children in this country – like, so it was said, their counterparts in the USA – were being allowed to 'divorce their parents'. There quickly followed the case of *Re T* (1993), in which an adopted girl of 13 sought a residence order to enable her to live with members of her birth family. She had taken advantage of an amendment made to the rules of court in 1992 which enables children of sufficient understanding to institute or defend Children Act proceedings by instructing a solicitor directly, rather than finding a suitable adult who is prepared to act on their behalf. The Court of Appeal gave guidance on a number of issues. First, it emphasized the absence of a rigid statutory definition of 'sufficient understanding':

> Different children have differing levels of understanding at the same age. And understanding is not absolute. It has to be assessed relatively to the issues in the proceedings. Where any sound judgment on these issues calls for insight and imagination which only maturity and experience can bring, both the court and the solicitor will be slow to conclude that the child's understanding is sufficient.

Second, it issued a warning to the Family Division (where, it will be recalled, applications for leave should be heard) that leave should not be granted to children without a proper investigation of the circumstances:

> Section 10(8) clearly envisages the court being under a duty to be judicially satisfied as to the child's understanding before granting leave . . . Each case will have to be looked at independently on its merits, and the court will have to be alert to detect instances where leave cannot conscientiously be given without more detailed evidence, or without an opportunity being afforded to any person who

might be able to assist the court in regard to an appreciation of the child's powers of understanding to make their views known before the application is granted.

This was, in effect, a second brake being created for children's applications. More were to follow. In *Re C* (1993) a girl of 14 sought leave to apply for a residence order enabling her to live at the home of a friend and a specific issue order enabling her to go on holiday to Bulgaria with the friend. As in *Re AD* (above), local authority social workers had suggested that the girl consult a solicitor. In rejecting the girl's application, the judge expressed in the clearest terms his antipathy towards the whole exercise:

> I am sure everyone will agree that it is a great pity that a child, albeit one aged nearly 15, should be involved in legal proceedings in this way . . . Not only do I see no identifiable advantage to C in my making [a residence] order, but I suspect that there might be possible disadvantages because it would enshrine in a court order *a state of affairs that, in my view, ought better to be resolved by discussion between C and her parents than by an order of the court . . . C should be dealing directly with her parents and not seeking the intervention of the court.* (Emphasis added)

A few days later in another case called *Re C*, the High Court ruled that before adjudicating on a child's application for leave it should arrange for notice of the application to be served on all those with parental responsibility. This enables the child's parent(s) to try to block the proceedings at the outset.

If reported cases are anything to go by, these various decisions have succeeded in discouraging children's applications for section 8 orders. After the frenetic activity of 1993, when it seemed that a new family law industry was about to mushroom, we seem to have reached the position where such cases are quite rare. Whether or not this is a satisfactory state of affairs depends partly on one's perception of what the legal process has to offer. Many, perhaps, will agree with the spokesperson for the Children's Society who in 1992 was reported as saying that the society was saddened and surprised that these issues were being left to the blunt instrument of the courts.

Applications after adoption

Thirty years ago, the idea of a birth relative seeking a court order in respect of a child who had been adopted outside the family would probably have been dismissed as fantasy. Today, more openness pervades the adoption process and though such applications are not common, they are made occasionally and the courts are not wholly dismissive of them. The position under the Adoption Act 1976 is that once an adoption order is made, the birth parents cease to be parents in the eyes of the law. There is a wholesale transfer of parental responsibility to the adopter(s). Consequently, if a birth parent wishes to apply for a section 8 order – and in practice a contact order is the most likely – they will be treated for Children Act purposes as a non-parent and so will have to obtain preliminary leave from the court. Other birth relatives will, of course, be in the same position. In the case of *M v C and Calderdale Metropolitan Borough Council* (1992), the Court of Appeal confirmed that the birth parent of a child who has been freed for adoption – but not yet adopted – also requires leave to make an application for a section 8 order. On an application for leave, the criteria in section 10(9) will fall to be applied (for these, see page 50 above).

As one would expect, judges have pursued an extremely cautious approach to these applications. In *Re S* (1993) a birth mother whose child had been adopted after a contested hearing tried to re-establish contact two years later. In rejecting her application for leave, the High Court stated that in cases of this sort the Official Solicitor should be brought in as a respondent. In addition, the relevant adoption agency should be notified of the application, as should the adoptive parent(s), but only once a *prima facie* case for granting leave had been made out. All cases, it was said, should be heard in the High Court. As to the merits of the application, the judge noted that the court which had granted the adoption order could, if it had wished, have attached a contact condition to the order. Since it had not done so, the mother's application was bound to fail unless she could point to some fundamental change of circumstances. In the later case of *Re T* (1995) the Court of Appeal cast doubt on the procedural hurdles erected in *Re S*: there would be cases where the leave application could be handled appropriately in the lower courts. *Re T* was a case of open adoption where the adopters had agreed to face-to-face contact with the birth mother once a year. The Court of Appeal ruled that in these circumstances a formal contact order should not be attached to the adoption order because that would unnecessarily restrict the freedom of the adopters. However, the court indicated that if the adopters were to deviate from the agreed contact arrangements unreasonably, the birth mother would not have much difficulty in obtaining leave to apply for an order.

It is, perhaps, in open situations where the section 8 order jurisdiction is most likely to be of significance. This would appear to be confirmed by the Court of Appeal's decision in another 1995 case called *Re T*. Here, the adopters of three children had informally agreed at the time of the adoption that they would provide annual progress reports to the children's 20-year-old half-sister. When the time came, however, no progress report was produced and the sister accordingly sought leave to apply for a contact order so as to enforce the informal agreement. The Court of Appeal, seemingly sympathetic to the applicant's position, said that the adopters should be given eight weeks to provide reasons why they had not kept to the original agreement. If no reasons were forthcoming – or, one assumes, the proffered reasons were not adequate – leave to apply should be granted. The adoption agency (which had brokered the agreement) had argued that the court should refuse to interfere since it would give out the wrong sort of message: 'there is a real danger that prospective adopters would be deterred from entering into open adoptions, because of the fear of ensuing court proceedings'. The Court of Appeal disagreed. While the stresses and strains of bringing up adopted children might well require agreed contact arrangements to be suspended or even terminated, it was unacceptable for this to occur without some reasoned explanation, particularly where – as here – the type of contact envisaged was purely indirect. For the court to wash its hands of the matter might well lead to more adoption cases being contested by birth relatives.

These two decisions are of considerable significance in a climate which is broadly favourable to openness in adoption. Further litigation of this type is probably inevitable because openness, by its very nature, generates a greater risk of conflict between adopters and birth relatives. In practical terms, it means that adopters will need to be briefed very carefully about the long-term implications of understandings reached about future contact.

Applications by local authorities and voluntary organizations

The wording of section 10(2) of the Act enables applications to be made by these bodies, except that it is made clear that local authorities cannot obtain residence or contact orders. Leave should not be a great problem in these cases since the application will always be motivated by professional concerns for the child. The first reported case involving a local authority application for a section 8 order was *Nottinghamshire County Council v P* (1993). The authority, having for various reasons (including lack of resources) rejected the option of applying for a care order or supervision order, attempted to deal with a situation of serious sexual abuse by way of a prohibited steps order. This strategy came unstuck when the Court of Appeal ruled that the Children Act did not permit the authority to obtain section 8 orders which covered issues of residence or contact. The authority was pointed firmly in the direction of the public law provisions of the Act. It had obtained leave to apply for a prohibited steps order from a single magistrate on an *ex parte* basis (i.e. without notice to the parents) but the Court of Appeal stated that this was wholly inappropriate: such applications should be heard in the county court and on an *inter partes* basis.

In *Re R* (1993) a local authority successfully applied for a specific issue order which authorized a hospital to administer blood products to a child whose parents were Jehovah's Witnesses. There was no need for the public law provisions of the Act to be invoked here since the authority did not wish to obtain wide decision-making powers. It was a case of limited intervention. The judge stated that such applications should always be made to the High Court and that strenuous efforts should be made to achieve an *inter partes* hearing.

Section 9(1) of the Act prevents a prohibited steps order or a specific issue order being made in respect of a child in care (i.e. a child who is the subject of a care order). This restriction does not, however, apply to a child who is accommodated on a voluntary basis under section 20 of the Act, nor to a child who is the subject of a supervision order. In *Re H* (1995) the Court of Appeal approved the making of a prohibited steps order in a case where supervision orders had been made in respect of four children, the effect of the order being to prohibit the mother's former cohabitee from contacting the children. The court acknowledged that such orders might have to be made on an *ex parte* basis in urgent cases: 'the variety of circumstances in which a judge, in his discretion, might require to make an injunctive order for the protection of children is so great that it would be wrong for this court to say anything which might reduce the necessary flexibility of this important tool'.

Other aspects of non-parental applications

Many of the supplementary provisions mentioned in the last chapter apply equally to non-parental cases. Those worth noting are as follows:

- Section 8 orders can only be made in respect of a child over 16 where the circumstances are exceptional.
- Section 8 orders will cease to have effect when the child reaches the age of 16, unless the court orders otherwise.
- All section 8 orders may be varied or discharged by the court.
- Section 8 orders are automatically discharged if a care order is made.
- The special provisions aimed at curbing delays in legal proceedings are fully applicable.
- Family assistance orders may be made by the court, whether or not it makes a section 8 order. The person to be assisted may be a parent or guardian, anyone who is caring for the child or who holds a contact order, or the child himself.
- The court has the power to order that no further application is to be made in respect of the child without its consent. Many non-parental applicants need leave anyway, of course, but as we have seen, some do not. This provision can be used by the court to stop repeated applications by members of this group.

- No application can be made for a section 8 order, other than a residence order, in respect of a child in care. If a residence order is made, it has the effect of discharging the care order (see Chapter 10).
- The procedure for applying for section 8 orders which was summarized in Chapter 3 is equally applicable to non-parental applications.

Financial provision for the child's carer

Schedule 1 to the Children Act contains an elaborate set of provisions dealing with the financial support of children. These provisions, some of which may be relevant where a non-parent has obtained a residence order, are described in Chapter 18.

5

Local authority support for children and families

The scope of the present chapter

The title of this chapter is rather vague. What is 'support'? Local authorities could be said to 'support' children and their families in dozens of different ways, ranging from the provision of libraries to the inspection of shops. The title is in fact taken from Part III of the Children Act which contains an assortment of provisions – some general, some specific – whose unifying theme is the involvement of social services departments in child welfare work. Some of these provisions were drawn from previous legislation, others were new. Some of them impose obligations on local authorities, others merely give them powers exercisable at their discretion.

It might be thought that with a title such as this, Part III of the Act would contain virtually everything in the measure concerning local authorities and children. This is not the case, however: later parts of the Act deal with (among other things) care orders, supervision orders, emergency protection orders, community homes and the regulation of private fostering, all of them areas with a high degree of local authority involvement. To that extent, therefore, the title is misleading.

The diversity of the contents of Part III would make a single chapter devoted to all of it rather unwieldy. Its coverage in this book has therefore been split. Those sections which deal with the provision of accommodation for children – what used to be referred to as 'voluntary care' – are described in Chapter 6, while those sections which deal with the treatment of children who are the subject of a care order (for they also appear in Part III) are described in the care orders chapter (Chapter 10). The present chapter is concerned with the remaining provisions. Hiving off segments of this Part of the Act for separate treatment is probably inconsistent with the intentions of both the draftsman and the Department of Health. This is, perhaps, particularly so as far as the provision of accommodation is concerned, because the whole thrust of the Government's approach to 'voluntary care' arrangements was that they are merely one of a number of support services which are available from local authorities to families living in their area. Nevertheless, it is hoped that through this division, the reader will be in a better position to acquire a command of what the Act has to say.

Children in need

The legal definition

A notable feature of Part III of the Children Act is its recurring reference to 'children in need'. Great care must be taken with this statutory expression. It is couched in ordinary language and the general idea conveyed by it is fairly clear; but it is not what it seems because it comes along with a definition. In other words, it is not to be taken literally; it is a legal term of art which bears a restricted meaning whenever it appears in the Act. It is extremely important to remember this. A failure to read Part III with the definition firmly in mind will probably take the reader along the wrong track.

It is easy to miss the definition because it only appears once in the Act, in section 17(10). The definition is as follows:

a child shall be taken to be in need if –
(a) he is unlikely to achieve or maintain, or to have the opportunity of achieving or maintaining, a reasonable standard of health or development without the provision for him of services by a local authority under this Part;
(b) his health or development is likely to be significantly impaired, or further impaired, without the provision for him of such services; or
(c) he is disabled.

Three of the words used in section 17(10) are themselves defined. A child is 'disabled' if he is blind, deaf or dumb or suffers from mental disorder of any kind or is substantially and permanently handicapped by illness, injury or congenital deformity or such other disability as may be prescribed by regulations. 'Development' means physical, intellectual, emotional, social or behavioural development. 'Health' means physical or mental health.

Disabled children

One of the things which many will notice about this definition of children in need is its inclusion of the handicapped. This is a manifestation of the policy, originally proposed in the Child Care Law Review and subsequently adopted by the DH, of unifying the two former main streams of public child law; these were described as child care law on the one hand and health and welfare law on the other. The first was to be found largely in the Child Care Act 1980, many of whose provisions dated back to the Children Act 1948. The second was scattered throughout various pieces of legislation covering not just children but people of all age groups, e.g. the National Assistance Act 1948 and the Chronically Sick and Disabled Persons Act 1970. Child care law, understood in the above sense, embraced the voluntary reception of children ('orphans and deserted children etc.', in the words of the Child Care Act) into local authority care, but it also contained a strong preventive element whereby children living at home with their families were supported by the local authority. Health and welfare law opened up similar possibilities – support at home and care away from home – but the rules which applied were completely separate from, and arguably inferior to, the rules relating to child care. The DH view was that this dichotomy could not be justified and that a merger of the two streams of law would have positive advantages. This view is reflected in Part III of the Children Act and particularly in the definition of 'children in need'.

It is worth noting that the Government's policy did not go unchallenged. In its 1987 White Paper, the DH referred to:

> the reservations expressed by some that this would cause concern to those parents of handicapped and disabled children who provide expert and devoted care but from time to time need respite care provided by the local authority. This concern it was said flowed from the perception that reception into care by local authorities under the present legislation was frequently associated with parental shortcomings.

However, the Government held to its view, no doubt fortified by the support it got from organizations representing the handicapped. 'The intention', it said, 'is to ensure that in all cases the children concerned receive the standard of care and protection and professional review appropriate to their needs and that those ends are achieved where possible in a partnership with parents.'

Anticipated problems

A further, important, feature of the definition which should be noted is its inclusion of children who are likely to encounter difficulties, as well as those who already have them. The wording of paragraphs (a) and (b) of the definition makes this clear. As was said in Parliament, 'one has to see the child in his or her particular situation and ask: "Well, if nothing is done for that child by the local authority, is that child likely to attain a reasonable standard of development?"' This is a very good example of the need to have the definition in mind when operating the Act, because without it it would be a matter of doubt as to whether the words 'child in need' were sufficient to cover such children. Through its reference to likelihood, however, the definition puts the matter beyond doubt and paves the way for important preventive functions to be given to local authorities.

Children being looked after

It should also be noted that the definition is sufficiently broad to encompass children who are already in local authority accommodation, as well as children living outside. This, another example of the extended meaning of 'child in need', paves the way for rehabilitative work to be done.

Targeting resources

The creation of this statutory group of 'children in need' provoked mixed reactions. Some sought to argue that, while it was undoubtedly well intentioned, it would produce problems of interpretation and, equally importantly, would produce an unfortunate labelling effect. It was suggested that identifying a child as one 'in need' would reinforce negative feelings and lock the family into a 'stigmatized framework'. The Government's response, however, was that the definition would set a target for local authorities to aim for. As there would not be limitless resources available, services under Part III of the Act had to be targeted on those in greatest need. This has, of course, been a familiar argument for many years in a variety of contexts.

The remaining sections of this chapter contain details of the range of functions imposed on local authorities in relation to children in need. Each of these functions is hungry for resources and it was not therefore surprising to find, soon after the Act's implementation, some hard-pressed authorities attempting to contain them by adopting a restricted interpretation of 'need'. The 1991 DH Guidance sought to deal with this by stating:

> because the definition is in the Act, a local authority cannot lawfully substitute any other definition for the purposes of Part III . . . It has three categories: a reasonable standard of health or development; significant impairment of health or development; and disablement. It would not be acceptable for an authority to exclude any of these three – for example, by confining services to children at risk of significant harm which attracts the duty to investigate.

Challenging a decision about 'need'

Should the members of a child's family wish to challenge formally the decision of their local authority that the child is not 'in need' for the purposes of the Act, the correct procedure to use is judicial review. As is explained elsewhere in this book (see page 100), this is a mechanism which requires the complainant to show that the decision is flawed on account of some error of law or some procedural lapse. If grounds are made out the High Court can (not must) set aside the decision. In *Re J* (1995) a child of 17 sought to challenge an adverse decision of the local authority by way of a specific issue order (on which see Chapter 3). The High Court confirmed the availability of judicial review but rejected the option of a specific issue order since the question whether a child is in need does not relate to any aspect of parental responsibility.

The provision of services for children and families

The Children Act aims to set out the functions of local authority social services departments in relation to children in need. Given this aim, and given the special meaning which the term 'child in need' bears in the Act, it is not surprising to find a fairly long list of functions. What *is* perhaps surprising is the fact that these functions are not all laid out in the same corner of the statute. In order to make his work more intelligible, the draftsman decided to place at the forefront of Part III a section (section 17) which contains the *general duty* of local authorities. This is then supplemented, or filled out, by a number of *specific duties and powers* which have been consigned to Schedule 2, at the back of the Act.

Not everyone will agree with this sort of arrangement – there was certainly opposition to it in Parliament – but that is the way the Act turned out. It is important to remember that the provisions in a schedule of a statute are just as much law as the provisions in the sections. It is understandable how a schedule can come to be regarded as something akin to a second-tier form of law, but such an approach is misconceived. Certainly it would be a great mistake to look upon the contents of Schedule 2 to the Children Act as something peripheral; many would regard them as being among the most important provisions in the Act.

The general duty of the local authority

It shall be the general duty of every local authority (a) to safeguard and promote the welfare of children within their area who are in need, and (b) so far as is consistent with that duty, to promote the upbringing of such children by their families, by providing a range and level of services appropriate to those children's needs.

This is how section 17(1) of the Act reads. Inspired by the Child Care Act 1980 (now repealed), it is a provision of the very highest significance, opening up as it does a vast array of child-oriented social services work. The prime duty is that contained in paragraph (a). Paragraph (b) is a reflection of the view that, generally speaking, the interests of children are best served by their remaining with their families, but this is only generally speaking and so the Act does not require the local authority to promote this where it would be inconsistent with the child's welfare.

The section envisages that the duty will be discharged by the provision of an 'appropriate' range of services. At first sight, it seems as though the provision must come from the local authority but section 17 goes on to state that the authority may make arrangements for others to act on its behalf. Furthermore, it is required to 'facilitate' the provision by others, including in particular voluntary organizations, of relevant services. This is a statutory acknowledgement of the very great part that voluntary bodies play in family support work. The extent of joint action by the local authority and the voluntary sector is left to be arranged locally, so variations will occur.

The problem with a statutory provision like section 17(1) is that its language is so open. What *are* the services which are to be provided? What exactly does 'appropriate' mean? What will promote the welfare of children in need (as defined)? The short answer to such questions is that there is no single right answer. The reality is that section 17(1), though couched in the language of duty, gives local authorities a very considerable degree of discretion in deciding what, if anything, to do. The duty is, in a sense, more political than legal. This is not to say that it has no place in a Children Act. Clearly, the point it is making is fundamental. It is just that, as a vehicle for ensuring that things get done (and get done consistently throughout the country), its value is limited. It leaves a great deal – and some might say too much – to the will and determination of those in charge of the local authority. But this may be an unfair argument. After all, section 17(1) is only a lead-in to the specific duties and powers set out in Schedule 2. What of them?

The specific duties and powers in Schedule 2

Schedule 2 contains 11 sets of provisions, each of which is seen as furthering in its own way the overall objective established by section 17(1). There is provision in the Act for the Government, with Parliament's approval, to amend these provisions, so that the legislation can reflect any new social services practices which may develop in the future in relation to children in need, and this power was exercised in 1996 to add a new paragraph relating to children's services plans (see below). The 11 matters dealt with are as follows.

Identification of children in need and the provision of information

Every local authority is required to take reasonable steps to identify the extent to which there are children in need (as defined) within its area. It must also publish information about the services relevant to such children which it provides and, where appropriate, which others – including in particular voluntary organizations – provide. It must take such steps as are reasonably practicable to ensure that those who might benefit from the services receive the information relevant to them.

The DH Guidance states that any publicity materials produced should take account of ethnic minorities' cultural and linguistic needs and the needs of those with sensory disabilities in the audience to whom the materials are addressed. 'As far as possible', it says, 'the relevant publicity should encourage parents to seek help if it is needed.'

Formulation of children's services plans

In 1996 the DH made an order which added new provisions to Schedule 2. Its effect was to require every local authority to review its provision of support services under Part III in consultation with other agencies and then prepare and publish a plan for the future. These tasks were to be completed by 31 March 1997. The change was made in the hope that the emphasis on inter-agency collaboration which is found in the child protection arena would be adopted in family support work. It had been recommended in the Utting Report *Children in the Public Care* (1991) and also in the Audit Commission Report *Seen But Not Heard* (1994).

Maintenance of a register of disabled children

Every local authority is required to keep a register of disabled children within its area. We have seen that section 17 of the Act contains a definition of 'disabled'. The register is designed to facilitate service planning and monitoring. The Guidance suggests that social services departments (SSDs) in conjunction with LEAs and health authorities draw up a common register to assist collaboration. It points out that registration is voluntary on the part of parents and children and not a precondition of service provision and goes on to state: 'it should be made clear that the register has no connection with child protection registers and that child protection registration is an entirely separate process'.

Assessment of children's needs

The local authority may assess the needs of any child who appears to be 'in need' within the meaning of section 17 at the same time as any assessment is carried out under other legislation (e.g. the Education Act 1996).

Referring to disabled children, the Guidance states:

> in the past assessments have tended to be undertaken separately by the relevant departments. This Act makes it possible to bring together in one process assessment for several different services where this is appropriate and in the child's best interests. Such collaboration should in future ensure that all authorities see children 'in the round', whether their particular needs are for educational or health or social care. It should ensure that parents and children are not subject to a confusing variety of assessment procedures.

Prevention of neglect and abuse

Every local authority is required to take reasonable steps, through the provision of services, to prevent children within its area suffering ill-treatment or neglect. 'Ill-treatment' is defined elsewhere in the Act so as to include sexual abuse and forms of ill-treatment which are not physical (e.g. emotional abuse). If a local authority believes that a child within its area is likely to suffer harm but lives or proposes to live in another local authority's area, it must inform the other authority.

Provision of accommodation to protect children

Where it appears to a local authority that a child is suffering, or is likely to suffer, ill-treatment at the hands of another person who is living with him, and that other person proposes to move from the premises, the authority is empowered to assist with the obtaining of alternative accommodation. This was a late addition to the Act which arose out of the debates on emergency protection orders. It is discussed, along with more recent provisions concerning exclusion requirements, in Chapter 8 (see page 137).

Provision for disabled children

Every local authority is required to provide services designed to minimize the effect on disabled children within its area of their disabilities and to give such children the opportunity to lead lives which are as normal as possible.

Provisions to reduce the need for legal proceedings

Every local authority is required to take reasonable steps designed to reduce the need to bring proceedings for care or supervision orders with respect to children within its area, or criminal proceedings against them, or wardship proceedings, or any family proceedings which might lead to them being placed in the authority's care. It is also required to take steps designed to encourage children within its area not to commit criminal offences and steps designed to avoid the need for children to be placed in secure accommodation.

Provision for children living with their families

Every local authority is required to make such provision as it considers appropriate for the following services to be available with respect to children in need within its area while they are living with their families: (a) advice, guidance and counselling; (b) occupational, social, cultural or recreational activities; (c) home help; (d) facilities for, or assistance with, travelling to and from home for the purpose of taking advantage of any other service provided under the Act or of any similar service; (e) assistance to enable the child concerned and his family to have a holiday.

Family centres

Every local authority is required to provide such family centres as it considers appropriate in relation to children within its area. A 'family centre' for these purposes is a centre at which the child, his parents and any other person who has parental responsibility for him (e.g. the holder of a residence order) or who is looking after him, may (a) attend for occupational, social, cultural or recreational activities; (b) attend for advice, guidance or counselling; or (c) be provided with accommodation while he is receiving advice, guidance or counselling.

Volume 2 of the Guidance contains some useful material on this topic. It points out that the duty created by the Act is not confined to children in need.

Maintenance of the family home

Every local authority is required to take reasonable steps, where any child in need within its area is living apart from his family, to enable him to live with his family or to promote contact between him and his family, if, in its opinion, it is necessary to do so in order to safeguard or promote his welfare. This duty does not extend to children in local authority accommodation (other provisions cover them).

These are wide-ranging and ambitious provisions which enable a great deal of supportive, preventive and rehabilitative work to be done by local authorities in conjunction with voluntary organizations and others. As with section 17(1), however, although the language of duty is employed extensively, the qualifications inserted – 'as they consider appropriate' – and the bland nature of many of the duties – 'shall take reasonable steps' – ensure that local authorities retain a large measure of freedom to decide how exactly the functions in question will be discharged. The range, and level, of services will consequently vary from area to area, with different matters being given different priorities. Nor does the Act (or the Guidance) dictate the manner in which social work support is to be delivered. Different practices can therefore be developed.

The enforcement of duties

The question is sometimes asked about public duties of this sort: what can be done if the local authority fails to discharge them? In recent years much has been accomplished by the High Court by way of improving and extending its special jurisdiction of judicial review over public agencies. In principle, this jurisdiction is available for the enforcement of public duties. Cases have shown, however, that the judges are reluctant to intervene in situations which involve duties framed in less than very specific language. Such cases often contain controversial political elements, such as the allocation of scarce resources, of which the courts are understandably wary. In an extreme set of circumstances, where, say, a local authority has done nothing at all to implement a duty, a judge might be prepared to act. Otherwise, the tendency, so far as broad duties are concerned, is to leave the matter to the authority's discretion (see, for example, the *Barnet* case noted below at page 74). As a result, 'enforcement' can only be pursued through whatever non-legal channels might be available.

It was suggested during the Parliamentary debates on the Act that the Government should be given power to establish minimum standards for local authorities in relation to their work under Schedule 2. This was resisted. Local authorities, it was said, are accountable to their local electorate and are responsible for making their own decisions according to their priorities and the particular needs and circumstances of their area. This is one matter, then, on which central government is prepared to adopt a hands-off approach. Such support for local government autonomy may be warmly welcomed, but the fear in some quarters was that it would only serve to perpetuate perceived inadequacies in some of the country's social services departments.

What the Government *did* agree to, however, was the inclusion in the Act of a provision giving the DH a 'default power'. This is contained in section 84. It enables the Secretary of State to declare a local authority to be in default with respect to any duty imposed by the Act, and to give directions (enforceable in the High Court) for the purpose of ensuring that the duty is complied with. The power can only be exercised where the DH is satisfied that the local authority has failed, without reasonable excuse, to comply with the duty in question. Experience of default powers in other fields (e.g. education) shows that government departments use them very infrequently. They are heavy-handed instruments, with a considerable potential for exacerbating delicate central–local relationships. Those thinking of utilizing this particular complaints machinery should bear this in mind.

A more fruitful option, perhaps, will be the internal complaints procedure which each local authority has had to establish under section 26 of the Act. This procedure – discussed in Chapter 6 – is available to all children in need and their families, whether or not the children are being looked after by the authority, and as we have just seen, several of the functions specified in Schedule 2 are aimed directly at them.

Assistance in kind and assistance in cash

Section 17(6) states that the services provided by a local authority in the exercise of its functions in relation to children in need 'may include giving assistance in kind or, in exceptional circumstances, in cash'. This power is not new, as it existed under the Child Care Act 1980 and before that under the Children and Young Persons Act 1963. However, some new supplementary provisions were added: first, assistance may be unconditional or subject to conditions as to the repayment of the assistance or of its value (in whole or in part); second, the means of the child and his parents must be taken into account before assistance is given or conditions imposed; and third, no repayment will be due from a person at a time when he is in receipt of income support, family credit, disability working allowance or an income-based jobseeker's allowance.

The power of a local authority to provide this sort of assistance has unquestionable value. But the high discretionary element means that problems over its implementation are inevitable. Three matters in particular were highlighted in the debate on the Children Act, each of them concerned with cash payments: the enormous variations which existed between local authorities, the low amount of the average payment, and the misunderstandings – in essence, unwarranted rigidity – of social workers caused by the use of the expression 'exceptional circumstances'. These points were all accepted by the Government but, basing its case on the recommendations of the Child Care Law Review, it argued that the existing statutory wording was the best formula available. It was especially reluctant to see the 'exceptional circumstances' criterion disappear, on the grounds that relaxation could push local authorities into an income-maintenance role which is more properly assigned to the social security system.

Day care for the under-fives and supervision of schoolchildren

Section 18 of the Children Act deals with the important question of day care. Opinions vary as to the extent to which public authorities should have obligations in this area and so the terms of the section were always going to be contentious. In the result, the Act draws a distinction between children in need (as defined) and other children.

As regards children in need, the section imposes a *duty* on the local authority to provide (and this can be done through other organizations) such day care for those aged five or under who are not yet attending school as is appropriate. 'Day care' for these purposes is defined as 'any form of care or supervised activity provided for children during the day (whether or not it is provided on a regular basis)'. Under Schedule 2 to the Act, a local authority, in making these arrangements, must have regard to the different racial groups to which children within its area who are in need belong. This provision is clearly designed to ensure that all sections of the community are properly catered for (see also Chapter 17).

A similar duty extends to those children attending school: every local authority is required to provide for children in need within its area who are attending any school 'such care or supervised activities as is appropriate' outside school hours or during school holidays. 'Supervised activity' means an activity supervised by a responsible person.

As regards children other than those 'in need', section 18 refers to a *discretion* to provide day care or supervised activities. Whether or not any initiative is launched is accordingly a matter for each individual authority.

The provisions of section 18 have given a higher statutory profile to day care, and they enable many imaginative schemes to be devised and supported. In this sense, they represented a step forward. An important question remained, however: would the necessary political will, together with the release of adequate resources, be forthcoming? It is true that in relation to children in need, the Act imposes obligations on authorities, not simply discretions. These obligations, moreover, are framed in objective terms ('as is appropriate' and not, as in the initial version of the Children Bill, 'as they consider appropriate'). As with section 17 and Schedule 2, though, it is difficult to see coercive measures being taken against an individual authority. This would appear to be confirmed by the High Court's decision in *R v*

Barnet London Borough Council ex parte B (1993). In this case, six children
in need (acting through their parents) applied for judicial review of the local
authority's decision to close the day nursery which they attended. One of
the arguments put forward was that this decision was so unreasonable that
it fell within the concept of irrationality (one of the traditional grounds for
judicial review). In rejecting this argument, the judge stated that it was
essentially a matter for each local authority's discretion how it discharged
its responsibilities. He said that section 18 'allows a local authority a measure of judgment and discretion in a field in which they have considerable
expertise, and in which they are entitled, indeed bound, to have regard to
the financial implications of the way in which they fulfil their statutory
duty . . . The weight which a local authority should give to the general
circumstances of children in need for whom it must provide day care one
way or another, when balancing them against its financial and budgetary
constraints, must be a matter for its judgment and experience. It is certainly
a matter upon which the court would rarely be competent to intervene on
the ground of irrationality'.

In an attempt to maintain the high profile, however, the Government put
into the Act a section (section 19) which requires each authority to review
the provision which it makes under section 18. These reviews are to be
conducted with the education department and are to take place every three
years. The form a review takes is a matter for the authorities concerned but
they are bound to 'have regard to' (this does not mean accept) any representations made by a health authority and any other relevant representations. And once the review is concluded, the results, together with any
proposals, must be published as soon as is reasonably practicable. Volume
2 of the Guidance contains detailed suggestions relating to the conduct of
section 19 reviews.

It should be noted that sections 18 and 19 do not deal simply with local
authority provision. They also contain rules concerning the provision of day
care by the private sector. These rules are described in Chapter 15.

Charges for local authority services

Section 29 of the Act enables a local authority to charge for any service it
provides under section 17 or section 18, other than advice, guidance and
counselling. Those who can be charged are the child's parents, the child
himself (if 16 or over) and any member of the child's family if the service is
in fact provided to that person with a view to promoting the child's welfare.
There is power to waive part or all of the charge where the means of the
payer are deemed insufficient and in any event no one is liable to pay at a
time when he is receiving income support, family credit, disability working
allowance or an income-based jobseeker's allowance.

Co-operation between authorities

In an attempt to ensure a properly co-ordinated approach by public agencies, section 27 of the Act expressly authorizes local authorities to request help from other councils and from health authorities in the discharge of their functions under Part III. The agency whose help is sought is under an obligation to comply with a request 'if it is compatible with their own statutory or other duties and does not unduly prejudice the discharge of any of their functions'. Inter-agency co-operation, like co-operation between individuals, is difficult to achieve by legal methods alone (a matter discussed in Chapter 7). To an extent, therefore, and bearing in mind the rather loose language which it employs, section 27 is another of the Children Act's more symbolic provisions.

The courts gave limited consideration to the terms of section 27 in the case of *R v Northavon District Council ex parte Smith* (1994). Here, the social services department was faced with a family about to be evicted from their home. The department was asked to exercise its power under section 17(6) to pay a deposit and rent in advance on fresh accommodation but it refused. Instead, it requested the assistance of the housing authority under section 27. The housing authority also declined to assist, on the ground that it had already rejected the family's application for housing on account of intentional homelessness. The House of Lords ruled, first, that the housing authority's refusal of assistance had been based on its view that providing accommodation would 'unduly prejudice the discharge of functions' within the meaning of section 27, and second, that this was a legitimate response in the circumstances. The judges acknowledged that an aggrieved person or authority was entitled to seek judicial review of a section 27 decision but they expressed the hope that this would not happen frequently. They also urged social services authorities to work 'in a spirit of mutual co-operation rather than by an immediate formal request under the provisions of section 27'.

Part III in practice

Although at the time of writing the family support provisions of the Children Act have been in force for over five years, it is by no means easy to judge their effectiveness in practice. There are a number of reasons for this. First, there is the difficulty of finding a suitable yardstick by which to measure effectiveness. How, for example, should one measure the success of preventive work with a family? By reference to what standard does one measure the success of a respite care scheme for disabled children? Second, because of the considerable variation in local provision, 'successes' or 'failures' which are said to exist in one geographical area may not provide a true guide to the situation nationally. Third, the wide range of services and situations encompassed by the provisions of Part III makes generalization hazardous. It is very unlikely that progress in all of the areas mentioned in the provisions has been made at a uniform rate, even within individual authorities.

Despite the obstacles to understanding and analysis, some research evidence relating to Part III has emerged. The most recent summary of this appears in the *Report of the National Commission of Inquiry into the Prevention of Child Abuse*, published in October 1996 (HMSO). The Commission reported that issues relating to children in need had been raised in many submissions to it. These painted a generally depressing picture:

> The statutory requirement . . . to assess children in need and provide services to support them and their families through social services, educational and health provision, is not fulfilled in practice in England and Wales because of a tight rationing of resources . . . There is now a body of research and experience which shows that section 17 of the Children Act is largely unimplemented . . . A recurring theme [in the evidence] is that the Children Act has been grossly under-resourced . . . In practice, statutory authorities tend to define 'appropriate' in a manner that matches their resources rather than need.

It is fair to say that predictions along these lines were made by many commentators as soon as the Children Act was passed.

6

Provision of accommodation for children

Accommodation as a support service

Section 20 of the Children Act deals with the provision of accommodation for children by social services departments. It replaced the previous legislation (set out mainly in section 2 of the Child Care Act 1980) governing the reception of children into so-called 'voluntary care', a process which embraced some 20000 children each year.

Section 20 is located in Part III of the Act, which, as was seen in the last chapter, is entitled 'Local Authority Support for Children and Families'. Its appearance there, alongside sections dealing with preventive and supportive services and day care, is indicative of the approach which commended itself to the Child Care Law Review and subsequently to the Department of Health. This approach sees the provision by a local authority of accommodation for children as a valuable service which should be on offer, on a wholly voluntary basis, to families in difficulties, in exactly the same way as its other Part III services are. Using the accommodation service should, according to this view, be regarded positively, as a means of assisting the child; it should not be looked upon as evidence of parental failure but as evidence of a responsible attitude to the discharge of parental duties. The previous legislation was considered vulnerable to criticism through casting voluntary care in too negative a light: witness section 1 of the Child Care Act, which talked of promoting the welfare of children by diminishing the need to receive children into care. Wording of this sort, it was said, conveyed the wrong impression, the impression that being accommodated by the local authority was something to be avoided at all costs.

This emphasis on accommodation as a service, entered into freely with the child's family, has a number of implications but the most important is the elimination of all traces of compulsion from the service – no obstacles are to be placed in the way of families wishing to use it. If compulsory intervention is deemed necessary, then a court order must be obtained on one of the grounds set out in a completely separate part of the statute (Part IV). In order to emphasize the split with the compulsory procedure, separate terminology has been introduced: children 'in care' (according to section 105(1)) are those who are the subject of a care order made by the court, whereas children dealt with under section 20 are simply 'accommodated'.

The powers and duties under section 20

The principal accommodation obligation imposed by the Act is contained in section 20(1). It reads as follows:

> Every local authority shall provide accommodation for any child in need within their area who appears to them to require accommodation as a result of – (a) there being no person who has parental responsibility for him; (b) his being lost or having been abandoned; or (c) the person who has been caring for him being prevented (whether or not permanently, and for whatever reason) from providing him with suitable accommodation or care.

This provision is very similar to section 2 of the Child Care Act 1980. One difference, however, is its reference to children in need. The obligation is owed only to these children. As was seen in the last chapter, 'child in need' is a term with a special meaning and covers not simply those in what might be called social need, but also those who are disabled. This latter group of children has therefore been brought into mainstream child care law instead of being dealt with alongside adults in the health legislation. 'Parental responsibility' bears the meaning given to it by Part I of the Act (discussed in Chapter 2) and so paragraph (a) would normally refer to the birth parents of the child, or the mother if the child was born outside marriage. Finally, it will be noticed that the duty extends to children in need of any age – it is not restricted to those under 17, as was the duty under the 1980 Act.

In addition to creating the main duty in subsection (1), section 20 contains two other measures authorizing the provision of accommodation. The first (subsection (3)) covers children in need aged 16 or over whose welfare is considered 'likely to be seriously prejudiced' if accommodation is not provided. It is in fact cast as a duty, not just a discretion, and it appears in the Act as a result of uncertainty on the Government's part as to the extent of a parent's legal duty to accommodate a child who has reached the age of 16. To meet this possible problem, it was decided to provide a local authority safety-net for children of this age group who are not living at home. As with section 20(1), this is a service which is to be on offer, and so the child will not be compelled to accept it.

The other accommodation provision in section 20 is subsection (4). This enables (not requires) a local authority to provide accommodation for any child – whether 'in need' or not – if it considers that to do so would safeguard or promote his welfare, even though there is a person with parental responsibility who is able to accommodate him. Runaways could be covered by this power.

The parental veto

The accommodation service under section 20 is seen as a voluntary one. Hence:

> A local authority may not provide accommodation under this section for any child if any person who (a) has parental responsibility for him; and (b) is willing and able to (i) provide accommodation for him; or (ii) arrange for accommodation to be provided for him, objects. (section 20(7))

So the parents have a veto, as they did under the old law. This fundamental rule, however, does not apply in two situations. The first is where the child is over 16 and agrees to being provided with the accommodation. Here we have yet another illustration of the self-determination principle at work and the result of it is that a 16- or 17-year-old may admit himself to accommodation if the statutory conditions are satisfied. The second situation in which a parent is denied a veto is where a residence order has been made under Part II of the Act (or a care and control order has been made in wardship proceedings) and the holder of the order agrees to the provision of accommodation. The holder might be one of the parents themselves, but he might also be a relative or a foster carer. In any event, the parent without the order is unable to stop the holder arranging accommodation. This is a perfectly logical rule, because the central purpose of a residence order is to give the holder the exclusive power to decide where the child is to live. This can obviously include local authority accommodation.

It should also be noted that a veto is only given to a parent who is willing and able to provide or arrange for accommodation for the child. This qualification was inserted into the Act so as to prevent an estranged parent frustrating the other parent's plan to use the section 20 service by lodging an objection even though he himself has no intention of taking in the child. To deny the caring parent the service in these circumstances was thought to be wrong.

As far as children born outside marriage are concerned, normally only the mother has a veto. This is because only she will have parental responsibility. If the father has acquired parental responsibility in any of the ways mentioned in Chapters 2 and 3, it is a different matter.

Can the provision of accommodation be demanded?

Suppose a parent asks the local authority to provide accommodation under section 20(1) but the local authority refuses. Does the parent have any redress? It is true that, as a matter of strict law, section 20(1) is framed in terms of a duty rather than a discretion. This might suggest that legal enforcement is available. The problem is that the duty only arises where the child 'appears to them', i.e. the local authority, to require accommodation. Moreover, obtaining judicial enforcement will necessitate the parent showing that, contrary to the opinion of the authority, all the relevant conditions, such as the child being 'in need', are satisfied. This is no easy task. Probably the most that can be said is that if the local authority refuses accommodation for a wholly extraneous and irrelevant reason, the court might intervene on the application of an aggrieved party (and this can include the child himself in appropriate cases). But in any event, going to court (and in this type of situation it is by way of the special judicial review procedure in the High Court in London) is a very cumbersome and wearying business. It often creates more problems than it solves. It is, perhaps, a shade unrealistic to expect dissatisfied individuals to regard it as a viable method of achieving their objective. The exertion of pressure on management, members of the social services committee, Members of Parliament and the DH is likely to prove more efficacious in many cases. Nor should it be forgotten that the local authority's complaints procedure may be available (see page 96 below). Indeed, cases decided in the High Court since 1991 indicate that judicial review in this field should not be resorted to until the complaints procedure has been used.

Does the child have a say?

We have already seen that the parental veto disappears if the child is over 16 and he agrees to being provided with accommodation. This right to self-determination does not extend to the under-16s. If a child under 16 expresses a wish to go into accommodation but the parents disagree, compulsory powers will be needed if the child is to move. This will involve the local authority going to court and proving grounds for an order.

What of the child who opposes the idea of accommodation? The Children Act does not require the child's consent to be obtained before section 20 accommodation is provided. What it does is to require the child's views to be considered:

Before providing accommodation under this section, a local authority shall, so far as is reasonably practicable and consistent with the child's welfare – (a) ascertain the child's wishes regarding the provision of accommodation; and (b) give due consideration (having regard to his age and understanding) to such wishes of the child as they have been able to ascertain. (section 20(6))

Although the Act does not give the child a veto, in practice a veto there will certainly be – at any rate for the older child of 16 or 17 who can leave school and become self-supporting. The reason for this is that there is nothing to stop such a child leaving the accommodation which has been provided. To acquire the power to detain him, the local authority will need a court order granted under the compulsory provisions of the Act; if there are no grounds available for an order – and there may well not be any if the child has suitable alternative accommodation to go to – then the local authority is not really in a position to do anything. As was said by a Government minister in Parliament, the over-16s 'can always vote with their feet'. It was for this reason that no specific provision on the matter was included in the Act.

The position when accommodation is provided

The code of treatment

Once a child is provided with accommodation under section 20, there becomes applicable an important series of provisions in the Children Act covering all children who are, to use the words of the Act, 'looked after by a local authority'. The other major group of children caught by this expression consists of those who are subject to a care order. Insofar as the Act lays down a code of treatment common to those being cared for under both voluntary and compulsory arrangements, it is no different from the old law set out in the Child Care Act 1980. Indeed, there is also considerable similarity as far as the details of the code are concerned, since many of the provisions were lifted straight out of the 1980 Act. The opportunity was taken, however, of introducing some significant changes. The code of treatment is contained partly in sections 20–29 of the Act, partly in Schedule 2 and partly in various sets of regulations made by the DH. Set out below is a commentary on the main features of this code, looked at from the particular perspective of the child in section 20 accommodation and his family.

The general welfare duty

The general duty of a local authority has remained the same: to safeguard and promote the child's welfare (section 22(3)). The following observation from the Government may serve to put this laudable provision into some perspective:

> It must be recognized that local authorities have to discharge their legal responsibilities within the limits of the resources available, so that the best for any individual child or group of children may simply not be available or available only at considerable cost to other children or to other client groups whose needs may be just as great.

The local authority is to make such use of services available for children cared for by their own parents as appears reasonable (also section 22(3)).

The concept of 'welfare' as it is used in section 22(3) is not defined. Nor does the welfare checklist contained in section 1(3) of the Act apply: this is directed only at courts (though of course there is nothing to stop a local authority from bearing in mind the matters referred to). A checklist of sorts does, however, emerge when other provisions within Part III are examined. An assortment of sections and subsections singles out a range of matters which the local authority is required to take into account when looking after a child. These matters are described in detail below but by way of summary we may note the following:

- The wishes and feelings of the child
- The wishes and feelings of the parents and other interested persons
- The child's religious persuasion, racial origin and cultural and linguistic background
- The particular needs of a disabled child.

It is an interesting exercise to examine the origins and aims of these respective checklists. Although the picture is not entirely clear, it would appear that, whereas the welfare checklist in section 1(3) was thought by the Law Commission to reflect the existing practice of the courts, the rather sprawling collection of factors applicable to local authorities owes its existence to a perception within the DH that social services departments across the country were giving insufficient attention to them – hence the need for express statutory provisions. The result, in terms of coherence and comprehensiveness, is not altogether satisfactory.

Consulting the child

The local authority has a duty to ascertain the wishes and feelings of the child before making any decision concerning him and to give due consideration to them, having regard to his age and understanding (section 22(4)).

Consulting the parents

The terms of section 22(4), noted above, also apply to the child's parents (this includes the unmarried father, whether or not he has acquired parental responsibility). This is obviously a key partnership provision of the 1989 Act. Should the parents feel that proper consideration has not been given to their views – whether they relate to a decision about the type of placement, the frequency of visits or anything else to do with the child – they are not without remedies. They can utilize (among other things) the section 26 complaints procedure or, if they have parental responsibility, they can simply remove the child from the accommodation. These matters are considered below.

Consulting other people

Section 22(4) acknowledges that persons other than parents may be important figures in the life of the child. It imposes a duty to consult any non-parent who has parental responsibility for the child (e.g. the holder of a residence order) and any other person whose wishes and feelings the local authority considers to be relevant. Due consideration is to be given to the wishes and feelings of such people.

Religion, racial origin and cultural and linguistic background

Section 22(5)(c) requires the local authority, when making a decision with respect to a child being looked after, to give due consideration to the child's religious persuasion, racial origin and cultural and linguistic background. Although the introduction of this provision into our public child law was widely welcomed, a number of important issues are left unanswered. The duty of the local authority is to give 'due consideration' to these factors. This is not a particularly restricting exercise. No indication is given of the weight to be attached to religion, ethnicity and language, nor are any initial presumptions set out. The result is that different local authorities are able to maintain different policies on the treatment of children from minority groups while at the same time proclaiming an adherence to the terms of the legislation. For example, the Act certainly does not require children to be placed with families of the same ethnic group, but there is nothing to stop local authorities adopting a policy along these lines if that is considered beneficial. It would be argued that in doing so, the local authority is not only giving 'due consideration' to the child's racial origin, it is also safeguarding and promoting his welfare, as required by section 22(3). Indeed, the DH itself has provided support for this approach in its 1991 Guidance. According to Volume 3 of this:

> It may be taken as a guiding principle of good practice that, other things being equal and in the great majority of cases, placement with a family of similar ethnic origin and religion is most likely to meet a child's needs as fully as possible and to safeguard his or her welfare most effectively. Such a family is most likely to be able to provide a child with continuity in life and care and an environment which the child will find familiar and sympathetic and in which opportunities will naturally arise to share fully in the culture and way of life of the ethnic group to which he belongs.

This passage is in fact a repeat performance of part of a letter sent to SSDs by the Social Services Inspectorate in 1990, following well publicized same-race controversies in London. The DH is certainly not intending to thrust a rigid policy upon local authorities – indeed, the Guidance goes out of its way to discourage rigidity – but the general emphasis is unmistakeable.

Selecting the placement

Section 23(2) states that a local authority shall provide accommodation for a child by:

(a) placing him with a family, a relative or any other suitable person;
(b) maintaining him in a community home;
(c) maintaining him in a voluntary home;
(d) maintaining him in a private children's home;
(e) maintaining him in a home provided in accordance with arrangements made by the DH; or
(f) making such other arrangements as seem appropriate.

The choice of placement is left to the discretion of the local authority, although the specific reference in paragraph (a) to fostering by relatives was designed to highlight the advantages (well documented in the research) of such arrangements. The DH Guidance states (in Volume 3) that placement with a relative will often provide the best opportunities for promoting and maintaining family links in a familiar setting. Although welfare considerations should be central to the decision-making process, the cost factor clearly cannot be ignored. In *R v Kingston-upon-Thames Borough Council ex parte T* (1993), the local authority agreed to provide section 20 accommodation for a 14-year-old emotionally abused child but the particular placement offered did not meet with the family's approval. The family's preferred placement – in a special unit run by a voluntary organization –

had been rejected by the authority partly on the grounds of cost. Following a challenge instituted by the family, the High Court ruled that the financial constraints affecting the authority were legitimate factors to take into account. The balancing of welfare and cost was essentially a matter for the authority and the court would only intervene in the event of a perverse decision (which this one was not).

It will be noticed that section 23(2)(f) is a residual provision which enables the local authority to arrange a placement of a type which is not referred to in any of the previous paragraphs. An example of 'other arrangements' is a hospital placement and the case of *R v Kirklees Metropolitan Council ex parte C* (1993) illustrates the breadth of power created by the Act. There, a violent and disruptive child of 12 had been transferred by the local authority from a children's home to a psychiatric hospital where she was kept for 16 days in an adult ward. There was no question of the child suffering from mental disorder, nor were any of the procedures under the Mental Health Act implemented. The expressed purpose of the placement was to facilitate an assessment of the child's needs in a way which had not been possible at the children's home. A claim against the local authority for false imprisonment was dismissed by the court: in legal terms the authority had simply used its statutory discretion to change the child's accommodation.

Placing the child near home

Whatever type of accommodation is provided, the local authority should ensure that it is near the child's home so far as this is reasonably practicable and consistent with his welfare (section 23(7)). This is one of a number of provisions aimed at preserving family links. Another one is described in the next paragraph.

Accommodating siblings

Section 23(7) also states that where the local authority is providing accommodation for a sibling of the child, they are to be accommodated together, so far as this is reasonably practicable and consistent with the child's welfare. The proviso at the end is important and has the effect of avoiding the creation of an absolute duty to be followed in every case.

Accommodating disabled children

Section 23(8) is devoted to accommodated children who are disabled – and it should be remembered that 'disabled' has a special meaning in the Act (see page 63 above). The local authority is under an obligation to secure that the accommodation which it provides for such a child 'is not unsuitable to his particular needs', but again this is subject to the 'so far as is reasonably practicable' proviso. Volume 6 of the DH Guidance contains much useful material on accommodation for disabled children.

The effect of section 23(8) was considered by the Court of Appeal in *R v Brent London Borough Council ex parte S* (1993), a case in which the grandparents of a 13-year-old autistic child claimed that accommodation which had been offered to them under section 20 was inadequate. The court stated that the wording of the Act seemed to be designed to avoid placing an unrealistically heavy burden on local authorities:

> the accommodation to be secured is not required to be suitable to the particular needs of the child, but only to be not unsuitable, and the duty to secure even that is qualified by what is reasonably practicable . . . so long as the council is doing the best they can, within the bounds of what is reasonably practicable, to secure not unsuitable accommodation, [we] do not think that they are in breach of their statutory duty.

Contact and the promotion of family links

Schedule 2 to the Children Act contains provisions (in paragraph 15) which are of considerable importance concerning the subject of contact between the child and his family. These provisions create a number of obligations, one general, the others specific. The general duty is imposed on the local authority and requires it to endeavour to promote contact between the child and his parents, any non-parent having parental responsibility for him, any relative and any friend or other person connected with him, unless such contact is not reasonably practicable or consistent with his welfare. The wording of this duty is designed to serve a number of purposes. First, and most obviously, it aims to encourage in a positive fashion the promotion of links between the child and his family on the grounds that this is, in most cases, the best way of furthering the interests and welfare of the child. From this point of view, it is at one with section 23(6) of the Act, which requires the local authority to make arrangements, subject to considerations of practicability and welfare, to enable a child being looked after to live with his family or a friend.

A second purpose is to acknowledge that in some cases, contact is either not a viable proposition (because, for example, the parents have disappeared or have refused to co-operate) or not a desirable one. Hence we have the familiar words 'reasonably practicable' and 'consistent with his welfare'. The use of the word 'endeavour' is also designed for this purpose:

according to the Government, it 'implies the idea of continuing to work at it in the hope that ultimately it will prevail'.

The specific duties are concerned with the notification of addresses and they work in both directions. Each of the parents has an obligation (under-pinned by criminal penalties) to keep the authority informed of his or her address. A non-parent with parental responsibility for the child is under the same obligation. The other side of the coin is that the authority must take 'such steps as are reasonably practicable' to secure that these parties are kept informed of where the child is being accommodated (which, it will be recalled, must normally be a place near the child's home).

Contact disputes concerning accommodated children can easily arise. As previously indicated, a dissatisfied parent is able to use the complaints procedure which the Act required to be set up; he is also able to remove the child from the accommodation. A further manoeuvre which is available (and this applies to non-parents too) is to seek a contact order from the court under Part II of the Act (see Chapters 3 and 4). Such proceedings, though, would do little to promote the partnership philosophy which sup-posedly permeates section 20 arrangements. Consequently, they should be viewed with caution.

Volume 3 of the DH Guidance contains a chapter devoted to contact with children being 'looked after' (this expression, it will be recalled, covers care order children as well as those being accommodated). The advice set out in it is, in effect, an expanded version of the Code of Practice on Access to Children in Care which was issued by the Department under the old law in 1983.

In order to sustain the viability of contact arrangements, Schedule 2 to the Act preserved local authorities' power to make payments to parents and others in connection with visits to, or by, their children (paragraph 16).

Independent visitors

If communication between the child and his parents (or a non-parent with parental responsibility) is infrequent or non-existent, or if there have been no visits to them or by them for a year, the local authority must appoint an independent visitor for the child, whose function is to visit, advise and befriend the child (Schedule 2). This provision is based very largely on section 11 of the Child Care Act 1980, but whereas section 11 was only concerned with care order children, the new obligation extends to all children who are being looked after by a local authority. An appointment does not have to be made, however, if it would not be in the child's best interests. Furthermore, a child with sufficient understanding has a veto.

The question of independent visitors is also the subject of a chapter in Volume 3 of the Guidance. This deals with such matters as recruitment, training and support, visits, advising and befriending, and relationships between the visitor and the local authority. The Definition of Independent Visitors (Children) Regulations 1991 describe those types of individual who are not to be regarded as independent for the purposes of Schedule 2.

Operating the placement

Most children who are accommodated under section 20 are placed with foster carers or placed in a children's home (a home run by the local authority itself or by some other organization). These types of placement are the subject of detailed regulations and guidance issued by the DH. Fostering is covered by the Foster Placement (Children) Regulations 1991 and Volume 3 of the Children Act Guidance, while residential care is covered by the Children's Homes Regulations 1991 and Volume 4 of the Guidance. As the Guidance states (Volume 3, paragraph 3.1), foster care is frequently the preferred way of providing care for children who need to be looked after by a local authority and Chapter 17 of this book considers the statutory framework of fostering in more detail.

Selecting secure accommodation

Although the elaborate network of provisions in the regulations and guidance concerning children's homes is beyond the scope of this book, the issue of secure accommodation within residential care merits some attention, partly because of its gravity and partly because the courts are often involved in the decision-making process. For a local authority to restrict the liberty of a child it is looking after is self-evidently a very serious step to take, and since 1983 restrictive conditions have been required to be satisfied before a secure placement is selected, including in some circumstances the granting of a court order. Under section 25(1) of the Children Act secure accommodation (defined in the section as 'accommodation provided for the purpose of restricting liberty') may be used only if it appears (a) that the child has a history of absconding and is likely to abscond from any other description of accommodation and, if he absconds, he is likely to suffer significant harm, or (b) that if he is kept in any other description of accommodation he is likely to injure himself or other persons. This provision applies to children accommodated under voluntary arrangements just as much as to those in compulsory care. According to the Child Care Law Review:

> About 10 per cent of admissions to secure accommodation are of children received into care, who form 5 per cent of those in secure accommodation at any one point. It has been questioned whether local authorities should be able to place children presently received

into care in secure accommodation. However, children in the care of local authorities may be particularly needy and vulnerable whatever the route by which they entered care, and temporary containment will in a few cases be desirable without needing to take over parental powers in order to do so.

Section 25(1) tells only half the story of secure accommodation, however, because the Government retained the power to make regulations in the area. These were made under the title of the Children (Secure Accommodation) Regulations 1991 and they replaced the regulations made under the old law in 1983 and 1986. Amendments to the 1991 regulations were made in 1992, 1995 and 1996. The broad effect of the regulations is that the maximum period beyond which a child may not be kept in secure accommodation without the authority of a court is an aggregate of 72 hours (whether or not consecutive) in any period of 28 consecutive days. No child under 13 can be placed in secure accommodation without the prior approval of the DH and such approval can be given subject to special conditions.

Applications can be made to a court (normally a magistrates' court) for authority to retain a child in secure accommodation and such authority can last for up to three months initially and thereafter for periods of up to six months. These applications are 'specified proceedings' for the purposes of section 41 of the Act and therefore a guardian ad litem will normally be appointed to represent the interests of the child (see further, Chapter 13). There are also special rules concerning legal aid and legal representation for the child (section 25(6)). The courts have experienced difficulty in defining their proper function when hearing a secure accommodation application. The most problematic question has been whether or not the welfare principle contained in section 1(1) of the Act is applicable (as, of course, it is in most other Children Act applications). Section 25(3) states that it is the duty of a court hearing a secure accommodation application 'to determine whether any relevant criteria for keeping a child in secure accommodation are satisfied in his case'. The 'relevant criteria' are those set out in section 25(1) – a history of absconding, etc. Section 25(4) states that if the court decides that any such criteria are satisfied, it *shall* make an order authorizing the child to be kept in secure accommodation and specifying the maximum period for which he may be kept there. It is the use of the word 'shall' which has caused problems of interpretation, for it appears to leave the court no discretion and accordingly no opportunity to consider welfare factors. And yet it seems perverse for a court to ignore such issues when dealing with a vulnerable teenager. Moreover, the mandatory appointment of a guardian ad litem would seem to suggest that the child's welfare was intended to be a critical factor. The DH 1991 Guidance certainly reflects this view.

An opportunity to examine and rule upon these matters was taken by the

Court of Appeal in *Re M* (1994), a case which did in fact concern an accommodated child. The child was a boy of 14 who had been accommodated since the age of nine on account of being beyond parental control. He had persistently absconded from children's homes, had displayed violent and disruptive behaviour and had taken drugs. He had a history of school exclusion and had been prosecuted for a variety of criminal offences. The local authority applied for a secure accommodation order and this was granted by the magistrates, the authorization to last for three months. On appeal, the Court of Appeal noted that a local authority, when selecting a secure placement for a child, will have to consider not only the section 25(1) criteria but also its general duty under section 22(3) to safeguard and promote the welfare of the child. Since the court's role in a section 25 application is, in effect, to review the local authority's decision, it would be inconsistent with the purpose of the section for the court to operate on a different basis. Consequently, welfare is relevant to a section 25 application, though it is not paramount and the welfare rules in section 1 of the Act (including the checklist) are not applicable. The welfare of the child is therefore one of the 'relevant criteria' for the court to consider under section 25(3) and according to the Court of Appeal it is an important consideration. The court acknowledged that there will be cases where the child's welfare is outweighed by other considerations, such as the need to protect the public. This is explicitly recognized by the Act itself, for section 25(1)(b) refers to a situation where a secure placement needs to be selected because if the child were placed elsewhere he would be likely to injure other persons.

Further control of local authority behaviour in relation to secure placements has been achieved by the provisions in the regulations which require the appointment of at least three people (including one independent person) to review the child's situation regularly. Their specific function is to ascertain the wishes and feelings of the child, his parents and other interested parties and then consider whether or not (a) the section 25(1) criteria continue to apply, (b) the placement in such accommodation continues to be necessary and (c) any other type of accommodation would be appropriate.

The use of secure accommodation by local authorities has continued to give rise to anxiety among commentators, especially since the 'pin down' controversy in Staffordshire. The DH in its Guidance (Volumes 1 and 4) has emphasized the extreme care which needs to be taken:

> Restricting the liberty of children is a serious step which must be taken only when there is no genuine alternative which would be appropriate. It must be a 'last resort' in the sense that all else must first have been comprehensively considered and rejected – never because no other placement was available at the relevant time, because of

inadequacies in staffing, because the child is simply being a nuisance or runs away from his accommodation and is not likely to suffer significant harm in doing so, and never as a form of punishment. Secure placements, once made, should be for only so long as is necessary and unavoidable.

It has also reminded SSDs of their obligation (referred to in the last chapter) to include secure accommodation in their preventive work under Schedule 2 to the 1989 Act.

According to section 25(9), 'this section is subject to section 20(8)'. This lapse into legalistic drafting disguises the rule that persons with parental responsibility may remove the child from secure accommodation where this has been provided in pursuance of voluntary arrangements. Not every parent will agree with the local authority having recourse to a locking-up device for their child, no matter how persuasive the social workers are, and this provision makes it clear that they have the ultimate remedy – explored in more detail later in the present chapter – of removal at their disposal.

Protecting the public

The local authority has power to take measures to protect the public even though they may be inconsistent with its general welfare duty to the child (section 22(6)).

Financial contributions by parents

Section 29 and Schedule 2 to the Act preserved the arrangements under which parents are liable to contribute towards the maintenance of the child while he is being accommodated by the local authority. The provisions are more or less the same as those previously in force, and so deal with matters such as contribution notices and court orders. These provisions are unaffected by the Child Support Act 1991, which has no application to children being looked after by a local authority. The collection of contributions is not an uncontroversial matter, of course, and the case for abolition was strongly pressed in Parliament in 1989. Perhaps not surprisingly, the Government resisted the proposal.

Emigration

The power to arrange for the child's emigration was retained by Schedule 2 to the Act. The procedure was changed, however. The previous legislation required the consent of the DH to be obtained in each case before emigration took place. The Children Act created two separate procedures, one for care order children (on which see Chapter 10) and one for those provided with accommodation. As far as the latter group is concerned, the local authority is authorized to arrange for emigration provided it has the approval of every person who has parental responsibility for the child.

Making plans and avoiding drift

In the wake of the Children Act came a new emphasis on planning within social services departments, the expressed purposes of which were to safeguard and promote the child's welfare, to prevent drift and to help to focus work with the family. This emphasis came as no great surprise because the Government's White Paper of 1987 contained clear indications of a future initiative in this direction. What was, perhaps, a surprise was the fact that the Act itself lacked any specific provisions on the matter, leaving regulations and guidance to do what was necessary.

The starting point of our consideration of planning must be *The Care of Children*, principle 32 of which states that 'planning is a central responsibility for all agencies providing services to children and their families'. It goes on to say that the following elements are important:

(a) Planning must take the other principles into account.
(b) Assessment must precede planning.
(c) Plans should be regularly reassessed both informally and at reviews and case conferences.
(d) Clarity and effective communication are essential and written agreements are likely to be the most effective method of achieving this.
(e) The goal must be inherent in the plan and clearly stated.

Principle 32, as can be seen, covers all family services. For more detailed material on planning and accommodation, we must turn to the Arrangements for Placement of Children (General) Regulations 1991. These regulations, as their title suggests, are general in scope in the sense that they extend to all types of local authority placement, including foster care and residential accommodation. Their main objective is to ensure that children being looked after are the subject of proper individual plans ('arrangements' is the word used in the regulations). Once made, a plan will have to be reviewed on a regular basis under the review regulations noted below. The result is that the placement of an accommodated child is regulated in law by the Children Act itself and various sets of regulations (e.g. those concerning plans, reviews and foster care) plus, of course, the guidance from the DH.

According to the 1991 regulations, before placing a child the local authority shall make immediate and long-term arrangements – in writing – for that placement and for promoting the welfare of the child. Formulating a long-term plan before placement is not always possible and the regulations provide that in this case the plan should be made as soon as reasonably practicable after it. Reflecting the partnership philosophy, regulation 3 goes on to say that the arrangements 'shall so far as reasonably practicable be agreed by the responsible authority with (a) a person [not 'every person'] with parental responsibility for the child or (b) if there is no such person the person who is caring for the child'. This is to be done before placement if possible. If the child in question is 16 or over, the regulations require the agreement to be made with him.

The effect of these provisions , as explained in Volume 3 of the Guidance, is first, that there must be a written plan for the child, and second, that this plan should form the basis of a written agreement with the parents or the child's carer or the child himself. The agreement therefore incorporates the detail of the plan and the regulations provide for the formal notification of these to all relevant persons and organizations. Informal explanation to the parents and the child is also urged by the Guidance, as is an indication as to who is responsible for implementing the various elements of the plan.

The regulations do not require the agreement to be signed but the DH encourages joint signature as an indication of commitment to the plan. Practitioners should not be led astray by the use of the expression 'agreement', still less by the fact that it has been signed. Both the local authority and the parents will, of course, be expected to do their best to adhere to the terms agreed. At the end of the day, however, the agreement will not be absolutely binding. From the local authority's point of view, its overriding obligation is that contained in section 22(3) of the Act – to safeguard and promote the child's welfare – and if it feels that this duty demands changes in the treatment of the child, then it should act accordingly, even if the agreement does not provide for them. From the parents' point of view, the provision of section 20 accommodation does not alter the fact that they retain parental responsibility for the child. The local authority lacks it. In the final analysis, therefore – and as we shall see shortly, the Act expressly confirms this – the parents may bring the whole arrangement to an end simply by removing the child from the accommodation. The existence of an agreement with the social services department will not prevent this – not in law at any rate. It may be hard for social workers to swallow this, particularly in cases where the agreement has been a long time in the making, but if the essential feature of the section 20 service is its voluntariness, which it is, then there is no room for compulsion at any stage.

What can one expect to find in plans and agreements? The answer is supplied partly by the regulations, partly by the guidance and partly by the Act. The regulations require the local authority to have regard to three sets of 'considerations' when making arrangements. The first set is 'general' and consists of the following:

1 Whether the authority should seek a change in the child's legal status.
2 Arrangements for contact, and whether there is any need for changes in the arrangements in order to promote contact with the child's family and others so far as is consistent with his welfare.
3 The authority's immediate and long-term arrangements for the child, previous arrangements in respect of the child and whether a change in those arrangements is needed and consideration of alternative courses of action.
4 Whether an independent visitor should be appointed if one has not already been appointed.
5 Whether arrangements need to be made for the time when the child will no longer be looked after by the authority.
6 Whether plans need to be made to find a permanent substitute family for the child.

The second set of considerations covers health and the third covers education. In addition to all this, the regulations prescribe 'matters to be included' in accommodation arrangements where practicable. These are as follows:

1 The type of accommodation to be provided and its address together with the name of any person who will be responsible for the child at that accommodation.
2 The details of any services to be provided for the child.
3 The respective responsibilities of the authority and the child, his parents and any non-parent with parental responsibility.
4 What delegation there has been by the parents to the authority of parental responsibility for the child's day-to-day care.
5 The arrangements for involving the parents and the child in decision-making.
6 Contact arrangements.
7 The arrangements for notifying changes in the plan to interested parties.
8 In the case of a child aged 16 or over, whether section 20(11) applies (this covers accommodation despite parental opposition).
9 The expected duration of arrangements and the steps which should apply to bring the arrangements to an end, including arrangements for rehabilitation.

All of these matters are explored in the Guidance, which points out that the regulations are not intended to be exhaustive. Nor do they repeat things which have already been said in the Act itself. The needs of the child arising from ethnicity and culture are a good example: they are mentioned in section 22(5) of the Children Act and accordingly fall naturally for consideration at the planning stage. There is no need for repetition in the regulations. As far as contents of plans are concerned, therefore, the effect of the provisions is to require local authorities to adhere to a prescribed core whilst enabling them to use their discretion in supplementing it.

Finally, it should be noted that the arrangements regulations (as amended in 1995) make special provision for cases involving a series of short pre-planned placements (e.g. for respite care). If certain conditions are present, these can be treated as a single placement so that only the one plan will be needed.

Reviewing the arrangements

The review of cases within the local authority has continued to be subject to government regulations (under section 26). The legal position here was rather odd before the Children Act because although the DH was given regulation-making powers as long ago as 1975, it never actually used them. This led to wide and unsatisfactory variations in local authority practice. Everything changed, however, as a result of the Review of Children's Cases Regulations 1991 and the associated guidance (Volume 3 in the Children Act series).

Under the regulations, each case is first to be reviewed within four weeks of the date upon which the child begins to be looked after by the local authority. The second review is to be carried out not more than three months after the first and thereafter reviews are to be carried out not more than six months after the date of the previous one. The Guidance emphasizes that the frequency of reviews required by the regulations is the minimum standard: 'a review of the child's case should take place as often as the circumstances require.'

The precise format of a review is a matter within the authority's discretion, except that two schedules to the regulations prescribe 'elements to be included in a review' and 'considerations to which authorities are to have regard'. The 'elements' are as follows:

1 Keeping informed of the arrangements for looking after the child and of any relevant change in the child's circumstances.
2 Keeping informed of the name and address of any person whose views should be taken into account in the course of the review.
3 Making necessary preparations and providing any relevant information to the participants in any meeting of the authority which considers the child's case in connection with any aspect of the review.
4 Initiating meetings of relevant personnel of the authority and other relevant persons to consider the review of the child's case.
5 Explaining to the child any steps which he may take under the Act including, where appropriate (a) his right to apply, with leave, for a section 8 order, (b) (this applies only to care order cases and is described

in Chapter 10), and (c) the availability of the authority's complaints procedure (see below for this).

6 Making decisions or taking steps following review decisions arising out of or resulting from the review.

The 'considerations' are broadly the same as the 'general considerations' set out in the arrangements regulations (see page 94 above for these). All these prescribed matters are designed to supplement the general welfare provisions of the Children Act itself.

Involving the child and his family is obviously a crucial matter in a review and the regulations attempt to ensure good practice in this respect. First, they state that before conducting any review, the authority must, unless it is not reasonably practicable to do so, seek and take into account the views of the child, his parents and any non-parent with parental responsibility. They must be given written details of the authority's review procedure. Second, the regulations require the authority to involve (again, so far as is reasonably practicable) these people in the review 'including, where the authority consider appropriate, the attendance of those persons at part or all of any meeting which is to consider the child's case'. The Guidance states that only in exceptional cases should a parent or child not be invited to a review meeting. Finally, the authority is required to notify them of details of the result of the review and of any decision taken in consequence of it.

The regulations also deal with health matters and they make special provision for cases where accommodation is provided for a series of short periods at the same place (e.g. for respite care).

Redressing a grievance: the complaints procedure

One feature of the Children Act which received a particularly detailed examination in Parliament was the collection of provisions in section 26 concerning local authority complaints procedures. The former position was that there was no legal requirement for a social services department to establish a formal procedure for handling complaints about child care decisions. The nearest the law came to it was the issue in 1983 of the DH Code of Practice on Access, which encouraged local authorities to develop 'clear procedures which will enable parents to pursue complaints about access and ask for decisions to be reviewed' and urged them to inform parents of the existence of such procedures. Unhappily, progress was slow. Indeed, the view was expressed in Parliament that 'there is a tremendous reluctance to set up a complaints procedure in most social services departments, and even when complaints procedures exist they are rarely publicized'.

In the absence of any systematic internal machinery, parents and their children, relatives, foster carers and others with a grievance were faced with the prospect of badgering whoever they could manage to get hold of, whether it was a social worker, manager or councillor. This was clearly unsatisfactory. There were always external mechanisms, of course (e.g. the media, MPs, the courts and even the Local Ombudsman) but knowledge of them and of how to use them is scanty, to say the least, and their efficacy cannot be guaranteed.

The question of complaints was considered by the House of Commons Social Services Committee and subsequently as part of the Child Care Law Review. The end product of these developments was section 26 of the Children Act. The first part of the section deals with reviews and this has already been described. Subsections (3) to (8) deal with complaints. According to these provisions, every local authority shall (so they have had no choice in the matter) establish a procedure for considering any representations – this rather legalistic expression specifically includes complaints – made to it by any child it is looking after, his parent(s), any non-parent having parental responsibility, any local authority foster carer or 'such other person as the authority consider has a sufficient interest in the child's welfare to warrant his representations being considered'. This last term was put into the section in order to cover complaints from people such as relatives, doctors and teachers; it also covers social services staff who wish to raise matters on the child's behalf.

Under the procedure, complaints and other comments may be made about 'the discharge by the authority of any of their functions under this Part in relation to the child'. 'This Part' means Part III of the Act, taken with the accompanying Schedule 2 set out at the back of the Act, so any matter mentioned in Part III or Schedule 2 can be made the subject of a complaint. Such a complaint can therefore concern the placement of the child, the treatment he is getting there, the contact arrangements which have been made, the charges which have been imposed on the parents, the depth of social work support being given, the breaking of any agreement made with the authority, and so on.

Complaints under the statutory procedure can be made by a variety of adults, including foster carers. They can also be made by the child himself. Children's complaints obviously have to be handled in an especially sensitive manner. As the House of Commons Social Services Committee pointed out in its report:

> For children, it is of particular importance to provide a channel which enables complaints to be made without destroying any relationship of trust with a social worker or foster parent.

The need for an independent element in the complaints procedure which was advocated by the Child Care Law Review is reflected in section 26(4), which requires the local authority's procedure to provide for the participation of at least one person who is neither a member (i.e. a councillor) nor an officer of the authority. This is, in fact, all that the Children Act says about the precise mechanics of the complaints procedure. Subject to the independent person requirement, it looks as though the authority is completely free to decide who shall hear the complaint and in what manner. However, in common with so many areas covered by the Act, complaints procedures are regulated by government rules and these rules, together with the associated guidance (in Volume 3 of the Children Act series), inevitably have the effect of reducing the options open to local authorities. The Representations Procedure (Children) Regulations 1991 aim to establish minimum standards and they have been framed in such a way as to enable authorities to operate their Children Act procedure in tandem with the one set up to cover other social services functions under the National Health Service and Community Care Act 1990.

The effect of the regulations is that a two-stage complaints procedure must be offered. The first stage consists of the authority considering the complaint with an independent person and formulating a response within 28 days (the independent person taking part in any discussions about what action, if any, is to be taken). The regulations require the authority to notify the results of the review within the 28 days to the complainant, the child (unless the authority considers that he is not of sufficient understanding or it would be likely to cause serious harm to his health or emotional condition), the independent person and any other person thought to have a sufficient interest in the case. The complainant must be told of his right to have the matter referred to a panel under stage two of the procedure.

If the complainant informs the local authority in writing within 28 days that he is dissatisfied with the proposed result of the review, he can ask that the matter be referred to a panel. The panel, which is to consist of three people (at least one of them independent of the authority), is required to meet within 28 days of the complainant's request. The function of the panel is to consider any oral or written submissions that the complainant or the authority wish to make and any submissions from the independent person who sat at stage one (if different), and then decide on its recommendations. These are to be committed to writing within 24 hours and communicated to the authority, the complainant and other interested parties. Procedure before the panel is at the panel's discretion except that the regulations provide for the complainant to be accompanied, if he wishes, by another person of his choice, who may speak on his behalf. The Guidance urges that the meeting is conducted in as informal an atmosphere as possible. Once a complaint has been heard by the panel, the local authority (assisted by the independent member) has to decide what to do about it. Section 26(7) imposes two obligations here. One is to have 'due regard' to the findings of those considering the complaint. This does not mean that the local authority must abide by the recommendations of the complaints panel; it simply means that the recommendations must be looked at and not ignored. (In *R v Brent London Borough Council ex parte S* (1993) the Court of Appeal acknowledged that it could not compel a local authority to accept panel recommendations. It went on to say, however, that it would be an unusual case when an authority acted contrary to the recommendations.) The second obligation is to notify in writing – if this is practicable – the complainant, the child (if he has sufficient understanding) and such other persons as appear to be likely to be affected, of the authority's decision in the matter and its reasons for taking that decision, together with any action which it has taken or proposes to take. The requirement to give written reasons for a decision, albeit after a complaint has been lodged, was a great step forward in achieving procedural fairness for consumers of social services. It is a practice which has been followed for a long time by many authorities and it is good to see it enshrined in legislation.

Another welcome feature of section 26 is subsection (8), which requires every local authority to give publicity to its complaints procedure. It has a considerable amount of discretion here, however, since the duty is to give 'such publicity as they consider appropriate'. Much depends on the social services department approaching the subject in the right spirit. According to the Guidance, 'the publicity should be framed in terms that make clear that the procedure is a part of the local authority's commitment to partnership . . . All the material should present a positive view of the use of the procedure and seek to diminish fears that invoking the procedure will cause problems for a complainant in their day to day contact with authorities' staff'. This approach is also reflected in a provision in the regulations which requires an authority to offer to a complainant 'assistance and guidance' on the use of its procedure. In addition to the obligation under section 26(8), it is worth remembering the impact which the other aspect of section 26 – concerning reviews – may have here. It has already been seen that regulations have been made regarding reviews; those regulations require the authority to inform the child on review of any steps he may take under the Act. This includes the possibility of making a complaint.

One important matter addressed in the Guidance, but not in the legislation, is the meaning of the expression 'complaint'. The Guidance states that 'it is not intended that all problems that arise in the day to day handling of child care services should automatically be elevated to the status of a complaint. A matter which is promptly resolved to everyone's satisfaction when drawn to the attention of an officer of the authority is not something that requires referral to the procedure'. While acknowledging (perhaps unhelpfully) that the precise meaning of complaint is a matter for interpretation by the courts, the DH has offered its own definition: 'a "complaint" is a written or oral expression of dissatisfaction or disquiet in relation to an individual child.' In the *Brent* case (above) a foster carer had written to the council's chief executive claiming that the council was not taking a particular problem seriously. Although the letter did not mention the complaints procedure – indeed, the foster carer was unaware of its existence – the Court of Appeal stated that the council should have recognized the letter as a 'representation' within the meaning of section 26(3). Consequently, the complaints procedure should have been activated.

Redressing a grievance: judicial review

Unlike the local authority's internal complaints procedure, judicial review in the High Court is not mentioned at all in the Children Act. This does not mean, however, that it has no application to the treatment of children being looked after. Judicial review is a mechanism which is available to any person with a sufficient interest who claims that a public authority (such as a local council) has failed to adhere to the statutory regime to which it is subject. It is, in other words, a method by which members of the public can seek to ensure that public bodies observe the law. Since Parliament, through Part III of the Children Act, has imposed on social services departments a legal framework relating to the way in which accommodated children are to be treated, it follows that the judicial review remedy will, in principle, be available if the code of treatment is infringed. As a result of the way judicial review has been developed by the judiciary in modern times, 'infringement' for these purposes includes the following:

- Failing to discharge a duty imposed by the legislation
- Exercising a discretion perversely (not simply 'wrongly')
- Exercising a discretion without considering all the relevant factors
- Exercising a discretion having considered irrelevant factors
- Adopting a procedure which is unfair to the individual(s) concerned
- Misconstruing the legislation.

If the applicant succeeds in establishing any of the above-mentioned grounds, the High Court may in its discretion set aside the decision which has been made (thus requiring the local authority to reconsider the case) or, if it is a case of failure to carry out a duty, order the authority to rectify the omission.

In order to deter hopeless or inappropriate claims, Parliament has provided (in section 31 of the Supreme Court Act 1981) that an applicant for judicial review must obtain preliminary leave from the High Court. In the context of grievances concerning 'looked after' children, this procedural obstacle is very important, particularly because the judiciary has developed a principle that leave to apply for judicial review should not normally be granted if there are other, more suitable, methods of redress which have not been pursued by the applicant. Since section 26 of the Children Act requires the local authority to offer a complaints procedure in respect of children being looked after, it is easy to argue that an aggrieved individual should use this procedure before resorting to judicial review and in *R v Kingston London Borough Council ex parte T* (1993) the High Court accepted the argument. Having noted the scope of the complaints procedure as well as its speed, convenience and cheapness, the judge stated that 'the door of the court is the last door that should be opened'. He did not appear to attach much weight to the argument that the complaints procedure is internal to the local authority (and therefore not entirely independent) and only results in recommendations, not binding decisions.

The Looking After Children Forms

The Dartington Social Research Unit, in association with a number of child care agencies and universities, has produced for the DH a series of forms and other documents which are designed for use by social workers, parents and others who have an interest in a child being looked after by a local authority. Eleven forms have been published by HMSO, including Assessment and Action Records, Essential Information Record, Placement Plan, Care Plan, Review of Arrangements and Consultation Papers. This exercise is not purely administrative: the very nature of the documentation is calculated to remind practitioners of the legal framework within which they are obliged to operate.

Removal from accommodation

From a legal point of view, this is one of the most problematic aspects of the Children Act. As has been pointed out, it was central to the Government's approach to section 20 accommodation that it is a support service on offer to families on a voluntary basis. This means that if those with parental responsibility for the child object, the service is not to be provided, and, as we have already seen, that is just what the Act says. The adoption of such an approach, however, must also mean that if those with parental responsibility wish to resume caring for the child, then they should be allowed to do so. And again, this is just what the Act says, in section 20(8):

> Any person who has parental responsibility for a child may at any time remove the child from accommodation provided by or on behalf of the local authority under this section.

This subsection is completely unambiguous. Putting it plainly, it means that the child's parent, or a non-parent with parental responsibility, can lawfully enter the accommodation in question at any time, seize the child and take him home. There are, however, two exceptions, which mirror those that apply to parental objections to the provision of accommodation. The first concerns children over 16, the second concerns the situation where a residence order is in force and the holder agrees to the provision of accommodation. In both sets of circumstances, section 20(8) does not apply.

The general rule contained in section 20(8) effected a substantial change in the law, and there lies the cause of the problem. The former position was that where the child had been in 'voluntary care' for six months, the local authority could demand 28 days' notice of removal from a parent. In that 28-day period, the authority could prepare the child for a return home. It could also, though, take steps to acquire compulsory powers over the child. This 28-day rule, created amid controversy by the Children Act 1975, has been scrapped. Such a move was not recommended by the Child Care Law Review, which referred to research by Olive Stevenson showing that the rule was being 'sparingly and sensibly applied'.

However, the DH in its 1987 White Paper took the view that the 28-day rule was incompatible with the concept of voluntary partnership between local authorities and parents, and should accordingly disappear. Where action to delay or prevent a return home was thought essential to protect the child from harm, it considered that the local authority's power to obtain an emergency protection order from a magistrate and the powers of the police would be a sufficient safeguard. It also envisaged that the parents and the authority would enter into an agreement at the outset about the child's upbringing and that this would deal with the question of giving notice of intended removal from accommodation. 'If the local authority cannot reach agreement on terms which they believe are in the child's best interest,' it stated, 'then they can reserve the right to withdraw their services to the child and family.' Section 20(8) faithfully reflects the White Paper's approach.

Now it is true that emergency protection orders (EPOs) and the powers of the police are available in cases where there is reasonable cause to believe that the child is likely to suffer significant harm. And it is also true that in many cases an agreement will have been reached with the child's parents under which they are to give so many hours' or days' notice of removal of their child. This matter is specifically addressed in the Arrangements for Placement Regulations, as we saw earlier. All this, however, has not satisfied a number of commentators and interested groups. What can be done if a parent, in spite of their 'agreement' with the authority, suddenly, and perhaps after a long period of care, turns up at a foster home or a children's home and demands the return of the child there and then, citing for good measure section 20(8) of the Children Act? In this sort of situation, it is not a complete answer to talk in terms of obtaining an EPO or bringing in the police: these procedures take time and statutory grounds need to be shown. Nor is it against the law for a parent to break any agreement made with the authority: the only sanction for non-compliance is a withdrawal of the offer of the accommodation service, hardly a satisfactory response in the situation under discussion. Some have therefore argued that a provision along the lines of the 28-day rule should have been retained.

It is only fair, however, to point out the arguments in favour of the Government's approach. In the first place, the 28-day rule did not apply to all children in voluntary care, only to those in care for six months or more. So it is not quite correct to portray the 1989 Act as bringing about a complete reversal of the previous law. Secondly, it cannot seriously be disputed that a barrier such as the old one is logically incompatible with the concept of a voluntary support service, no matter how much one bases the argument on the welfare of the child and the need to prepare him for a return to the family. As such, it has the capacity to discourage families from using the service. It is also worth remembering that this barrier is not encountered in private law. As was said in Parliament: 'if I leave my child with a relative and go along to pick up the child I would be surprised if I had to give 24 hours' notice. Very often I would give such notice, but there would be no requirement upon me to do so.' Why should the position be different where the child is in public accommodation?

There is no easy answer to these problems. While section 20(8) is a perfectly logical reflection of the voluntary service philosophy, difficulties are bound to arise in practice. Some have suggested that SSDs may be less inclined to offer accommodation and more inclined to resort to compulsory intervention. Furthermore, social workers and foster carers are placed in a tricky position if a parent does turn up in inappropriate circumstances. The clear wording of the Act suggests that they must stand aside while the parent reclaims the child.

On this point, it is worth returning to consider the extreme, but by no means unknown, situation where the parent is clearly not in a fit state to care for the child because, for example, he is heavily intoxicated. We know that an application can be made for an EPO and we know that the police can be asked to exercise their powers to prevent harm being done to the child, but can the child simply be withheld from the parent? The previous law was not at all clear but there were indications that reasonable preventive measures could lawfully be taken. However, there is now a specific provision in the Children Act which may be capable of dealing with the matter. This is section 3(5). It has already been mentioned in Chapter 2 in relation to unmarried fathers but it has possibly greater relevance to the present discussion. Section 3(5) reads as follows:

A person who does not have parental responsibility for a particular child but has care of the child may (subject to the provisions of this Act) do what is reasonable in all the circumstances of the case for the purpose of safeguarding or promoting the child's welfare.

In fielding the argument centred on the unfit but demanding parent, the Government cited this provision to back up its claim that the social worker or foster carer, faced with an on-the-spot decision, is not powerless. Indeed, it was quite specific on the point during the Parliamentary debates:

> I consider that a foster parent would be able to prevent a parent who, by reason of alcohol or drugs, was in no fit state to remove the child from doing so. The combination of that power [under section 3(5)] and the emergency protection order should be sufficient to deal with any difficult situation which may occur.

Section 3(5) was not drafted with only local authorities in mind. It was suggested by the Law Commission as a general provision in child law; hence its appearance at the beginning of the Children Act. However, its wording might be thought to lend support to the Government's view. At this stage, though, we encounter a technical legal argument which may have the effect of undermining that view. The argument derives from the fact that section 3(5) is expressed to apply 'subject to the provisions of this Act' – in other words, it is subordinated to any other section or subsection which runs in the opposite direction. Section 20(8) is just such a provision, providing in the clearest possible terms for an unrestricted parental power to remove the child from accommodation. Consequently, the arguments based on section 3(5) may be unsound. Until the courts rule on the combined effect of section 20(8) and section 3(5), the legal position is unhappily obscure.

If the arguments based on section 3(5) do ultimately prevail, then 'unfit' parents may be kept at arm's length by the local authority. But while solving one problem, this creates others. For how long may the authority hold on to the child? Can the parents be kept away indefinitely? Can the authority retain the child on grounds unconnected with the parents' physical capacity to care, e.g. because a removal from accommodation would be emotionally upsetting for the child? It is a pity that the answers to important questions such as these remain unclear.

Help on leaving accommodation

The section 20 service is available for children right up to the age of 18. There is, in addition to the functions already described, a discretionary power to provide accommodation for those between 16 and 21 in any community home which takes children over 16, if the local authority considers that to do so would safeguard or promote their welfare. As we have seen, however, by the time they reach the age of 16, children acquire in effect the right to discharge themselves from accommodation.

The acute problems of many of the children who leave local authority care were highlighted during the passage of the Children Act. Their problems could be said to fall into two broad categories, although they are certainly linked. The first problem is that of attracting emotional support from the SSD. The second concerns material support. Legislation aimed at ensuring this support is not new: the Child Care Act 1980 contained specific provisions on the subject. However, these were described as 'weak and confused', and consequently productive of wide variations in practice, by the House of Commons Social Services Committee in its 1984 report, and this diagnosis was endorsed by both the Child Care Law Review and the DH in its White Paper. The result of this dissatisfaction was a new set of provisions, collected in section 24 of the Children Act.

Preparing for departure

The first of these provisions, section 24(1), is concerned not so much with the child who has left accommodation, but with all children currently being looked after by the local authority. It requires the authority to advise, assist and befriend them with a view to promoting their welfare when they cease to be looked after by it. This may be regarded as a direct response to the problem identified by the House of Commons Committee, whereby young people, particularly those in community homes, are released from care with insufficient preparation for life in the world outside. As the Child Care Law Review pointed out, however, this duty should not be regarded as simply requiring the provision of an end-of-stay package: 'the foundations for leaving care rest on the quality of the young person's experience throughout his or her stay in care and on the effectiveness of reviews'.

Needless to say, the nature of the preparatory work will vary according to the characteristics of the child and the circumstances of the case, e.g. whether he is returning to his family, or staying in his present accommodation, or becoming fully independent, and so on. The 'assistance' which is given may be in kind or, in exceptional circumstances, in cash (subject to the usual conditions, referred to below). Volume 3 of the DH Guidance states that 'well before a young person leaves care, a continuing care plan should be formulated with him'. Parents, foster carers and other agencies may also have a role to play here. The reference to a care plan ties in with both the Arrangements for Placement Regulations and the Review Regulations: aftercare is included in their lists of relevant considerations. The Guidance also suggests that each SSD should provide an easy-to-read guide to its services, and other agencies' services, for young people when they leave care.

Advice and assistance after departure

Section 24(2) was the new provision concerning those who have left accommodation. The 'target group' consists of persons under 21 who were provided with section 20 accommodation at some time between the ages of 16 and 18 but who are no longer so accommodated. Section 24 imposes a *duty* on the local authority to advise and befriend any member of this group, provided certain conditions are fulfilled. These are:

1 The authority knows he is in its area.
2 He has asked the authority for help.
3 It appears to the authority that he is in need of advice and being befriended.

In addition to the duty to advise and befriend, there is a discretionary *power* to give assistance. At this point, the section brings into play the usual rules governing the provision of 'assistance', so that assistance given to the under-21s may be in kind, or in exceptional circumstances, in cash; it may be unconditional or subject to conditions as to repayment (in whole or in part); the means of the recipient must be taken into account; and no repayment can be demanded if he is receiving income support, family credit, disability working allowance or an income-based jobseeker's allowance.

Several things need to be noted about these provisions. First, their operation depends on the local authority acquiring knowledge that a person qualifying for help is in its area. Two further aspects of the Act should assist in this respect: section 24 requires every authority to inform another authority if a person it is advising under the section (and this includes those about to leave care) proposes to live in the area of that other authority; and Schedule 2 requires every authority to publish information about the services provided by it under section 24 and to take reasonable steps to ensure that those who might benefit from the services receive the information relevant to them.

Secondly, the duty only arises if a request is made. There is no question of thrusting advice, friendship and the rest down the throat of an unwilling recipient. Some young people who are leaving, or who have left, local authority accommodation may not want help from that particular quarter. For the same reason, there is no legal obligation on the authority's part to track down members of the target group and offer help. How exactly an authority responds to any request will obviously depend on the circumstances and, to a large extent, the judgment of the social worker. The nature of the response may also depend, heavily, on the state of the authority's budget. The provision of assistance, including cash in 'exceptional circumstances', to the under-21s on a discretionary basis gives rise to exactly the same problems as does its provision to children in need as part of a preventive strategy and to children being prepared for leaving care: different interpretations, leading to different policies based on different philosophies.

Accommodation and training

Section 24 empowers local authorities to give assistance to the persons described above by contributing to accommodation expenses incurred in connection with employment, education or training. It also empowers them to make grants to enable these persons to meet expenses connected with education and training. Assistance with education and training can last beyond the age of 21.

Complaints procedures

In 1990 section 24 was amended by Parliament so as to require every local authority to establish a complaints procedure available to persons qualifying for advice and assistance under the section. This amendment meant that the 1991 Representations Procedure Regulations could extend to the aftercare functions of SSDs as well as their other support functions. The result is that young people who fall within the scope of the section can, if they wish, ventilate any relevant grievance against their authority via the two-stage procedure described on pages 96–100.

The impact of section 24

Few would seek to argue that section 24 (together with the particularly extensive guidance prepared by the DH) has not brought about a more coherent statutory framework for local authority involvement in aftercare. Nor can it be denied that the voluntary sector makes an outstanding contribution in this field. But massive problems remain. Shortages of housing, employment opportunities and money continue to afflict many of those leaving care, resulting in some cases in personal tragedy. Research carried out after the Children Act has revealed the following disturbing patterns:

- 38 per cent of young people in prison have spent some time in local authority accommodation
- 30 per cent of young, single, homeless people have spent some time in local authority accommodation
- 80 per cent of care leavers are unemployed two years after leaving care
- Two-thirds of care leavers have no GCSE qualifications
- One in seven females leaving care is either pregnant or already a mother.

Many would argue that these problems are not unavoidable. Valiant attempts were made during the Parliamentary debates on the Children Act to strengthen the law in favour of care leavers even further. Particular emphasis was given to the adverse effects of the new social security regime introduced during 1988. This, it was said, had a severe impact on young people living apart from their families; for children leaving care, the impact was especially hard. The Government resisted these attempts. Its argument was that the scope and purposes of the Act did not embrace alterations to housing law, social security law or any other branch of law which concerns the population generally, as opposed to children. Such an approach enabled the DH to deflect the pressure for change onto other parts of the Government. While it is true to say that the issue of aftercare has received a generally higher profile since the 1989 Act, evidence of the necessary political will and commitment to appropriate levels of public expenditure remains elusive.

Aftercare for other children

This chapter is primarily concerned with those children provided with accommodation under section 20. Section 24 has been described with these in mind. It should be noted, however, that the provisions of section 24 also apply, with some variations, to care order children, children looked after in the private sector and children accommodated in certain health establishments.

The acquisition of control by the authority

Circumstances will arise where the local authority feels that, in accordance with its general duty to safeguard and promote the child's welfare, it should acquire firm control over the future upbringing of the child. Indeed, the question of the child's legal status and any necessary change in it should remain clearly in view because of the requirements, noted earlier, which are imposed by the regulations concerning plans and reviews. Although in providing accommodation under section 20 the authority will inevitably be intimately involved in the day-to-day care of the child, without more its power will be qualified, especially by the statutory right of the parents to remove the child from the accommodation. How may firm control be acquired?

It was a fundamental objective of the Children Act to bring about a situation whereby parental responsibility (i.e. parental rights) can only be acquired by a local authority through the medium of a court order. Under the previous law, authorities which had received a child into care were in a position to acquire 'the parental rights' through a resolution passed by the council (section 3 of the Child Care Act 1980). This machinery was heavily criticized, not so much because it was being misused by authorities but on grounds of principle. It came to be accepted on virtually all sides that to allow the State to deprive parents of their rights by an essentially adminis-trative device was wrong. Accordingly, the parental rights resolution has become a thing of the past. To acquire compulsory powers, the local authority has to go to court. This is an absolute rule: it applies whether the parents consent or not.

Since 14 October 1991 there have been two ways, and only two ways, in which local authorities have been able to acquire long-term parental responsibility. The first is by obtaining a care order. The second is by obtaining, with the consent of a parent or guardian, an order under the Adoption Act 1976 freeing the child for adoption. In addition to these methods, short-term parental responsibility may be obtained through an emergency protection order. Such an order will sometimes, of course, be a precursor to a care order. These three procedures are dealt with in later chapters.

While the abolition of the parental rights resolution procedure has been widely welcomed as a matter of principle, difficulties in practice have arisen out of restricting local authorities which want control to care and freeing-for-adoption proceedings. There are cases where the authority wishes to get into a position in which it can take decisions in relation to a child whom it is accommodating but feels that a care order or a freeing order is either not obtainable or not desirable. It may, for example, wish to consent to important medical treatment or to some leisure activity, but feel that, not having parental responsibility, it cannot do so. If those who do have such responsibility, i.e. the parents, are not available or are not competent to consent, what is the authority to do? The case of *Birmingham City Council v D* (1994) illustrates the problem. Two children aged 5 and 6 were being accommodated under section 20 following the death of their mother. Their father, who had not married the mother, had declined any responsibility, and placements within the extended family had broken down. The local authority sought care orders in respect of the children, arguing that the absence of parental responsibility in any person or body imperilled their welfare. It contended that the powers that would flow from a care order were essential if it was to cope properly with unforeseen situations. The High Court rejected the application on the grounds that the threshold criteria contained in section 31 of the Act (on which see page 155 below) were not made out. Parliament had made express provision for orphans in section 20 and it would be wrong to strain the language of section 31 in order to deal with unspecified events in the future.

Two solutions to the above-mentioned problem are offered by the Children Act. One is for the local authority to apply to the court under section 10 for a specific issue order (described in Chapters 3 and 4). Getting directions from the court via such an order will clearly provide the necessary legal justification for taking the action in question. The second solution is for the authority to go ahead with the action and, in the event of its legality being questioned, seek to rely on section 3(5) of the Act. As we saw earlier, this states that a person caring for a child may do what is reasonable in all the circumstances of the case for the purpose of safeguarding or promoting the child's welfare. These two approaches may not be as satisfactory as the granting of parental responsibility to the authority but they may at least offer a way out of some awkward situations.

The acquisition of control by individuals

Just as the local authority can gain parental responsibility in respect of the accommodated child, so can individuals. Foster carers and relatives, for example, have the opportunity of applying for a residence order under section 10 of the Act, in much the same way as they could apply for custodianship under the old law. As was seen in Chapter 4, however, the Children Act draws a distinction between those non-parents who are entitled to seek a residence order and those who must first obtain the leave of the court. Moreover, in the case of foster carers, there may be a requirement to obtain the consent of the authority. Volume 2 of the DH Guidance states that if there is no one with parental responsibility and no suitable carer, the local authority will need to consider how best to provide the child with someone to exercise such responsibility. As it points out, this may mean that the authority should assist another appropriate person to obtain a residence order.

Apart from a residence order, an adoption order can be sought in respect of the accommodated child. Here, of course, the consent of the parents will need to be obtained, unless there are grounds for dispensing with it. Finally, it should not be forgotten that where the child has no parent with parental responsibility, the court may appoint an individual – but not the local authority – to be the child's guardian under section 5 of the Act (see Chapter 2).

7

Compulsory powers: investigation and intervention

For decades English law has enabled public agencies, especially local authorities, to take action so as to acquire the exclusive right to care for a child, either temporarily or permanently. By the 1980s, however, the law relating to compulsory intervention had become a statutory jungle whose rationale was impossible to discern. The impenetrable mass of legislation may have been a delight for some academics but it was a nightmare for practitioners, and the need for comprehensive reform was almost universally recognized. As far as this branch of child law is concerned, the Children Act had two fundamental objectives:

1 To restate the rules relating to public agency intervention in clear and straightforward terms.
2 To give all the parties (and this includes the child) a fairer deal than they got before.

The rules contained in the Act which are concerned with compulsory powers are to be found mostly in Parts I, IV and V. Schedule 3 acts as a supplement to Part IV. These rules establish a framework for intervention. Many of them are quite detailed, but in some cases (needless to say) the Act leaves the detail to be supplied by government regulations. The features of this framework were derived in the main from the Child Care Law Review of 1985 and the DH White Paper of 1987. However, the 1988 Butler-Sloss report into child abuse in Cleveland and other ad hoc inquiry reports also had some impact.

As has been said, it was one of the Act's principal objectives to restate the rules in a clear manner. What the Act does *not* do, however – and in this respect it is no different from the previous legislation – is to tell public agencies when to use them. It makes available to social workers, police officers and others a range of tools which are seen as appropriate and necessary for child protection work; it requires specified conditions to be fulfilled before action can be taken; it imposes procedural safeguards for the parties when action is taken; but it gives no orders about the employment of this machinery. The use of the statutory procedures is a matter left to the judgment and discretion of the agency and those working alongside it. There is no question of the statutory machinery having to be used in any given situation: the law's requirement is simply that the discretion is exercised in good faith, after a consideration of all the relevant factors. As the DH put it in 1988, in the context of child abuse:

> Not all cases can or should come before the court. Each case is unique and it would be difficult to set out in detail factors that could influence this decision. In broad terms, the decision about court action is likely to be based on the nature of the abuse, the circumstances of the incident and the response of the parents, the initial assessment of parental ability to change, their acceptance of responsibility or acknowledgement of problems and their willingness to co-operate with the helping agencies. *(Protecting Children: A Guide for Social Workers undertaking a Comprehensive Assessment)*

There is no objection to a particular agency establishing a formal policy on the use of compulsory procedures. Experience has shown that such a device can produce positive benefits in terms of open, consistent and rational decision-making. But to remain within legal bounds, a policy must not be over-rigid; in other words, it must not preclude the examination of each case on its merits.

The tools given to agencies by the 1989 Act are five in number: the emergency protection order, the child assessment order, the police protection power, the care order and the supervision order. These five methods of compulsory intervention are described in the following chapters of this book, and in the order in which they have just been set out. This is not the order in which they appear in the Act but it may be thought appropriate to look at these methods in a temporal framework, recognizing the fact that applications for care orders and supervision orders are sometimes preceded by the granting of the emergency and assessment orders.

The effect of this regime has been to consign to history the compulsory power provisions of the Children and Young Persons Acts 1933 and 1969 and other statutes. In addition, the use of wardship by local authorities – of growing importance during the 1980s – has been severely restricted.

Inter-agency co-operation

In her report into the child sexual abuse crisis in Cleveland, Lady Justice Butler-Sloss stated that:

> The reasons for the crisis are complex. In essence they included: lack
> of a proper understanding by the main agencies of each other's
> functions in relation to child sexual abuse; a lack of communication
> between the agencies . . .

Following such damning findings, it was inevitable that the need for effective inter-agency working would receive an even higher profile than normal
leading up to the Children Act. Of course, the exposure of poor relationships between different child care agencies was nothing new. It had been a
depressingly prominent feature of numerous child-oriented inquiries and
reports over the years. But the scale of the intervention which occurred in
Cleveland, combined with the ensuing publicity, guaranteed that this issue
would be highlighted. As with certain other aspects of child protection
work, however, it is far easier to demonstrate past failings in co-operation
than it is to construct a foolproof framework for the future. It is, moreover,
particularly difficult to enshrine such a framework in law: this is partly
because of the enormous variations in the types of case which can occur in
practice and partly because of the differing ways in which the structures and
traditions of agencies up and down the country have developed over the
years.

The upshot of this difficulty is that co-operation between agencies has
tended to be dealt with, not through the medium of legislation, but through
the issue of guidance and advice. The Children Act did nothing to disturb
this tradition. The furthest it goes is to authorize a local authority – not
require, be it noted – to call upon other authorities to assist it while conducting enquiries with a view to possible action in support of a child (section
47(9)). As in the past, therefore, local authorities and other institutions
have to be relied upon to abide by the spirit, if not the letter, of documents
issued by the DH and other co-ordinating bodies. In this context, mention
should be made of the publication entitled *Working Together*. First issued
by the DH in 1988 to coincide with the release of the Cleveland Report, it
was revised in 1991 to take account of the legal changes introduced by the
Children Act. Further revisions are planned for 1998 so that issues arising
since the Act's implementation can be addressed. According to the document's preface, it:

> consolidates previous guidance on procedures for the protection of
> children and recommends developments aimed at making these more
> effective. It takes into account the requirements of the Children Act
> 1989 and lessons learned from individual cases which have caused
> public concern, as well as examples of good practice provided by a
> number of agencies. It does not attempt to provide guidelines on the
> practice of individual professions in the recognition of child abuse or
> subsequent care or treatment but is concerned with inter-professional
> and inter-agency co-operation.

Of course, child care work, and therefore child care law, does not cover just child abuse. There are plenty of children's matters not touched upon in *Working Together*. But it is an important example of the sort of official guidance which can be given to individuals in the field, with a view to achieving an effective multidisciplinary approach. The document contains much detailed advice relating to the management of child abuse cases, ranging from the holding of inter-agency child protection conferences and the designation of key workers to the operation of child protection registers and the formation of Area Child Protection Committees. It is, in addition, careful to emphasize the various contributions which professionals, those in the voluntary sector and members of the general public can make to the successful handling of child abuse cases. Clearly, these are all important matters. None of them, however, is mentioned in the Children Act and anyone who takes a look at *Working Together*, or any other piece of official guidance, should quickly appreciate the impracticality of transforming its contents into fixed legal rules.

Those working with the 1989 Act should therefore understand that it needs to be read, not on its own, nor simply in conjunction with the many sets of government regulations which have been issued, but alongside all the relevant non-legal material as well. This may be confusing but unfortunately it is unavoidable.

The investigation stage of intervention: the statutory duty of the local authority

Compulsory intervention under the Children Act can be directed towards children who are already being looked after by a local authority or other agency, as well as those presently living 'on the outside'. For those already in agency accommodation the investigation and assessment of the child's needs and general situation should take place as a matter of course, as part of the overall continuing welfare responsibility owed by the agency. Such assessment should obviously include a consideration of whether or not an application for compulsory powers is needed (indeed, this question is expressly mentioned in the review regulations). This assumes, of course, that the risk of harm to the child arises from a source external to the agency. If a suspicion of abuse revolves around the child's foster carer or an employee of the agency itself, then the investigation provisions described below will apply.

For children on the outside, whether living with their families or not, section 47 imposes a specific duty on the social services department to make, or cause to be made (i.e. arrange for others to do the job) 'such enquiries as they consider necessary to enable them to decide whether they should take any action to safeguard or promote the child's welfare'. This duty is triggered by the department having reasonable cause to suspect that a child who lives, or is found, in its area 'is suffering, or is likely to suffer, significant harm'. 'Harm' is a central concept in the compulsory power sections of the Children Act and, as will be seen in Chapter 10 (see page 156), is defined expansively so as to cover ill-treatment or the impairment of health or development. Whether or not there is reasonable cause to suspect significant harm is wholly dependent upon the particular circumstances. It is a matter for professional judgment. There is, however, a provision buried at the back of the Act which should not be overlooked in this context. Schedule 2, which is devoted to local authority support for children (see Chapter 5), states that where a local authority believes that a child within its area is likely to suffer harm but lives or proposes to live in the area of another authority, that other authority must be informed of the details. Where this information is transmitted, the receiving authority may feel that section 47 should be put into effect.

The local authority's duty, then, is to make enquiries to enable it to decide whether it should take any action. 'Action', for these purposes, can embrace many things, of course, and may simply involve the provision of advice and information (not necessarily by the authority) to the child and/or his carers. At the other end of the spectrum there is the compulsory intervention machinery, and this is expressly mentioned in section 47: 'the enquiries shall, in particular, be directed towards establishing whether the authority should make any application to the court'. If, on the conclusion of the enquiries, the authority decides not to apply for an emergency protection order, a child assessment order, a care order or a supervision order, it must consider whether it would be appropriate to review the case at a later date, and if it decides that this would be appropriate, it must fix a date for that review. Despite the express reference in section 47 to these compulsory orders, there is no automatic connection between the two. In many cases, the only action necessary will be the offer of voluntary support services under the 'children in need' sections of the Act (described in Chapters 5 and 6). Section 47 enquiries therefore have a close link with Part III of the Act. If the enquiries are conducted in the right manner (see the section on partnership below), working with the family under Part III should not prove impossible: investigation and support are not mutually exclusive.

As previously mentioned, the Act empowers the local authority to call upon others to assist it during the enquiry process. These others are: any other SSD, any local education authority, any local housing authority, any health authority, and any person specified by government regulations for the purposes of the section. They must all assist the investigating department unless this would be unreasonable in all the circumstances. The list of consultees is obviously not exhaustive. The police and the probation service, for example, are only missing from the list for technical reasons. Where the child is ordinarily resident in the area of another local authority, that other authority must be consulted; and where it emerges that there are matters connected with the child's education which should be investigated, the LEA must be consulted. (Volume 1 of the DH Guidance states that this may include such situations as the child's non-attendance at a named school, the fact that the child is not registered at any school, or where the school raises questions about the child's behaviour.)

Apart from the duty to see the child – discussed below – this is as far as the Act goes in terms of directing the course of an investigation. But the Act is only part of the picture: nationally agreed guidelines, such as those contained in *Working Together*, *Protecting Children* and the *Memorandum of Good Practice on Video Recorded Interviews*, and locally agreed procedures, need to be borne in mind at all times, because it is likely that very detailed 'rules' concerning investigations will be set out in them. This is certainly true of *Working Together*, Part 5 of which discusses the investigatory functions not just of the SSD, but also of the NSPCC and the police, and emphasizes the need for enquiries to be pursued on a multi-agency, multidisciplinary basis, with relevant information being shared at all times.

Seeing the child

According to *Working Together*, the prime tasks of an investigating agency are:

- to establish the facts about the circumstances giving rise to the concern
- to decide if there are grounds for concern
- to identify sources and level of risk
- to decide protective or other action in relation to the child and any others.

The refusal of the child's carer to allow agency representatives to see the child, which will almost certainly have the effect of blocking the investigation, was an eventuality which was bound to generate discussion in the context of the Children Act. One of the reasons for this was the publicity given to the Kimberley Carlile case and the ensuing inquiry report (*A Child in Mind*, 1987). This case contained many different strands of child care issues but it is likely to be remembered as the one in which the social worker carrying out a visit to the family home was permitted to view the child only through a small glass panel in a door. The breaking of the Doreen Mason case in December 1988, shortly after the introduction of the Children Bill, only served to highlight the importance of the access issue, because there too social workers had been obstructed.

A direct result of this concern was that, in contrast to the previous legislation, specific references to access were incorporated in the Children

Act. Some of them relate to emergency protection orders and child assessment orders – indeed, the child assessment order owes its existence largely to the issue. The relevant provisions are discussed in subsequent chapters but for the moment it will be sufficient to mention what section 47 of the Act has to say about the denial of access and information during a local authority investigation.

The section states first of all (section 47(4)) that where enquiries are being made, the local authority shall take such steps as are reasonably practicable to obtain access to the child or to ensure that access to him is obtained on its behalf by an authorized person, unless it is satisfied that it already has sufficient information about him. So there is a statutory assumption that the child will be visited by, or on behalf of, the SSD. If the child's carer is obstructive, section 47(6) comes into play: where any local authority officer or authorized person is refused access to the child or is denied information as to his whereabouts, the authority shall apply for an emergency protection order, a child assessment order, a care order or a supervision order unless it is satisfied that his welfare can be satisfactorily safeguarded without its doing so.

This latter provision is the nearest the Act comes to telling a local authority when to embark on compulsory intervention procedures. While it is framed as a duty, there are two important discretionary elements. First, proceedings do not need to be taken if the local authority considers that the welfare proviso at the end is satisfied. For example, it may be that action to be taken by the police is regarded as a sufficient response to the problem, at least for the time being. Second, even if proceedings are to be taken, the local authority has a choice as to which form of compulsory order to apply for. The combination of these two qualifications does obviously give the investigating team considerable room for manoeuvre. At the same time, however, the wording of the provision remains strong and reflects the view of the Government and others that the frustration of a local authority child abuse investigation is a matter to be taken extremely seriously. As the Social Services Inspectorate put it in 1995: 'The importance of seeing and communicating with the child or young person cannot be over estimated. The reasons for this should be explained to adult carers and they should be helped to understand the responsibility of the statutory agencies to pursue allegations thoroughly' (*The Challenge of Partnership in Child Protection: Practice Guide*).

Questions may arise as to the meaning of 'access' in this context. Suppose the social worker is asked to stay on the doorstep while the child is brought to the top of the stairs? Is access being granted or denied? Many other scenarios can easily be envisaged. It is suggested that 'access', interpreted in the light of the purposes of the Act and its background, must mean face-to-face contact (but not a physical examination) which lasts for a reasonable time. If the child's carer does not satisfy the investigating team on this score, it may be felt appropriate to warn him of the effect of the Act and the possible consequences of his intransigence.

Examination and assessment of the child

Gaining access to the child in an investigation is vital. But what about the allied matter of medical and similar examinations? Can the child's carer be instructed by the investigating team to present the child to a health service professional? Here, too, the public has been made aware by events such as the Carlile case of the difficulties, practical and legal, caused by obdurate families. The effect of the Children Act has been to make available a wider range of compulsory measures in the event of a total and unreasonable refusal by the carer to co-operate. Social workers are not given the power to carry out forcibly an examination themselves, nor have they the power to order an examination; but they are given the power to seek such an order from the court. This can be done either as part of an emergency protection order, or under a child assessment order, both of which are discussed in the following chapter. Having such remedies available should enable the investigators to exert considerable pressure on the carer. After all, there is little difference in purely practical terms between a social worker making and then serving a medical examination order on a person, and giving him a letter stating that an emergency protection order or child assessment order will be sought if the child is not presented to a doctor within 24 hours.

Partnership during an investigation

Partnership with parents and other family members has been one of the most heavily emphasized messages emanating from the DH in the post-Children Act period. The concept of partnership, though not expressly mentioned in the Act itself, can be detected in many of its provisions and it *is* expressly mentioned in the DH guidance, including *Working Together*. As far as section 47 investigations are concerned, the most detailed official advice on working in partnership is contained in *The Challenge of Partnership in Child Protection: Practice Guide*, produced by the Social Services Inspectorate in 1995. This document sets out the reasons why partnership is important, describes the fundamental principles involved, and offers advice on how partnership can and should operate in practice. It acknowledges, realistically, that full partnership is not always possible (because of the hostility of the parents, for example) and observes that the presence of particular factors may preclude any attempt to adopt at the outset an open approach to the family (e.g. suspected Munchausen Syndrome by Proxy or organized abuse).

Investigations into alleged sexual abuse

Child sexual abuse is a major social evil. The damage sexual abuse can cause to a child's emotional and psycho-sexual development is incalculable. It can and frequently does result in repetition of abusive behaviour in adulthood. By like token, however, there are few things more destructive of family life and relationships than a false allegation of sexual abuse.

These words are taken from the judgment of Mr Justice Wall in the important case of *Re A and B* (1994), and although the sentiments they express are certainly not new, they encapsulate some of the immense difficulties confronting practitioners who are called upon to investigate an allegation or suspicion of sexual abuse. Despite the attention lavished on this subject in recent years, section 47 of the Children Act does not refer expressly to it. Sexual abuse is in fact treated by the Act (in section 31(9)) simply as a form of ill-treatment – and therefore harm – alongside physical and emotional abuse, with no special provision for it made at all. The evidential difficulties associated with sexual abuse investigations, however, certainly mark them out as different and these have been fully addressed outside the legislation, especially in the *Cleveland Report* of 1988 and the *Memorandum of Good Practice on Video Recorded Interviews* of 1992. Further advice is to be found in the SSI's *The Challenge of Partnership in Child Protection: Practice Guide* (1995).

In *Re A and B* (above), the mother of a young child made a series of complaints to the local authority concerning possible sexual abuse by her husband. There followed a series of interviews with, and physical examinations of, the child after which she was referred to the Great Ormond Street Hospital, the social worker writing to the hospital: 'A is a five-year-old girl who has been sexually abused by her father. She is in need of assessment with a view to therapeutic relief'. In dismissing all these allegations of abuse, the judge stated that it was a matter of considerable concern that elementary errors of investigation had been committed by the police and the local authority as late as 1992, some four years after the publication of the Cleveland guidelines. In this case, the initial enquiries had been undertaken by an inexperienced social worker whose training had been minimal, and by a police officer whose training was also suspect. Both of them had approached the investigation with a closed mind and they had subjected the child to repeated and unwarranted interviews. The judge made the following observations on the question of the social worker's role in a joint police/social services investigation:

1 Where there is a police investigation into an allegation of abuse the social worker's ability to discuss the case with the alleged abuser is

inhibited until such time as the alleged abuser has been interviewed by the police.

2 Every encouragement should be given by local authorities to the members of the police child protection team to proceed with expedition and to interview the alleged abuser at the earliest opportunity. It is quite proper for the local authority to make it clear to the police that delay in interviewing the alleged abuser is hampering its work with the family.

3 Even where there is a police investigation, there is no good legal or social work reason why the social worker should not make contact with the alleged abuser so that he can be given any available information which does not prejudice the police investigation and so that he himself can give the social worker any information he feels relevant to the welfare of the child. The social worker can make it clear that until the police investigation is complete he or she cannot discuss the specific allegations. But this is no reason for not making contact.

4 Many suspected abusers suffer a legitimate sense of grievance when they are not only denied contact with their children but are given neither the reason for the denial of contact nor the detail of the allegations made against them. The sense of grievance is gravely exacerbated where the suspect with good reason feels there is a presumption of guilt against him and that the local authority is pursuing its investigation with a closed mind.

Further important guidelines were laid down in the case of *Re D* (1994). It was stated that whenever possible conversations or interviews with a child who may have been the victim of sexual abuse should be videoed. Any allegation by a child which is relied upon and which has not been videoed will inevitably carry less weight in subsequent court proceedings, because the court will not be able to assess the allegation for itself. Where a video recording of an interview is not possible, a tape recording should be considered. Such a recording is second best but is infinitely preferable to no contemporaneous recording at all or to an attempt at a contemporaneous note. An alleged disclosure to a foster carer is less likely to carry significant weight in a court than is a statement by a child to an experienced and skilled interviewer. If a medical examination of the child is to be carried out, it is preferable that the child's medical record and background history is produced before the doctor proceeds with the examination. Such information is essential if a balanced and reliable medical opinion is to be given.

Investigations during private law proceedings

The case of *Re A and B* (1994), noted above, arose out of an application by a father for a contact order made during divorce proceedings. Concurrently with the father's application to the court, a joint police/social services investigation was being carried out following allegations of abuse made by the mother. The father's application was filed with the court in May 1992 but was not determined until April 1994, a delay described by the judge as wholly unacceptable and attributable to poor case management at the county court level. The judge proceeded to lay down the following guidelines for situations such as this, which were subsequently endorsed by the Children Act Advisory Committee:

1 The Children Act imposes a duty on the court to be proactive in children's cases in drawing up a timetable to ensure that the issues in the case are resolved without delay.

2 In private law cases where the local authority is undertaking a section 47 investigation, it is of the utmost importance that the court takes a proactive co-ordinating role. The role of the court should complement the role of the local authority.

3 Directions appointments with the court are of vital importance. The court must take a firm grip of every child case: it must build in reviews of progress and set stringent timetables.

4 Section 7 of the Act (which deals with welfare reports to the court) should be used imaginatively to keep the parties informed of the progress of the section 47 investigation and the material available to the local authority.

5 The local authority should normally make the author of the section 7 report available to be called as a witness by the court at any important hearing at which oral evidence is required.

6 An order for a court welfare officer's report should normally form part of a detailed order for directions which includes the filing of evidence and provision for a hearing date.

7 The parties and the court should direct their minds at the earliest possible opportunity to the need for expert evidence. Where expert evidence is required, precise and structured directions about it should be part of the stringent planning and timetabling process.

8 Whilst inviting co-operation, the court should not hesitate to use its powers to compel the release of documentation from the local authority and the police which is necessary for the proper determination of the proceedings.

It is clear from these guidelines that while the courts do not have the power to give instructions to local authorities as to the way in which they carry out section 47 investigations, they are able to influence both the duration and the course of such investigations where private law proceedings are in train. This is due to the rather fortuitous wording of the welfare report provisions of section 7 (on which see Chapter 13).

Investigations: applying the brake

All child protection work involves taking risks. Social services departments, which have been given lead responsibility in this field, discharge their responsibilities against a background of two widely supported principles, each of which contains a substantial risk element:

- the State has a duty to intervene to protect children from harm
- the State should promote the welfare of children by respecting the integrity of the family.

Balancing these principles has, of course, always been part of the social worker's task. But today, when child protection work is carried out under the most intense media spotlight and in a climate which favours deregulation, success in accomplishing the task is arguably more difficult than ever. The provisions of section 47 of the Children Act, described above, were generally very well received, as were the guidelines contained in the revised edition of *Working Together*, and considerable effort was expended in training child protection workers in this new regime. The practical operation of these provisions, however, has generated concern at government level and has led to controversy and, regrettably, confusion.

In June 1995, the DH published *Child Protection: Messages from Research*. This report, which sought to summarize the findings of a number of research studies commissioned by the Department, concluded, among other things, that a significant number of section 47 investigations undertaken by SSDs (25 000 out of a total of 160 000 each year) do not result in clear findings of maltreatment or neglect. It referred to the criticism that 'many investigations are undertaken, many families are visited and case conferences called but in the end, little support is offered to the family'. Many, if not most, of these investigations cause anxiety to the child and his family – whether or not abuse or neglect is present – and the report seemed to suggest that there was a case for local authorities to reassess their approach to section 47:

> Protection issues are best viewed in the context of children's wider needs. It is important to ensure that inappropriate cases do not get caught up in the child protection process, for this could have several undesirable consequences. Of particular concern is the unnecessary distress caused to family members who may then be unwilling to co-operate with subsequent plans . . . For children who have been grossly injured or sexually abused, swift child rescue, sometimes using emergency powers, will be necessary. However, the research evidence suggests that, for the majority of cases, the need of the child and family is more important than the abuse or, put another way, the

general family context is more important than any abusive event within it.

Launching the publication of the report, the then Minister of Health was reported as calling for a 'lighter touch' in investigations. He said:

> We need just as many investigations of the serious cases, but we need to use the other enquiries for going into a family and enquiring how they are getting on, so that today's problem doesn't become tomorrow's crisis.

Statements such as these are problematic, for a number of reasons. From a purely legal point of view, they are at variance with the terms of section 47 and *Working Together*, which impose a duty to investigate upon reasonable suspicion and require social workers to take all referrals seriously. Secondly, the alleged distinction between 'investigations' and 'enquiries' – a distinction persistently drawn in *Messages from Research* – is not supported by the wording of the Act. Making enquiries about a matter is an investigation. Investigations can be carried out under numerous provisions of the Children Act, not just section 47 (e.g. section 17 in relation to children in need). A third, and obvious, problem is that such statements assume omniscience on the part of the social worker. Establishing that a child has been 'grossly injured or sexually abused', or that his case is 'serious', is something that can often only be done *after* an investigation. The severity of harm is not always self-evident at the point of referral.

As for the exhortation of a 'lighter touch', the argument seems to be that in the interpretation and application of section 47 and the accompanying guidance, too low a threshold has been employed by social workers, resulting in too many families becoming enmeshed in the child protection process. (According to *Messages from Research*, 'too many minor cases were rigorously investigated with the result that a large number of minnows, which later had to be discarded, got caught up in the protection net'.) The fallacy in such an argument is the failure to consider the terms of section 47 which, like the earlier provisions in the Children and Young Persons Act 1969, are highly susceptible to different interpretations. This has always been acknowledged. The concepts of 'significant harm' and 'reasonable suspicion' – like those of 'abuse' and 'neglect' – are open-ended and, to an extent, value-laden. A crucial element in their interpretation and application must be the perceived expectations of the general public and the media, who in recent years have seemed unwilling to tolerate any margin of error. Viewed in this light, the published statistics are not particularly surprising. They, and the defensive practice which possibly underlies them, may be an inevitable consequence of the current social and political climate.

Those charged with the task of revising *Working Together* will therefore have their work cut out in devising a form of words which deals more effectively with all these factors.

A further point needs to be made. There seems to be an assumption in some quarters that there are two distinct responses to a referral: first, treating it as a 'child protection' matter (or dealing with it 'under a child protection banner', as *Messages from Research* puts it) and second, treating it as concerning a child in need. The Children Act does not support such a distinction. While it is true that 'Protection' is dealt with in Part V of the Act and 'Local Authority Support' is dealt with in Part III, there are firm links between the two sets of provisions so that they should be considered as a whole. The clearest example of such a link is section 47(3)(a). This states that enquiries carried out when there is reasonable cause to suspect harm shall be directed towards establishing whether the authority should make any application to the court, or *exercise any of their other powers under this Act*. These 'other powers' include the children in need powers under Part III of the Act, which can be exercised alongside, as well as instead of, formal intervention. If it is true, as *Messages from Research* strongly suggests, that too many families who are investigated fail to receive the support services they require, that points to a problem with policies and resources for children in need; it does not necessarily indicate that too many investigations are taking place.

Court-ordered investigations under section 37

Section 37 of the Children Act makes provision for child protection investigations following a direction by a court which is dealing with family proceedings. The rules relating to such investigations are completely separate from those in section 47. They are described in Chapter 10 of this book (see page 163 below) but the following points of difference may be noted here:

- the local authority has no choice but to investigate once a court invokes section 37
- the court may only exercise the power when hearing family proceedings
- a section 37 investigation is subject to statutory time limits
- a guardian ad litem may be appointed once the section 37 power has been exercised
- an interim care order or supervision order may be made by the court at the same time as the section 37 direction
- none of the provisions of section 47 (e.g. those requiring the child to be seen) applies to a section 37 investigation.

8

Emergency protection orders and child assessment orders

Introduction

This chapter is devoted to two completely separate types of court order. This may seem a strange sort of arrangement, but the connections between the two orders are such as to make it appropriate to treat them together. We enter an area of controversy at this stage, because whereas the need for an emergency protection order (EPO) was never doubted by those involved in the reform of child law, the child assessment order (CAO) entered life without a universal blessing. Significantly, perhaps, the CAO was not part of the package recommended by the Child Care Law Review in 1985; nor was it endorsed in the government White Paper of 1987. It was mentioned in the 1988 Butler-Sloss report into the Cleveland affair but the inquiry came out firmly against it. And it did not appear in the Children Bill when the Bill was first presented to Parliament. It is therefore hardly surprising that its eventual emergence in the Act was troubled.

The EPO and the CAO have various things in common. Both are forms of compulsory intervention aimed at protecting children. Both are available only through the court system. Both are short-term measures which may or may not lead to an application for a care order or a supervision order. Note the contrasting features, however. The EPO is available from a single magistrate, whereas the CAO is only obtainable from a full court. The EPO is available on an *ex parte* basis, i.e. without a hearing at which the parents are able to be present. The CAO can only be made after a full hearing (*inter partes*, in legal terms, as opposed to *ex parte*). It is not therefore ('emphatically not', according to Volume 1 of the DH Guidance) aimed at emergencies. Most importantly, the EPO authorizes the removal of the child from his carer into any suitable accommodation. The CAO will not normally go this far. For this reason, the CAO is undoubtedly the lesser order. The challenge for child protection professionals is to recognize when to use, and when not to use, each one.

The emergency protection order

The discredited place of safety order

The EPO was designed to replace the place of safety order. Under the previous law, there were at least five separate statutory procedures whereby a place of safety order could be made. All these procedures were swept away by the Children Act. The place of safety order was the subject of a number of criticisms. Its name was said to conceal the fact that it was, or should have been, aimed only at emergencies; it could last for 28 days, an excessively long period; the legal position of the various parties during the place of safety period was unclear; and there was no effective right of challenge available to the child's family. These faults were all contained in the legislation and could therefore be corrected fairly easily. What was perhaps more difficult to adjust was the way in which the legislation was actually used in the field. Here, too, there were criticisms, not least in relation to the events in Cleveland during 1987: the place of safety order positively dominated the 300-page report compiled by Lady Justice Butler-Sloss. This searching examination of child protection practices in one small part of the country guaranteed the order and its successor the very highest of profiles during the passage of the Children Act.

The need for caution

The Cleveland affair is often cited as a leading example of over-zealous public officials initiating compulsory intervention prematurely. Whether this description is justified is a question which has been keenly debated but in a sense the answer does not matter because the undeniable effect of the events was to alert both the caring professions and the general public to the dangers inherent in the summary removal of children from their families. This sense of unease, which had been curiously absent from public debate in the years before Cleveland, assumed sizeable proportions during 1991 due to the developments in Rochdale and Orkney. In those cases, the parents' grievances were compounded by the fact that their children had been taken away in a 'dawn raid' on their homes.

The fact that these two unfortunate episodes occurred after the Children Act had been passed but before it was brought into force meant that, while it was too late to change the law, it was not too late for suitably worded guidance to be issued. This was done, in *Working Together*. In the Introduction, the DH warns that 'although there is an obvious need to act with speed and decisiveness in cases where there is reasonable cause for suspicion that a child may be in acute physical danger, the potential for damage to the long-term future of the child by precipitate action must always be considered. There must be confidence that agencies will act in a careful measured way when suspicions are brought to their attention'. Later on, when considering stages of work in individual cases, the document emphasizes that all referrals must be taken seriously. In addition, however, 'it is important in all these cases that the public and professionals are free to refer to the child protection agencies without fear that this will lead to uncoordinated and/or premature action'. These statements can be regarded as direct responses to the Rochdale and Orkney cases.

The same can be said of the guidance in *Working Together* concerning 'dawn raids'. Referring to joint police/SSD operations, it states:

> In many cases there will be no need to remove a child and simultaneously arrest a suspect living in the same home. In other cases, however, particularly those involving several children and adults in different households, it may be important to prevent suspects from communicating with each other or destroying evidence. In those cases it may be necessary for co-ordinated police action, distressing though this may be, at a time of day when the whole family is at home. In other cases, although early morning police action might secure better forensic evidence, such action may not be crucial to the overall welfare of the child(ren) and should not therefore be part of the plan for investigation.

It will be observed that this passage does not seek to prohibit early morning action; such a restriction would be contrary to common sense. What it does is to underline the need for caution during every stage of a case involving removal.

The range of applicants for an EPO

Anybody could apply for a place of safety order under the previous law, and the Children Act did nothing to change the position: section 44(1) refers to an application made by 'any person'. So that social workers, police officers, health visitors, teachers and other professionals continue to have ready access to the courts.

It should be noted that section 52 of the Act enables regulations to be made providing for a transfer of responsibilities under an EPO to the local authority within whose area the child is ordinarily resident. This will, of course, only be relevant in those cases where the applicant for the order was not that authority. If such a transfer does take place, the authority will be treated as though it had applied for the order: so it will acquire decision-making power (and duties) in the case and the original applicant will lose it. The procedure is laid down by the Emergency Protection Order (Transfer of Responsibilities) Regulations 1991. These require the SSD in question to be satisfied that a transfer would be in the child's best interests. The original applicant must be consulted and a number of specified considerations must be taken into account (including the ascertainable wishes and feelings of the child). There are also requirements concerning official notification of the transfer.

A link exists between section 52 and the investigation provisions of section 47. We saw in the last chapter how section 47 requires a local authority investigation to be undertaken where significant harm is suspected. It imposes a similar requirement where an authority is informed that a child who lives, or is found, in its area is the subject of an EPO. According to section 47(3), the enquiries shall, in particular, be directed towards establishing whether it would be in the child's best interests for him to be in the authority's accommodation. The need for a transfer will therefore have to be addressed. It may be asked: how will the authority come to learn of the EPO? The answer is that the rules of court require the applicant to serve a copy of the order on it within 48 hours.

The grounds for an EPO

The grounds for an EPO are set out in section 44(1). According to this, the court may make an order if, but only if, it is satisfied that:

(a) there is reasonable cause to believe that the child is likely to suffer significant harm if (i) he is not removed to accommodation provided by or on behalf of the applicant; or (ii) he does not remain in the place in which he is then being accommodated;

(b) in the case of an application made by a local authority, (i) enquiries are being made under section 47 and (ii) those enquiries are being frustrated by access to the child being unreasonably refused to a person authorized to seek access and the authority has reasonable cause to believe that access to the child is required as a matter of urgency; or

(c) in the case of an application made by the NSPCC (i) it has reasonable cause to suspect that a child is suffering, or is likely to suffer, significant harm; (ii) it is making enquiries with respect to the child's welfare; and (iii) those enquiries are being frustrated etc. (as in (b)).

The section makes it clear that 'a person authorized to seek access' means an officer of the local authority or someone authorized by the authority to act on its behalf, or the NSPCC.

As can be seen, the Act sets out three distinct grounds for an EPO. When it was first presented to Parliament, the Children Bill contained only ground (a), the so-called general purpose ground. Grounds (b) and (c), which are concerned with the blocking of official child protection enquiries through the denial of access to the child, are a reflection of the great importance which the DH attaches to this particular issue. We have seen in Chapter 7 how section 47 of the Act virtually directs a local authority to seek compulsory powers where access is refused to an investigating team; and we shall see later in the present chapter how the issue of access played a part in the creation of the child assessment order. This need to see the child is one of the clearest messages which the Act sends out to social workers.

Several points concerning the interpretation of section 44(1) need mentioning here. As far as paragraph (a) is concerned, its forward-looking wording is a distinct improvement on the old law, as is its express reference to the situation where the child needs to stay put (as opposed to being removed). Volume 1 of the Guidance rightly emphasizes that past or present significant harm is relevant only to the extent that it indicates that the child is likely to suffer significant harm in the near future. The expression 'significant harm' is a crucial one and occurs in several places in the Act. Its meaning is discussed in Chapter 10 (see page 156).

With regard to paragraphs (b) and (c), the reason for their appearance in the Act has already been explained. While anybody may apply for an EPO under paragraph (a), paragraphs (b) and (c) are reserved for the use of social services departments and the NSPCC. It will be noticed that paragraph (c) refers to the NSPCC having reasonable cause to suspect significant harm, while paragraph (b) does not mention harm. The difference is more apparent than real, however, because the local authority enquiries referred to in (b) are themselves conditioned on a reasonable suspicion of harm (see Chapter 7).

'Access' is not defined in the Act but, as stated in Chapter 7, it is suggested that it involves face-to-face contact with the child which lasts for a reasonable time. It would seem that the contact does not need to be in the child's home.

Grounds (b) and (c) refer to access being 'unreasonably refused'. Whether or not this condition is satisfied is ultimately a question of fact for the court or magistrate to decide. As the Guidance states, refusal of a request to see a sleeping child in the middle of the night may not be unreasonable, but refusal to allow access at a reasonable time without good reason could well be. Social workers should be aware of the need to explain their position in calm and clear terms to the child's carer and to produce official identification. If their request to see the child is mismanaged, his carer might be fully justified in adopting a negative approach.

The court's discretion

As with the other types of compulsory intervention, the court is not obliged to grant an application for an EPO. The court (or magistrate), guided by the welfare principle set out in section 1 of the Act, will need to consider carefully whether the order is available (i.e. have grounds been made out?) and whether making it would be better for the child than making no order at all. Needless to say, this should not be a mere rubber-stamping exercise (a point hammered home in the aftermath of the Cleveland affair). Concern was expressed during the 1980s about the use of place of safety orders in non-emergency situations, and the hope was that social workers and the courts would be aware of the dangers of such a practice. As the Child Care Law Review commented: 'An EPO should not become a matter of course where care proceedings are a likely option'.

The checklist of factors set out in section 1(3) of the Act (discussed in Chapter 3) does not strictly speaking apply to EPO applications, on account of the urgency of the cases, but elements of it are used in practice.

The legal effect of an EPO

As previously explained, the precise legal consequences of a place of safety order were unclear. The EPO provisions of the Children Act address this question directly.

The first legal consequence (under section 44(4)) is that the order operates as a direction to any person who is in a position to do so to comply with any request to produce the child to the applicant. Disobedience of this deemed direction can be punished as a contempt of court and those who know where the child is should be made aware of this if they prove obstructive.

The second, and critical, consequence is that the applicant may lawfully remove the child from his present residence to other accommodation or prevent his removal from his present residence (e.g. a hospital or a foster home). Anyone who intentionally obstructs the exercise of this power commits a criminal offence. An important feature of this provision is that it gives the applicant a discretion: in other words, the applicant does not have to exercise the power to remove or detain. Indeed, section 44(5) states that the power shall only be exercised 'in order to safeguard the welfare of the child'. This flexibility is essential if social workers and other professionals are to respond to what are often rapidly changing circumstances. An obvious example is where a suspected abuser leaves the family home between the time of the application for the order and the time when the social worker arrives at the doorstep. Another is where the suspected abuser is prepared to give an undertaking to leave the home or comply with an exclusion requirement which has been attached to the EPO (see page 137 below). Where the child is removed, Volume 1 of the Guidance suggests that the child is entitled to an explanation of why he is being taken from his home and what will happen to him.

Similarly, there is discretion to backtrack once the power has been used: if it appears to the applicant that it is safe for the child to be returned, that action should, under section 44(10), be taken. By the same token, however, if circumstances again change while the order is in force, the power to remove can be reactivated. The child's carers (or would-be carers) should be told at the outset, and in clear terms, how the making of an EPO gives the applicant full power to determine the child's place of residence for the duration of the order.

Many children removed under EPOs are placed in local authority accommodation. Where this occurs, the child is within the category of those being 'looked after'. The significance of this is that the code of treatment set out in Part III of the Act (and supplemented by regulations concerning plans, reviews, placements and complaints procedures) becomes applicable (except for the parental contribution rules). This code, which is of course heavily influenced by the partnership philosophy, was described in Chapter 6. Its overall effect is to encourage parental participation in the discussions concerning the child's treatment.

The third legal consequence of an EPO is that it gives the applicant parental responsibility (i.e. parental powers and duties) in respect of the child. Doing this does not deprive the parents of their parental responsibility – as we saw in Chapter 2, only adoption has this effect – but it does give the holder of the EPO legal authority to take decisions concerning the child while he is under protection. However, we are dealing here with a short-term measure; for the holder to take a decision with long-term implications would clearly be inappropriate. The Children Act attempts to cover this point by stating (section 44(5)) that the holder 'shall take and shall only take such action as is reasonably required to safeguard or promote the welfare of the child (having regard in particular to the duration of the order)'. This is a trifle vague, of course, and it probably leads to variations in practice, but given the variety of situations encountered it is the best that can be achieved in a statute.

Two specific aspects of parental responsibility are dealt with by special provisions: contact and medical examinations. These matters, which caused great problems in the Cleveland affair, are discussed in the following sections.

Contact

The effect of the Act has been to clarify and improve the position of parents and others connected with the child, following the exercise of emergency protection powers. The provisions are modelled on those pertaining to care orders, so there is a statutory presumption (section 44(13)) in favour of contact. The applicant is to allow the child 'reasonable contact' with: the parents (this includes the unmarried father), non-parents with parental responsibility, anybody living with the child prior to the order, anybody holding a contact order and anybody acting on behalf of these people. There is no indication in the Act as to what is reasonable.

Should the applicant wish to restrict contact or stop it completely, the court can be asked to give appropriate directions, either at the time the EPO is made or subsequently (section 44(6)). Conversely, the court can at any stage issue directions – with conditions attached, if necessary – in favour of contact with any person. This facility may be of help to those family members who are unhappy with the amount of contact being offered by the holder of the EPO. Any direction as to contact can be varied subsequently.

These provisions on contact are not the only ones which need to be borne in mind. As was explained earlier, if a child is removed under an EPO into local authority accommodation, he becomes subject to the code of treatment set out in Part III of the Act. This code contains contact rules too (see Chapter 6).

Medical examination and assessment

Commenting on the uncertainties surrounding the place of safety order legislation, the Cleveland inquiry team said:

> We would suggest that an initial examination to ascertain the health of a child would be within the authorisation of the agency under the order, and in a case such as physical injury, X-rays and any consequential necessary treatment would follow. It would not however in our view include repeat examinations for forensic purposes or for information gathering rather than for continuing treatment. Such examinations would require the consent of the parents. A situation might well arise and indeed did arise in Cleveland where there were excessive numbers of medical examinations of certain children. Some control over examinations in the present climate is now highly desirable . . .

The Children Act introduced such control. Section 44(6) states that where the court makes an EPO it can give such directions (if any) as it considers appropriate with respect to the medical or psychiatric examination or other assessment of the child. Such a direction may be to the effect that there is to be no examination or assessment, or none without the court's consent. Furthermore, a direction can be given at any time while the EPO is in force and can be varied by the court. Finally, when making an EPO, the court can direct that the applicant, when exercising any powers, be accompanied by a doctor, nurse or health visitor (section 45(12)). Such a person could conceivably conduct an examination of the child if the circumstances were deemed appropriate, although the environment might well be a difficult one.

A very important qualification of the above rule is contained in section 44(7): the child may refuse to submit to an examination or an assessment if he is of sufficient understanding to make an informed decision. The same qualification is to be found in the provisions relating to interim orders and child assessment orders. It represented a victory for those who champion the rights of children and their right to be treated wherever possible in the same way as adults, and it prevailed over the argument that in some cases the child's 'refusal' is not completely genuine but a product of parental pressure. Many doctors can be expected to err on the side of caution in applying this provision. In 1989 the then Minister of Health said that 'even if it were deemed that [he] was not a child with full understanding of the process, I do not believe that any medical practitioner would carry out a medical examination if a child resisted it. I believe that that would be in line with what we know about medical ethics'. In such cases, it becomes a matter of persuading the child rather than compelling him.

The DH, in its Guidance, suggests that as a matter of good practice a local authority applying for an EPO should always seek directions on assessment or examination where this is likely to be an issue. It also expresses the hope that assessment arrangements can be agreed between the parties and points out that the court may direct (perhaps after a parental request) that the child's GP observe or participate.

The procedural aspects of EPOs

The Children Act is virtually silent on this matter, leaving it to be regulated by the rules of court. Although applications for EPOs can be made to the county court and the High Court, in practice most are made to the magistrates' court and it is therefore the Family Proceedings Courts (Children Act 1989) Rules 1991 which contain the key provisions on procedure. These enable applications to be made either at an ordinary sitting of the magistrates' court or to a single magistrate on an *ex parte* basis, but in the case of the latter the leave of the justices' clerk must first be obtained (this additional screening mechanism obviously necessitates close local liaison between SSDs and clerks). Consequently, some EPO applications are heard with the child's parents being present and some (in fact most) are not.

The 1991 rules prescribe an elaborate form for use in EPO applications and this obliges the applicant to supply to the court detailed information concerning the child, his family and his present circumstances. The completed form is served on the other parties (principally, those with parental responsibility for the child) either before the hearing or, in the case of an *ex parte* order, within 48 hours. In certain circumstances, persons without parental responsibility have to be notified of the application. This is the case, for example, if the child is presently living with relatives or friends of the family. Upon being notified, such persons can apply to become full parties to the case.

Section 41 of the Children Act provides for the appointment of a guardian ad litem (GAL) for the child in 'specified proceedings'. This expression is defined by the section so as to include EPO applications, thereby signalling the introduction of GALs into this type of litigation. This has been an important development with substantial practical implications and it is considered, alongside other GAL matters, in Chapter 13 of this book. For present purposes, it needs to be borne in mind that a guardian, if appointed, will be in a position to exert a significant influence on the course and outcome of the proceedings. The same goes for any solicitor appointed by the GAL (or the court) to act as an advocate for the child.

At the hearing, whether *inter partes* or *ex parte*, the magistrate(s) have to be presented with sufficient evidence to justify the making of the order. What sort of material is produced by the applicant will depend on the circumstances but the Act seeks to discourage, in the interests of the child, an over-rigid adherence to the strict rules of evidence. It provides (in section 45(7)) that the court may take account of any statement contained in any report made to it in the course of, or in connection with, the hearing, or any evidence given during the hearing, which is in the court's opinion relevant to the application. The significance of this is explained in the DH Guidance: 'this enables the court to give such weight as they think appropriate to any relevant hearsay, opinions, health visiting or social work records and medical reports'.

If an EPO is made, it is issued in a prescribed form. The form states the effect of the order (including any directions), the reasons for making it and its duration. The rules require an order made *ex parte* to be served on the other parties, and any person who has actual care of the child, within 48 hours. When served, these people will learn from the form and the accompanying notes something of their legal rights and duties, but they will nevertheless be advised to see a solicitor as soon as possible (the Guidance suggests that the SSD should consider making available similar written information in other languages where English is not the primary language of the families concerned).

The duration of an EPO

'An emergency protection order shall have effect for such period, not exceeding eight days, as may be specified in the order.' This is what section

45(1) provides. If the last of the eight days is a Sunday, or a bank holiday, or Good Friday or Christmas Day, the court can specify a period which ends at noon on the first later day which is not such a holiday. And if the EPO is made following the exercise of the police protection power (see Chapter 9) time starts to run from the first day of that period.

One extension of an EPO is possible, on application by a social services department or the NSPCC (section 45(4)). This can last for up to seven days. However, it is only available where the court has reasonable cause to believe that the child is likely to suffer significant harm if the order is not extended. If an application is made, it will be heard by the court on an *inter partes* basis (perhaps with a GAL in attendance). The hearing could be preceded by a preliminary directions appointment, a standard Children Act device whose purpose is to prepare the ground.

These rules inevitably have had the effect of putting social workers and their legal advisers under more pressure, in terms of looking ahead and preparing a case, than the previous 28-day provisions did. The DH in its Guidance remained optimistic, however: 'if there has been a genuine emergency and the authority believe care proceedings should follow it should normally be possible to proceed to satisfy the court as to the grounds for an interim order within the first period'. One determining factor may be the outcome of any challenge to the EPO which has been made (see below).

The parents' right of challenge

Section 45(8) corrected a major flaw in the previous law by introducing an effective right for parents and others to challenge the emergency removal of children. The challenge is by way of an application to the court to discharge the EPO, and the Act makes it available to the parents, non-parents with parental responsibility, any person who was living with the child prior to the order, and the child himself (who may, of course, act through a GAL).

The catch is that a challenge cannot be made (i.e. heard by the court) until 72 hours have expired. This mandatory period of delay was considered necessary so as to enable the holder of the order to assemble a case. Nor is a challenge possible if the aggrieved party was given notice of, and was present at, the hearing at which the EPO was made – only one right of reply is available. And there is no right to challenge an EPO which has been extended, because the parties will have had an opportunity to question the extension when it was ordered.

The DH in its Guidance states that it is not intended that 72 hours is the effective time limit by which the authority must complete its assessment if it is to contest a challenge: 'if an application comes to court for the discharge of an order after 72 hours and the assessment has not been completed the authority will advise the court accordingly and unless circumstances have so changed as to allay any concerns the authority may have had for the safety of the child it is unlikely that the court will agree to discharge the order'.

What if the EPO is refused?

There is no right of appeal against a refusal of an EPO or a refusal of an extension (section 45(10)). The unsuccessful applicant may be able to institute wardship proceedings as a way round this, except for local authorities, whose use of wardship is heavily circumscribed by the Act (see Chapter 14). Alternatively, the police can be asked to intervene under their protection power. This will only have a limited duration, however.

Because magistrates are not infallible, the denial of a right of appeal to unsuccessful local authorities is bound to result in some children losing the protection which they need. Calls for a review of the legal position were inevitable and in June 1995 these were made in the case of *Re P*, in which magistrates had refused an extension to an EPO despite strong evidence that the child's life was at risk from a mother subsequently diagnosed as suffering from Munchausen Syndrome by Proxy.

Supplementary powers: locating the child

Section 48 of the Act contains provisions aimed at the effective enforcement of EPOs.

- Where it appears to the court that adequate information as to the child's whereabouts is not available to the applicant but is available to another person, it may include in the EPO a provision requiring that other person to disclose, on request, what he knows. Disobedience of such a requirement can be punished as a contempt of court. The prescribed form for EPO applications contains a box designed for the insertion of supplementary powers such as this, and in fact the Guidance suggests that in cases where it is not known for sure that the child is at particular premises, courts should be asked as a matter of routine to attach an information direction to avoid unnecessary returns to court.
- An EPO can authorize the applicant to enter specified premises and search for the child. Anyone intentionally obstructing the applicant commits a criminal offence. Again, the Guidance advises that this type of authority be sought 'as a matter of course'.
- An EPO authorizing an entry and search may also authorize a search for other children believed to be on the premises. In these circumstances, the applicant may, if the other children are found, proceed as if an EPO had been made in respect of them too, provided he or she is satisfied that the statutory grounds exist. The court must be notified of what happens.

- The police can be brought in to assist in the exercise of EPO powers. This matter is dealt with in Chapter 9.

Supplementary powers: exclusion requirements

It has long been recognized that in a situation which is actually or potentially abusive to a child, an outcome that may be less damaging to the child is for the abuser to leave the child's home, as opposed to the child being removed. This option is, of course, conditional upon there being someone else in the home who can be trusted to provide the child with good enough parenting and appropriate protection from the abuser. It has always been possible for a local authority to negotiate a voluntary departure with an abusing party (perhaps under threat of the child's removal) and it has always been possible for an authority to provide material assistance to such a person. The Children Act contains explicit provisions on this matter: under paragraph 5 of Schedule 2, where it appears to a local authority that a child who is living on particular premises is suffering, or is likely to suffer, ill-treatment at the hands of another person who is living on those premises and that other person proposes to move from the premises, the authority may assist him to obtain alternative accommodation. Such assistance may be given in the form of cash (subject to the usual conditions regarding repayment – see page 72 above).

The DH has repeatedly drawn attention to the advantages of a negotiated departure. In Volume 1 of its 1991 Guidance, it stated that 'where the need for emergency action centres on alleged abuse of the child the local authority will always want to explore the possibility of providing services to and/or accommodation for the alleged abuser as an alternative to the removal of the child'. Four years later, in *The Challenge of Partnership in Child Protection* (1995), the SSI advised that 'wherever possible, an alleged abuser should be encouraged to move out of the home to avoid disruption to the child'. What the Children Act – as originally drawn up – did not do, however, was enable a local authority to obtain a court order compelling an actual or alleged abuser to leave. Such a reform was certainly discussed in 1989 but it was deferred pending the Law Commission's review of the domestic violence legislation.

The absence of express ouster provisions in the Act did not inhibit some lawyers in attempting to persuade the courts to find ouster powers by implication. In *Nottinghamshire County Council v P* (1993) the local authority sought to deal with a situation of persistent and gross sexual abuse by asking the court to make a prohibited steps order prohibiting the abusing father from residing in the same household as his children. The Court of Appeal rejected the application, stating that it was very doubtful whether a prohibited steps order could in any circumstances be used to oust a parent from the family home. In the later case of *D v D* (1996) the Court of Appeal stated bluntly that 'there is no jurisdiction to make an ouster order under the Children Act'. The effect of these rulings – which, it is submitted, were clearly correct – was that the enforced departure of an abusing party could be secured under civil law by two methods only:

1 An injunction granted on the application of the spouse or cohabitee of the abuser (under the Domestic Violence and Matrimonial Proceedings Act 1976).
2 An injunction granted by the High Court on the local authority's application under that court's inherent jurisdiction (this is explained in Chapter 14 below).

The first of these methods is referred to in the DH Children Act Guidance, which suggests that the local authority should explore it in appropriate cases; the second method is not mentioned, probably because its availability was not confirmed until the High Court's decision in the case of *Re S* (1993).

The law as stated above underwent change in the autumn of 1997. At that time, the Government implemented provisions in the Family Law Act 1996 concerning so-called exclusion requirements in emergency protection orders and interim care orders. The effect of these provisions, which were recommended by the Law Commission in 1992, is as follows:

• A court may include an exclusion requirement in an EPO if two conditions are satisfied (section 44A(1) of the Children Act, as inserted by the 1996 Act).
• The two conditions are (a) there is reasonable cause to believe that, if a person is excluded from the child's home, the child will not be likely to suffer significant harm even though the child is not removed (or does not remain where he is), and (b) another person living in the child's home is able and willing to give to him reasonable care and consents to the exclusion requirement. (There is an equivalent set of conditions where the EPO is granted on the 'frustrated access' ground.)
• An exclusion requirement may consist of one or more of the following: (a) a provision requiring the person in question to leave the child's home, (b) a provision prohibiting him from entering the home, and (c) a provision excluding him from a specified surrounding area (section 44A(3)).
• The exclusion requirement may be ordered to operate for a shorter period than the EPO itself (section 44A(4)).
• A power of arrest can be attached to the exclusion requirement (section 44A(5)). If this is done, the police may arrest without warrant any person whom they have reasonable cause to believe to be in breach of the requirement. Section 44A(9), which has been clumsily drafted, provides for the consequences of an arrest (e.g. bringing the person before a court

within 24 hours). Powers of arrest can be varied or discharged upon application (section 45(8B)).
- If the holder of the EPO removes the child from his home to other accommodation for a continuous period of more than 24 hours, the exclusion requirement automatically comes to an end, thus enabling the excluded person lawfully to return home (section 44A(10)).
- The court may accept an undertaking from the alleged abuser instead of ordering a formal exclusion requirement (section 44B). Breach of such an undertaking is punishable – for contempt – in the same way as breach of a requirement.
- The court may make a non-molestation order in respect of the child once it has made an exclusion requirement (section 42(2) of the Family Law Act 1996).

In recommending these changes, the Law Commission expressed the view that they would be an effective protection against child abuse in only a relatively small proportion of cases: 'the possibility of ousting the suspected abuser is probably most relevant in cases of sexual abuse or serious "one-off" incidents of violence'. While it is impossible to know how the new provisions will operate in practice, it is clear that they contain several points of difficulty:

1 If an exclusion requirement is included, it cannot last longer than the EPO itself unless an identical requirement is attached to an interim care order. Since interim care orders are temporary measures themselves (see Chapter 10), exclusion requirements should not be seen as a long-term solution to the child's predicament.
2 A requirement cannot be made unless another person in the child's household consents. This other person will, in practice, often be the child's mother. Such a prerequisite will, however, defeat the local authority in cases such as *Nottinghamshire County Council v P* (above), where the mother did not wish to see her husband excluded from the home.
3 There is a curious inconsistency between the grounds for an EPO and the conditions for an exclusion requirement. On the one hand, the applicant social workers will be arguing that an EPO should be granted because the child will suffer harm if he is not removed, while at the same time they will be arguing that an exclusion requirement should be made in order that the child may stay put. Whereas the statutory grounds for an EPO (contained in section 44) are based on the desired removal of the child, the statutory grounds for an exclusion requirement are based on the desired removal of someone else. And yet the two have to be applied simultaneously. This is the inevitable consequence of tying exclusion requirements to EPOs, instead of making them free-standing orders of the sort found in private domestic violence law.

4 Many applications for EPOs, and exclusion requirements, will be made *ex parte*. In these circumstances, the applicant may find it difficult to satisfy the court that another person in the child's household consents to the exclusion requirement.

5 The selection of an absolute 24-hour cut-off point where the child is moved may serve to constrain unduly the discretionary powers of the professional workers involved.

6 It goes without saying that some exclusions will result in wholly innocent people being compelled to leave their property. This is because at the EPO stage of a case the evidence is likely to be incomplete. It is, perhaps, worth making the point that in private domestic violence law the judiciary has for many years acted with extreme caution when faced with *ex parte* ouster applications.

The consequences of an EPO

There are, obviously, numerous possible consequences of EPO powers being used. It may be that an application for an interim care or supervision order will follow; it may be that the child will return home free of the threat of further intervention. It should be noted, however, that the making of an EPO must lead to an investigation by the local authority, whether or not it was the applicant for the order. This is required by section 47 of the Act, whose provisions were discussed in Chapter 7.

The child assessment order

The rationale of the CAO was explained by the Government to the House of Commons in the following way:

The difficulty is to know whether the emergency protection order is adequate or whether we require an additional order – a child assessment order – to run in parallel with it. There may be a repeated failure to produce a child and perhaps it cannot be asserted that the matter is quite so urgent that there is an immediate need to intervene to take the child away – it is at the heart of our concerns that the emergency protection order is used only in those very serious circumstances, so the issue is whether there should be a lesser order requiring the production of a child and one which allows for the assessment of the child to take place. Section 43 represents the best attempt that the Government can make to take on board the various views and produce an easy-to-use, readily explicable proposition, which has the proper safeguards that one would expect when any intrusion into the rights of parents over their children is considered.

The range of applicants for a CAO

Whereas anybody may apply for an EPO, only a local authority or the NSPCC can apply for a CAO (section 43(1)).

Grounds for a CAO

Under section 43(1), the court may make an order if, but only if, it is satisfied that:

(a) the applicant has reasonable cause to suspect that the child is suffering, or is likely to suffer, significant harm; and
(b) an assessment of the state of the child's health or development, or of the way in which he has been treated, is required to enable the applicant to determine whether or not the child is suffering, or is likely to suffer, significant harm; and
(c) it is unlikely that such an assessment will be made, or be satisfactory, in the absence of an order.

It will be noticed that the first condition is based on the applicant having reasonable cause to suspect. This may be contrasted with other conditions in the Act which refer to the applicant having reasonable cause to believe, e.g. in relation to EPOs. As for the third condition, Volume 1 of the DH Guidance suggests that the court hearing an application will expect to be given details of the investigation which preceded it and the way in which it arose, 'including in particular details of the applicant's attempts to be satisfied as to the welfare of the child by arrangements with the people caring for the child. If the court is not satisfied that all reasonable efforts were made to persuade those caring for the child to co-operate and that these efforts were resisted, the application is likely to founder on the condition'.

The section 43(1) criteria need to be considered by the court in conjunction with the welfare principle and the presumption of no order contained in section 1 of the Act.

The legal effect of a CAO

The sole purpose of a CAO is to bring about an assessment of the child, in order that the basic facts about his condition can be established. As was noted in Chapter 7, assessment is not the same thing as a social worker obtaining access to a child. It is symptomatic of the confusion which surrounded the creation of the CAO that some of its supporters saw it as a way of responding to denials of access. The Government met this concern by widening the grounds for an EPO, but it insisted that the CAO still had a place in the Act.

According to section 43(5), a CAO must specify the date by which the assessment is to begin and shall have effect for such period, not exceeding seven days beginning with that date, as may be specified in the order. According to the Guidance, the seven-day period was fixed 'with the intention of causing the least possible disruption to the child but allowing sufficient time for an assessment to produce the information required'. In fact, the duration of a CAO was the subject of extended haggling in Parliament between the order's supporters and its detractors. Members of the latter group expressed doubts as to whether a proper assessment could always be expected in a week and this point has since been conceded by the DH.

Section 43(6) states that it shall be the duty of 'any person who is in a position to produce the child' (this does not simply mean the parents, of course) to produce him to such person as may be named in the order and to comply with such directions relating to assessment as the court thinks fit to specify.

Section 43(7) expressly authorizes the assessment professional(s) to undertake the assessment in accordance with the terms of the order. This means that no parental consent is needed, provided, of course, that the assessment does not go beyond the proper boundaries. Doctors and other members of the assessment team need to take great care in adhering to the task described in the court's order.

Section 43(8) is an important, *Gillick*-inspired, provision. It enables a child who is of sufficient understanding to make an informed decision to refuse to submit to a medical or psychiatric examination or other assessment. Those engaged in assessment need to think long and hard before proceeding with a protesting child, even if there is a feeling that the seeds of the opposition have been planted by a suspected abuser.

Separation of the child and his family

Supporters of the CAO went out of their way to emphasize how different it would be from an EPO and, in particular, how the CAO would not involve the removal of the child from his family. 'Its prime virtue,' said the Kimberley Carlile inquiry team, 'would be that it would partake of none of the coercive nature of a removal and detention of a child from the child's parents and home . . . since the order would not physically order the detachment of the child from its parents, there should be no question of family trauma'. Things have not turned out quite like this. A CAO may well involve the separation of the child from his family, because not all assessments can be carried out at a doctor's surgery or a clinic: residence in a hospital may be necessary if a thorough assessment is to be undertaken.

This sort of scenario is explicitly mentioned in the Children Act. Section 43(9) states that:

> The child may only be kept away from home – (a) in accordance with directions specified in the order; (b) if it is necessary for the purposes of the assessment; and (c) for such period or periods as may be specified in the order.

The period specified cannot exceed seven days, of course, since that is the maximum duration of a CAO. And the specifying will be done by the court, not the social workers. The inevitable result, however, is that there will be cases where the court orders the removal of a child into a health service establishment for a week. The parents will not lose parental responsibility but they will lose the child. In these circumstances, the differences between a CAO and an EPO may be difficult for them to appreciate. No question of family trauma?

A concession to family unity is made by section 43(10), which requires the court, where the child is to be kept away from home, to make such directions as it thinks fit with regard to the contact that the child must be allowed to have with other persons while away. The Guidance states that the court may consider that the parents or other persons closely connected with the child should be allowed to stay with the child overnight; the applicant for the order should therefore consider offering this facility when asking for a direction that the child be kept away from home.

Defiance of a CAO

The CAO requires the child's present carer to 'produce' him to a named person. The court's supplementary directions must also be complied with. Suppose the carer fails to co-operate? There are several possible responses to this:

- The authorities could choose to do nothing. This might apply if their fears about the child prove to be unfounded before the assessment is actually carried out.
- The carer could be threatened with sanctions for contempt of court.
- The authorities could apply, or threaten to apply, for an EPO. Such an order would give them the power forcibly to remove the child.

Action following the assessment

Again, there are many possible outcomes of an assessment. What ultimately happens will depend on two factors in particular: the conclusions of the assessment professional(s) and the degree of co-operation which can be expected from the child's carer. These factors will dictate what sort of action, if any, is needed. Further compulsory intervention may be high on the agenda (an outcome which the carer will have been acutely aware of from the beginning).

One problem area has been highlighted by critics of the CAO: what can be done to protect the child immediately if it becomes apparent during the assessment that serious abuse has been taking place? Obviously an EPO can be sought but that takes time. An alternative strategy is to summon the police and invite them to exercise their protection power (on which see Chapter 9). That apart, it has to be said that without clear statutory authority to detain the child, doctors and social workers are in a precarious legal position. It is worth remembering, however, that this is the case when abuse is detected during a 'voluntary' examination.

Procedure

The CAO machinery is not aimed at emergencies, and this is reflected in the procedural provisions. Under section 43(11), any person applying for a CAO shall take such steps as are reasonably practicable to ensure that notice of the application is given to various parties. These are: the child's parents (this includes the unmarried father), any non-parent having parental responsibility, any other person with whom the child is living, any person holding a contact order, and the child himself.

The procedure is further prescribed by the 1991 rules of court. CAOs are not available on an *ex parte* basis, so a full hearing, normally in the magistrates' court, is necessary, with the child probably being represented by a guardian ad litem and/or solicitor. The relevant application form has been constructed in such a way as to require the applicant to settle in advance the details of the proposed assessment (e.g. type, identity of assessor, location, duration, contact). Close liaison with the medical services is therefore needed well before the hearing.

The question of the child's attendance at the hearing is bound to arise in many CAO cases, especially as he has the statutory right to torpedo the entire exercise. This matter is governed by section 95 of the Children Act, a provision which in fact extends to all applications under Parts IV and V of the Act. It simply states that the court may order the child to attend such stage or stages of the proceedings as may be specified. However, the section has been supplemented by the rules of court. Under these, it is a function of the GAL (if appointed) to advise the court of the wishes of the child concerning attendance; attendance can be the subject of a direction given at a preliminary directions appointment; and the child must be excluded from a hearing if the court considers it in his interests, provided that he is represented by a GAL or solicitor. The overall effect is to make the child's attendance a matter for the court's discretion.

Variation and discharge

CAOs are amenable to variation and revocation. The procedure is spelt out in the rules of court.

Limits on the number of applications

Under section 91 of the Act, once a CAO application has been made, no further application can be made for six months without the leave of the court. This should be seen as an attempt to prevent the CAO being used oppressively.

CAO or EPO?

Ever since the CAO was first mooted, it has been recognized that its creation would throw up dilemmas for child protection workers. One of the main fears has been that social workers would, in an attempt to cause minimum damage to the family, go for the softer option – the CAO – and thereby do a disservice to the child who is in need of immediate removal from his home. The Kimberley Carlile inquiry team expressed this very clearly:

> The only worry that we entertain is whether there might not be a kind of bureaucratic magnetism about the lesser order. What we fear might happen is that social workers would too readily opt for the child assessment order in circumstances where their clear duty would be to apply for an emergency protection order. This real danger can be countered by social services directorates issuing clear instructions about the proper use of the two discrete orders. So long as social workers understand the different functions, there ought not to be any confusion about their use.

In 1989 opinions differed as to whether this view was overoptimistic. Certainly the Act contains no explicit guidance on how the choice between CAO and EPO (which, as we have seen, can itself contain directions for medical assessment) is to be made. However, what the Act does do is to acknowledge that applications for the wrong order will be made, because section 43(3) enables the court to treat an application for a CAO as an application for an EPO. It goes on to say (section 43(4)) that the court shall not make a CAO if it is satisfied that there are grounds for making an EPO and that it ought to make such an order rather than a CAO. Accordingly, social workers applying for CAOs may expect to be questioned very closely in court to see whether they have fallen victims to the bureaucratic magnetism described in the Carlile report.

The DH Guidance is alive to the problem of choice. It emphasizes that 'emergency action should not be avoided where disclosure of the abuse is itself likely to put the child at immediate risk of significant harm and/or where there is an urgent need to gather particular forensic evidence which would not otherwise be forthcoming in relation to the likelihood of significant harm'. It is noticeable, though, how its observations on the use of the two orders are qualified by words such as 'usually' and 'not necessarily'. These qualifications are unavoidable in this context but unfortunately they only serve to highlight the fine judgments which have to be made in child protection investigations.

There is another dimension to the dilemma, however. The Carlile inquiry envisaged the CAO as an order obtainable from a single magistrate without notice being given to the child's carer. That is not how things turned out: as we have seen, a CAO is available on an *inter partes* basis only. From the social worker's point of view, applying to a single magistrate, which is of course possible in the case of an EPO, may appear far more convenient and effective than having to go through a full hearing, with all the delays and complications which that can entail.

It is, perhaps, because of the procedural obstacles that the CAO has proved unpopular in practice. Whereas about 3000 EPOs are made each year, the annual number of CAOs is less than 100. It may be that the threat of seeking a CAO is used in some cases as a lever in negotiations between the local authority and the family; even so, the very small number of applications, which is inconsistent with the attention lavished on the CAO in Parliamentary debate, suggests that the legal framework needs to be reconsidered.

9

Police powers

Police involvement in child protection cases tends to be transient and sporadic, but it is none the less important. Like the previous child care legislation, the Children Act contains specific provisions relating to the police. These fall naturally into two categories: those which concern action taken on the initiative of the police, and those which concern the role of the police in assisting others.

The power of the police to act of their own motion

The lead provision here is section 46. This enables a constable (which in law means any police officer) simply to remove a child to suitable accommodation and keep him there; alternatively, a constable can take such steps as are reasonable to prevent the child's removal from his current accommodation (a removal from hospital is the obvious example of the sort of situation which Parliament had in mind here, and section 46 mentions this expressly). Once such action is taken, the child is said to be in 'police protection', and he can be kept there for up to 72 hours.

Other chapters of this book show how the police protection power can be used in a variety of situations, e.g. to preserve a placement in local authority accommodation or a certified refuge, or to give immediate protection following an examination under a child assessment order. Volume 1 of the DH Guidance refers specifically to the use of the power to protect runaways, glue-sniffers, children whose parents have abandoned them and children found to be living in unhygienic conditions. According to evidence given to a Parliamentary committee in 1995, section 46 is used almost routinely around Piccadilly Circus in London, where young children are seen wandering the streets; in other parts of London it is used about once a month.

It should be noted that the power given by section 46 is a power to remove or detain. This is quite distinct from a power to enter property, on which the section is silent. If a police officer wishes to exercise his power of protection but the child is on private property, he will have to look to some other provision for authority to enter the premises where the child is residing. In this connection, it is worth bearing in mind section 17 of the Police and Criminal Evidence Act 1984, for this permits a constable to enter and search any premises without a search warrant if his purpose is to save life or limb.

Clearly, the power to intervene under section 46 is a drastic one. It is not particularly novel, however, since a similar power was to be found in the Children and Young Persons Act 1969, although following the Review of Child Care Law the opportunity was taken to revise the rules. The police protection power is only available where a constable has reasonable cause to believe that the child would otherwise be likely to suffer significant harm. The expression 'significant harm' is defined in section 31 of the Children Act (see page 156 below).

What happens once the child is taken into police protection obviously depends on the circumstances, but whatever the situation, certain rules have to be complied with as soon as is reasonably practicable:

• The constable must inform the local social services department of the steps which have been (and are proposed to be) taken with respect to the child and the reasons for taking them.
• The constable must notify the social services department for the child's home area of his current place of residence (a statutory acknowledgement that the protection power is used on runaway children).
• If he appears capable of understanding, the child must be informed of the steps which have been taken with respect to him and the reasons for taking them, as well as the further steps which may be taken.
• The constable must take such steps as are reasonably practicable to discover the wishes and feelings of the child.
• The case must be inquired into by an officer designated for the purpose by the Chief Constable.
• If the child has initially been taken to accommodation which is not local authority accommodation or an approved refuge (on this, see Chapter 15), he must be moved to such a place.
• Certain persons must be informed of what has happened and why, and of what may happen. These are: the child's parents, any non-parent with parental responsibility, and any other person with whom the child was living immediately before being taken into protection. This duty links in with the family contact provisions noted below.

The position of the designated officer

It can be seen that once the police protection power is used, attention shifts to the designated officer and to the local social services department. As far as the former is concerned, he must carry out an inquiry into the case. Section 46(5) of the Act states that on completing this, he is to release the child unless he considers that there is still reasonable cause for believing that the child would be likely to suffer significant harm if released. If he decides to retain the child, the section permits him to apply, on behalf of the social services department for the child's home area, for an emergency protection order. In this way, continuity of care can be ensured. In the meantime, the designated officer, while not having parental responsibility, is empowered – indeed obliged – to do what is reasonable in all the circumstances for the purpose of safeguarding or promoting the child's welfare. The Act does not envisage any long-term decisions being taken.

Family contact during the police protection period is regulated by section 46(10). The designated officer is to allow five categories of individual such contact (if any) with the child as, in his opinion, is both reasonable and in the child's best interests. These categories are: the parents, any non-parent with parental responsibility, any person who was living with the child before the police action, any person holding a contact order, and any person acting on behalf of these persons.

The position of the social services department

What is the position of the SSD? If the above-mentioned rules are followed, the child may find himself at an early stage in departmental accommodation (unless of course the police protection consists of preventing, rather than effecting, the removal of the child). The DH Guidance states that no child taken into police protection need be accommodated in a police station: section 21 of the Children Act requires every local authority to make provision for the reception and maintenance of children in the category now under consideration. Once in such accommodation, the child falls within the provisions of Part III of the Act concerning children being 'looked after' by a local authority. Consequently, the code of treatment – described in Chapter 6 – will apply (except for the rules relating to parental contributions). As far as family contact is concerned, the department is in the same position as the designated police officer, so that a fairly wide discretion is given.

The SSD has more than just a duty to accommodate, however, because the exercise by the police of their protection power triggers off an obligation on the part of the department to mount an investigation into the child's case. This is laid down by section 47. According to this, the enquiries are to be directed in particular towards establishing whether it would be in the child's best interests for an emergency protection order to be sought.

The position of the parents

The position of the child's parents during the period of police protection – which, it will be recalled, can last for up to 72 hours – is inevitably rather weak. Although they have a statutory right to be informed of the situation, they lose whatever possession rights they had: a criminal offence is committed if they knowingly take the child away 'without lawful authority or reasonable excuse' (section 49). In practice, this means obtaining permission from either the police or the social services department. And although the Act refers to contact with the child, it is ultimately a matter of discretion for the authorities. Furthermore, there is no right of appeal against the exercise of their powers by the police. The only consolation is that the period of protection is relatively short. If it is followed by the making of an emergency protection order, the parents will be in a position to challenge that order (and it should be noted that in these circumstances the eight-day maximum duration of an EPO runs from the first day of police protection).

Police applications for emergency protection orders

Since EPOs can be made on the application of any person, it follows that they may be sought by the police. This subject is discussed in Chapter 8.

Criminal investigations

The Children Act does not seek to regulate the process of investigation by the police into alleged criminal offences committed against children. Such offences, and investigations that follow their commission, are dealt with by other legislation. However, because compulsory intervention by local authorities and the investigation and prosecution of suspects often coincide, the DH Guidance on the Children Act is careful to take account of the criminal dimension. At the investigation stage, agencies are expected to adhere to the guidelines laid down in *Working Together* (1991), a document which emphasizes the need to share information (even 'confidential' information) at all times. If a decision is made to record an interview with a child on video, the guidelines in the *Memorandum of Good Practice* (1992) should be followed.

In discharging their responsibility to bring offenders to justice, the police may wish to secure access to documents which have emerged during Children Act proceedings instituted by the local authority. Although the 1991 rules of court provide for the confidentiality of documents held by the court, they do enable the court to authorize disclosure on the application of an interested person. Cases decided in recent years reveal a willingness on the part of the judiciary to release relevant documentation to the police so that a criminal investigation can be pursued more effectively. The argument that a willingness to disclose leads to parents and others being less frank in their evidence has certainly been acknowledged but it does not appear to have been particularly successful.

In *Re F-S* (1988) – a pre-Children Act case – care orders were made in respect of 17 children following evidence of sexual abuse perpetrated by a large number of relatives. Although the trial judge had refused permission for a police officer to attend the hearing, she did grant an application at the end of the hearing that the local authority disclose to the police a transcript of her judgment together with all relevant documents and information in the authority's possession. This decision was upheld by the Court of Appeal, which emphasized the importance of making it possible for those who have apparently committed criminal offences to be investigated properly so that they may be brought to justice and so that other children unaffected by the care proceedings may be protected. Cases in the post-Children Act period have gone the same way. In *Re L* (1996) a police officer learned of the existence of a chemical pathologist's report while attending a child protection conference. The report had been compiled at the request of the mother's lawyers for the purposes of pending care proceedings and the House of Lords authorized its disclosure to the police, who wished to pursue a criminal investigation into the mother's past conduct. Lord Jauncey said: 'in proceedings of this nature it would be most unsatisfactory if the court having information that the mother might have committed a serious offence against the children whose welfare it was seeking to protect should be disabled from disclosing such information to the appropriate investigating authority'. In *Re EC* (1996) a police investigation into the death of a child following non-accidental injuries had reached an impasse but evidence emerging in the course of care proceedings in respect of the surviving sibling (including an admission of responsibility by the father) offered an opportunity to make progress. The police successfully applied for disclosure of the statements and evidence of the parents and other family members together with the evidence of medical experts. The Court of Appeal placed emphasis on the gravity of the circumstances.

The role of the police in assisting officials

The Children Act contains a number of provisions, modelled on previous legislation, under which the assistance of the police can be sought. The theme running through these provisions is the need to facilitate police involvement when the exercise of statutory powers by public officials, notably social workers, is being frustrated, or is likely to be frustrated. Knowing when police assistance will be helpful, and knowing when it will be counter-productive, are obviously matters for professional judgment, and not surprisingly the Act maintains a neutral stance: it makes assistance possible but does not compel its deployment. The Act (the relevant sections are 48 and 102) uses common criteria for the situations in which it authorizes the issue of a warrant of assistance: *either* it must appear to the court that a person attempting to exercise powers has been prevented from doing so by being refused entry to the premises concerned or refused access to the child concerned *or* it must appear to the court that any such person is likely to be so prevented from exercising powers. The situations in question concern the exercise of the following powers:

1 Powers under an emergency protection order.
2 Powers under Part VII (inspection by local authorities of accommodation provided by voluntary organizations).
3 Powers under Part VIII (inspection of private children's homes).
4 Powers under Part IX (inspection of private foster homes).
5 Powers under Part X (inspection of premises used for child minding or day care).
6 Powers under section 80 (inspection of children's homes etc. by the DH).
7 Powers under section 86 (inspection by local authorities of residential care homes, nursing homes and mental nursing homes).
8 Powers under section 87 (inspection of independent schools).
9 Powers under Schedule 3 (visits by and contact with a supervisor under a supervision order).
10 Powers under section 33 of the Adoption Act 1976 (visiting of protected children).

In each of these cases the court may direct that the constable concerned may be accompanied by a doctor, nurse or health visitor if he so chooses. The person applying for the warrant is entitled to accompany the constable, unless the court has directed otherwise. What the warrant does is to authorize (not compel) the constable to assist the applicant in the exercise of the powers concerned. This may involve the application of a certain amount of force. Once the assistance has been given, and entry to the property or access to the child secured, the situation may demand the exercise of other police powers, e.g. the power of arrest. The procedural aspects of warrant applications are governed by the 1991 rules of court. They allow such applications to be granted by a single magistrate on an *ex parte* basis and prescribe specific forms to be used. As far as EPO cases are concerned, the Guidance suggests that the applicant should consider at the time of the EPO application whether he or she needs to apply for a warrant: 'if any difficulties in gaining entry are foreseen, or if the applicant believes that he is likely to be threatened, intimidated or physically prevented from carrying out this part of the order, the possibility of simultaneously obtaining a warrant should always be considered'.

Police involvement in the recovery of abducted or missing children

Section 50 of the Children Act permits the court to make a 'recovery order' in respect of various types of child: those who are the subject of a care order or emergency protection order and those who are in police protection. The order can be made whenever there is reason to believe that the child has been unlawfully taken away, or is being unlawfully kept away, or has run away, or is staying away, from the person who for the time being has care of him under the relevant arrangements. The order can also be made if there is reason to believe that the child is missing. The effect of a recovery order is to authorize the removal of the child by, among others, the police. They may also enter any premises specified and search for the child. In addition, any person who has information as to the child's whereabouts is required to disclose that information to the police if asked to do so.

Section 50 is a useful provision but its scope is limited. It should be borne in mind, however, that it forms only one part of child abduction law. There is plenty of other legislation on the subject (e.g. the Child Abduction Act 1984). Nor should it be forgotten that the police are in the position of having special powers of entry and removal which are not dependent upon the existence of a court order; these powers could easily be exercisable with respect to abducted or missing children.

10

Care orders

Introduction

Part IV of the Children Act is entitled 'Care and Supervision' and, as the title implies, it contains provisions concerning care orders and supervision orders. Because the effects of these two orders are so different it is proposed to deal with them separately in this book. The present chapter is devoted to care orders.

In Part IV of the Act, the crunch question is reached, so far as State intervention in family life is concerned: in what circumstances are parents and other care-givers liable to have their children forcibly removed from their care, perhaps for good? The grounds for a care order are supremely important in the context of the Children Act, because the statute goes out of its way to channel all local authority applications for compulsory care through this procedure. No longer do separate grounds exist where care is being sought during matrimonial or other family proceedings. Nor is the wardship jurisdiction available, as it used to be, as a convenient method of bypassing the statutory procedure. All cases in which long-term intervention is being considered need to be studied with reference to Part IV.

In addition to the grounds for an order, other important questions arise. Who may apply for an order? What will the procedure be? What is the effect of a care order? What rights of appeal exist? All of these matters, and many others, were up for review and debate during the 1980s. The consequences may be seen in Part IV.

The centrality of the provisions of Part IV in the child protection context was reaffirmed in the case of *Nottinghamshire County Council v P* (1993), whose facts were summarized in Chapter 8 (see page 137). The Court of Appeal declared that the local authority's decision to deal with a case of serious sexual abuse by applying for a prohibited steps order was wholly inappropriate. It went on:

In cases where children are found to be at risk of suffering significant harm . . . a clear duty arises on the part of local authorities to take steps to protect them. In such circumstances a local authority is required to assume responsibility and to intervene in the family arrangements in order to protect the child. Part IV of the 1989 Act specifically provides them with wide powers and a wide discretion . . . It is to be hoped that . . . local authorities will recognize that where children are believed to be at risk of suffering significant harm, their appropriate avenue is via Part IV of the Children Act 1989 which is specifically designed to accommodate public law applications.

Applicants for a care order

Only a local authority or an authorized person can apply for a care order (section 31(1)). 'Authorized person' in practice means the NSPCC – expressly mentioned in the legislation – and if it proposes to make an application, it is required to consult the local authority in whose area the child is ordinarily resident. The Act, however, prevents the NSPCC from applying if the child is already the subject of an application for a care or supervision order; nor can it apply if the child is subject to a supervision order. In these situations, a local authority will by definition already be involved and accordingly intervention by the NSPCC would be inappropriate. The DH Children Act Guidance (Volume 1) advises that as a matter of good practice, the NSPCC should always keep the local authority informed of its concerns about children in the authority's area. Information and thinking should be shared as matters develop and the two organizations should seek to agree a course of action.

The children concerned

Any child under the age of 17 can be made the subject of a care order, with the exception of a 16-year-old who is married (section 31(3)). The Guidance points out that the court is likely to look 'particularly keenly' at a case for making an order for a young person who is approaching his 17th birthday.

The grounds for a care order

The threshold criteria

According to section 31(2), a court may only make a care order if it is satisfied:

(a) that the child concerned is suffering, or is likely to suffer, significant harm; and

(b) that the harm, or likelihood of harm, is attributable to (i) the care given to the child, or likely to be given to him if the order were not made, not being what it would be reasonable to expect a parent to give to him; or (ii) the child's being beyond parental control.

Four important definitions accompany section 31(2). 'Harm', according to section 31(9), means ill-treatment or the impairment of health or development; 'development' means physical, intellectual, emotional, social or behavioural development; 'health' means physical or mental health; and 'ill-treatment' includes sexual abuse and forms of ill-treatment which are not physical. In addition, section 31(10) states that 'where the question of whether harm suffered by a child is significant turns on the child's health or development, his health or development shall be compared with that which could reasonably be expected of a similar child'.

A great deal of thought went into the wording of section 31(2). It was based largely on the recommendations of the Child Care Law Review of 1985, which expressed the view that 'the primary justification for the State to initiate proceedings seeking compulsory powers is actual or likely harm to the child'. The Review rejected proposals to have a simple test based on the welfare of the child on the grounds that this would lead to widely varying and subjective interpretations and would fail to offer the right degree of statutory protection against unwarranted intervention. The welfare of the child is important and, as we shall see, it forms part of the decision-making process, but on its own it is not enough to justify intervention. Conditions of greater specificity are needed. It is for this reason that the contents of section 31(2) have come to be known as the 'threshold criteria'. As was explained by the House of Lords in the case of *Re H and R* (1995):

In section 31(2) Parliament has stated the pre-requisites which must exist before the court has power to make a care order. These pre-requisites mark the boundary line drawn by Parliament between the different interests. On the one side are the interests of parents in caring for their own child, a course which *prima facie* is also in the interests of the child. On the other side there will be circumstances in which the interests of the child may dictate a need for his care to be entrusted to others. In section 31(2) Parliament has stated the minimum conditions which must be present before the court can look more widely at all the circumstances and decide whether the child's welfare requires that a local authority shall receive the child into their care and have parental responsibility for him.

The meaning to be ascribed to statutory words and phrases is frequently a controversial matter and section 31(2) contains many nuggets for aficionados of textual interpretation. However much practitioners and policymakers might regret a descent into semantics, such an outcome was probably unavoidable once the decision had been taken to introduce a threshold criterion of harm. In a case heard shortly after the implementation of the Children Act (*Newham London Borough Council v AG* (1992)) the President of the Family Division of the High Court said:

> I very much hope that in approaching cases under the Children Act courts will not be invited to perform in every case a strict legalistic analysis of the statutory meaning of section 31. Of course, the words of the statute must be considered, but I do not believe that Parliament intended them to be unduly restrictive when the evidence clearly indicates that a certain course should be taken in order to protect the child.

The hopes expressed by the President in this case were, predictably, not fulfilled, as the litigation described below demonstrates.

'The child concerned is suffering significant harm'

When the Children Bill was first published, it provided for the making of a care order if 'the child concerned has suffered significant harm'. During the Parliamentary proceedings the past tense was changed to the present so as to prevent orders being made simply on the basis of harm suffered long ago. This change dealt with one problem but created another in its place: taken literally, the statute would require the applicant local authority to prove actual suffering at the time of the final hearing. If – as is invariably the case – the authority had taken steps to remove the child from a damaging environment well before such a hearing, it would be difficult, if not impossible, to prove that this condition was satisfied. A child who is living in a secure foster home is not usually suffering harm. This is exactly the situation which arose in *Northamptonshire County Council v S* (1992). There, the local authority sought care orders in respect of two children on the grounds of the mother's lack of parenting skills. By the time of the final hearing, the children had been in foster care (on a voluntary basis) for nearly a year and were making good progress. A similar scenario was evident in *Re M* (1994). The child's father had killed the mother and following the child's removal from home under emergency powers, the child had been looked after by a foster carer. By the time of the final hearing, the child had been in foster care for 16 months. In both of these cases the children had suffered in the past but in neither case were they suffering at the time of the hearing of the care order application. In the

Northamptonshire case, the High Court ruled that the words 'is suffering' in section 31(2) 'relate to the period immediately before the process of protecting the child concerned is first put into motion . . . That means that the court has to consider the position immediately before an emergency protection order, if there was one, or an interim care order, if that was the initiation of protection, or, as in this case, when the child went into voluntary care'. This approach was approved by the House of Lords in *Re M*. As a result, the way was clear to make care orders in each case (as indeed was done). Such an interpretation does involve doing violence to the words of the statute but the alternative, literal, approach – which had been favoured by the Court of Appeal in *Re M* – would have had bizarre consequences.

'The child concerned is likely to suffer significant harm'

This element of the threshold criteria represented an important breakthrough in our child care law, since it enables a court to make a care order solely on the basis of anticipated harm. This type of case was not properly catered for under the previous legislation, with the result that local authorities were driven to use the wardship jurisdiction of the High Court.

The word 'likely' has appeared in a variety of statutes over the years and its possible meanings have been considered by the courts on a number of occasions. The first reported case in which likelihood in section 31(2) fell to be considered was *Newham London Borough Council v AG* (1992). That was a very clear case of anticipated harm. The child was two years old and his mother was suffering from serious mental illness. She had neglected herself, had already physically ill-treated the child and had threatened to harm him again. The Court of Appeal noted that when a civil court is asked to make finding of fact – e.g. that a particular event 'happened' – it uses a 'balance of probabilities' test: if the evidence shows a balance in favour of the event having happened, then it is proved that it did in fact happen. This test cannot be used, however, when the court is looking to the future, as it is of course in 'likely to suffer' cases. The duty of the court, it was said, is to assess the risk to the child. In this case, there was ample evidence that there was a 'real significant likelihood of this child suffering significant harm'.

Three years later, in *Re H and R* (1995), the courts were presented with the opportunity to give rather fuller consideration to the issue of likelihood. In this case, care orders were sought in respect of three girls. The local authority's application was based on the alleged sexual abuse of the girls' older sister by their father, and it argued that in such circumstances they were likely to suffer significant harm. The county court judge, applying the traditional balance of probabilities test, stated that he was not satisfied that the older sister had been abused as alleged although he confessed that he was 'more than a little suspicious' that the allegations were true. Since the allegations formed the only basis of the local authority's case that the three children were at risk, the judge felt obliged to dismiss the application. This decision was upheld on appeal. The House of Lords ruled first that the word 'likely' in section 31(2) 'is being used in the sense of a real possibility, a possibility that cannot sensibly be ignored having regard to the nature and gravity of the feared harm in the particular case'. Likely does not mean probable because that would fix the threshold at an unacceptably high point. The second – and, on the facts of the case, crucial – ruling was that for a court to be satisfied as to the likelihood of significant harm, there must be facts from which the court can properly conclude that there is a real possibility of future harm. Unresolved doubts and suspicions cannot by themselves form the basis of a conclusion that the condition is satisfied. A decision on the likelihood of a future happening must be founded on a basis of present facts and the inferences fairly to be drawn from them, and an alleged but non-proven fact is not a fact for these purposes. In the present case, perhaps unusually, the local authority's application was based solely on the father's past abuse of the older sister (he did not have any history of abuse). Since that fact had not been proven, there was nothing to support a finding of likelihood of harm to the three younger girls. It would have been different had there been other proven facts indicating a future risk (and the House of Lords observed that 'the range of facts which may properly be taken into account is infinite').

The second ruling in this case was not unanimous: one judge in the Court of Appeal and two judges in the House of Lords supported the proposition that the courts should be able to find the likelihood condition satisfied merely on the basis of strong suspicion. They were concerned that the majority's approach would leave some children (such as the three in this case) without the protection they needed. The weakness of this minority position, however, is that it would create an unjustifiable inconsistency between the 'is suffering' condition – which everyone accepts must be based on proven facts – and the one covering likelihood.

'Significant harm'

'Harm' is defined expansively, particularly through its incorporation of impairment of development; but to give the court jurisdiction to make an order, it must be shown that the harm is 'significant'. *There is no definition in the Children Act of 'significant'*. This word was included in the statutory formula to emphasize the gravity of compulsory intervention and to warn the court that an order should not be made in trivial cases. Of course, it may be said that no harm suffered by a child is trivial, especially harm caused by physical violence or sexual abuse. It may also be said that no court would ever make a care order unless the case was a serious one. No doubt there is a lot of truth in this. The fact remains, however, that with the very broad meaning attributed to 'harm' in the Act, some sort of qualifying term is warranted to prevent unnecessary interference. At any rate, this was how the Government argued it. The Lord Chancellor put it this way:

> It is not proper to intervene on any level of harm. The fundamental point is that State intervention in families in the shape of the local authority should not be justified unless there is some level – 'significant' is a good word for it – at which significant harm is suffered or is likely to be suffered.

Whether or not the harm is 'significant' is ultimately for the court to decide, guided if necessary by relevant expert evidence. It will be noted that where the allegation is that harm is impairment of health or development – as opposed to ill-treatment – section 31(10) requires the child's actual or likely health or development to be compared with that which could reasonably be expected of a similar child, i.e. a child of the same age, characteristics, disabilities, etc. The degree of disparity between the child before the court and the hypothetical similar child will determine whether or not the harm is significant.

'Is attributable to'

Paragraph (b) of section 31(2) was described by one of the judges in *Re H and R* (above) as the 'causation' element of the threshold criteria. It requires the applicant local authority to prove that the significant harm – whether actual or anticipated – is linked to one of two specified situations (these are described below). If there is no such link, a care order cannot be made. This will be the case, for example, if the harm is attributable to the unavoidable actions of a third party.

'The care given to the child, or likely to be given to him if the order
were not made, not being what it would be reasonable to
expect a parent to give to him'

This element of the threshold criteria enables a care order to be made where the child has not been, or will not be, receiving proper parenting. It is the element most frequently used in practice (the alternative one, directed at children beyond control, is considered below). The applicant local authority and the court have to focus on the particular attributes of the child and measure them against the standard of parenting that can be offered by the care-giver (or prospective care-giver in an anticipated harm case). Different attributes obviously require different standards and the applicant has to prove a substantial shortfall in those standards to get its order. According to the DH Guidance, 'the court will almost certainly expect to see professional evidence on the standard of care which could reasonably be expected of reasonable parents with support from community-wide services as appropriate where the child's needs are complex or demanding, or the lack of reasonable care is not immediately obvious'. It should be observed that where the requirements of this element are satisfied, that in itself does not suggest any culpability on the part of the carer: it may simply be a case of him not having the necessary faculties to care for the child. Difficulties have arisen in 'likely to suffer' cases where a third party (e.g. a relative) has come forward with a request to assume future responsibility for the child. If such a person is, with the support of the parents, offering a decent home to the child, how can it be said that the child is likely to suffer significant harm attributable to the lack of reasonable care? This question fell to be considered in *Northamptonshire County Council v S* (1992). The magistrates felt that if the children were returned to their mother they were likely to suffer further physical and emotional harm due to her inadequate parenting. However, the grandmother of one of the children offered to take over his care and the magistrates had no doubts as to her qualities. Nevertheless they made a care order. Upholding this decision on appeal, the High Court ruled that the words of section 31(2)(b) relate to the parent or other carer whose lack of care has caused, or is likely to cause, significant harm: 'the care which other carers might give to the child only becomes relevant if the threshold test is met'. As with the meaning attributed to 'is suffering', this approach involves a departure from the plain meaning of the Act. It does, however, almost certainly reflect the intentions of the draftsman. In the case of *Re M* (1994), referred to earlier, the Court of Appeal adopted a rather different interpretation of section 31 and had regard to the standard of care which the child would receive from the third party who had come forward (in that case, the mother's cousin). The same stance was taken in the later Court of Appeal decision in *Re A* (1994). However, as both of these Court of Appeal decisions were overruled when *Re M* reached the House of Lords, the interpretation in the *Northamptonshire* case remains the authoritative one.

'The child's being beyond parental control'

Whether or not a child is beyond parental control is a question of fact. The fact that a child is beyond control does not in itself indicate an absence of reasonable parental care. The child's carers may actually be offering extremely reasonable care but may still be unable to prevent the child from inflicting significant harm on himself.

The threshold criteria and child protection registers

As noted in Chapter 7, the 1991 edition of *Working Together* (Part 6) contains guidance on child protection conferences and child protection registers. According to this guidance, the inclusion of a child's name on the register should normally only take place following a conference. Furthermore, before a child's name is registered 'the conference must decide that there is, or is a likelihood of, significant harm leading to the need for a child protection plan'.

This reference to 'significant harm' is understandable in a publication which seeks to take full account of the Children Act, but there is nevertheless some potential for confusion. Child protection registers operate on a wholly non-statutory basis: there is no legislation which governs them or even refers to them. Consequently, as a matter of law there is no point of connection between Part IV of the Act and Part 6 of *Working Together*. The latter document is not framed in technical terms like much of the Act and it is not subject to the Act's provisions concerning evidence, proof, procedure and the rest. This explains how it is that *Working Together* can suggest four categories of child abuse for the purposes of registration, categories which it freely admits 'do not tie in precisely with the definition of 'significant harm' in section 31'. They are: neglect, physical injury, sexual abuse and emotional abuse. Practitioners need to appreciate that registers and care order proceedings, though clearly linked in practice, remain distinct in law. The disjunction between the threshold criteria and the grounds for CPR entries will no doubt be addressed during the consultations leading up to the revision of *Working Together*.

When an application can be made

Section 31(4) states that an application for a care order may be made on its own or in any other family proceedings. By this, the Act simply means that an application can be made whether or not any other legal proceedings involving the family are on foot. If other 'family proceedings' are in train, the local authority or the NSPCC can seek to combine its case with them. As originally drafted, section 8(3) defined these 'other proceedings' as meaning:

1 Proceedings under Parts I and II of the Act (e.g. a guardian's application or an application for a section 8 order).
2 Proceedings under the Matrimonial Causes Act 1973 (divorce, nullity and judicial separation).
3 Proceedings under the Domestic Violence and Matrimonial Proceedings Act 1976 (injunctions).
4 Adoption proceedings.
5 Proceedings under the Domestic Proceedings and Magistrates' Courts Act 1978 (maintenance applications).
6 Proceedings under the Matrimonial Homes Act 1983 (applications concerning the occupation of the matrimonial home).

7 Proceedings under Part III of the Matrimonial and Family Proceedings Act 1984 (applications for financial provision following an overseas divorce).
8 Wardship and other proceedings under the so-called inherent jurisdiction of the High Court.

The recasting of our divorce and domestic violence laws by the Family Law Act 1996 means that, at some point in the future, some of the references in the above list will change. This will not, however, alter the substance of the legislation. Whether or not any of these family proceedings are in train at the time of the decision to seek a care order is, of course, purely a matter of chance, but if they are it will often make sense for the care order request to be handled by the same tribunal. Chapter 12 of this book explains how applications can be transferred between courts for the purposes of consolidation with other pending proceedings.

The discretion to apply for a care order

It was emphasized in Chapter 7 that the decision to invoke the compulsory intervention machinery is essentially a matter for the discretion of the agency concerned, guided no doubt by a multi-disciplinary case conference. It follows that neither the local authority nor the NSPCC can be compelled to institute care order proceedings. Nor can they be prevented from doing so (except that, as previously mentioned, there are certain restrictions on the NSPCC). There is a provision in the Act, however, which enables an instruction to be given to a local authority to *consider* the launching of proceedings. This is section 37, which is concerned with family proceedings, understood in the sense described above (i.e. divorce etc.), in which it appears to the court that it may be appropriate for a care order or supervision order to be made. In these circumstances the court can direct the local authority to undertake an investigation of the child's situation.

Where such a direction is given, the local authority is under a duty to consider whether it should (a) apply for a care order or a supervision order, (b) provide services or assistance for the child or his family, or (c) take any other action. The 1991 rules of court provide for the forwarding by the court of copies of any relevant documentary evidence which has been submitted in the family proceedings. The local authority is perfectly entitled to decide not to take legal action, but if that is its decision the Act requires it to inform the court of its reasons. The court must also be given details of any service or assistance which the local authority has provided, or will provide, for the family, together with details of any other action taken or to be taken. All this must be done within eight weeks of the direction unless the court otherwise directs. Finally, section 37 requires an authority which declines to seek an order to consider whether it would be appropriate to review the case at a later date and, if so, to fix a date for the review. Whether or not the local authority decides to apply for an order, it may find that the care of the child is temporarily thrust upon it anyway, because section 38 of the Act enables a court which orders an investigation to make an interim care order at the same time. This matter is discussed at page 201 below. Where a section 37 direction has been given and the court has made, or is considering whether to make, an interim care order, the proceedings become 'specified proceedings' for the purposes of section 41 of the Act, with the consequence that the court is obliged to appoint a guardian ad litem for the child unless satisfied that it is not necessary to do so in order to safeguard his interests (see further, Chapter 13).

Problems were experienced with section 37 in the early years of the Children Act. The Children Act Advisory Committee reported that the procedure was being misused in some parts of the country for a variety of reasons, e.g. to facilitate the introduction of a guardian ad litem into private law proceedings or to ensure the delivery of a welfare report more quickly than could have been obtained by using the court welfare service. Even where the procedure had been invoked properly, there had been difficulties: some local authorities had been unable to meet reporting deadlines and some had failed to communicate properly the results of their investigation. The Committee also expressed concern about 'circumstances in which a section 37 report has revealed serious parental deficiencies but nevertheless the local authority has declined to apply for a care or supervision order, thereby placing the court in difficulty'. In an attempt to ensure greater consistency, the Committee published Best Practice Guidance (Annual Report 1992/93, Annex 1 to Chapter 4). This was subsequently incorporated in the Committee's *Handbook of Best Practice in Children Act Cases* (1997).

The reference made by the Committee to situations in which the local authority decides not to initiate legal proceedings under section 31 was probably inspired by the case of *Nottinghamshire County Council v P* (1993). A number of strands of child law became entangled in that case, including prohibited steps orders, contact orders and ouster from the family home, and these have already been considered in this book (see pages 30, 137 and 154 above). For present purposes it is sufficient to note that the local authority, though very concerned about past and anticipated sexual abuse within the family home, declined to apply for a care or supervision order. Instead, it sought a prohibited steps order to exclude the father from the home. The county court judge, who clearly disagreed with this strategy, issued a section 37 direction but the local authority adhered to its view that section 31 proceedings were inappropriate. When the case reached the Court of Appeal the frustration felt by the judiciary was bluntly expressed:

> This court is deeply concerned at the absence of any power to direct
> this authority to take steps to protect the children ... The operation
> of the Children Act is entirely dependent upon the full co-operation
> of all those involved. This includes the courts, the local authorities and
> the social workers and all who have to deal with children. Unfortu-
> nately as appears from this case if a local authority doggedly resists
> taking the steps which are appropriate to the case of children at risk of
> suffering significant harm it appears that the court is powerless.

Although the incredulous tones of this passage might suggest otherwise, the
court's decision on the law was never really in doubt, for the wording of
sections 31 and 37 makes it absolutely clear that the initiation of Part IV
proceedings is a matter for the local authority alone. This allocation of
responsibility is consistent with the position once a care order is made,
when – as is explained below – the local authority possesses a large measure
of autonomy, but some people have evidently found this difficult to accept.

The processing of a care order application

The procedural aspects of legal proceedings can be dry and technical but
they are important. Their potential for determining the course which a case
takes is significant and often underrated and this is particularly so in care
order and other children's applications, which invariably take place against
a moving, rather than a static, background. The case of *Avon County
Council v N* (1995) provides a poignant example of how the outcome of a
section 31 application can be dictated by events occurring at the interim
stages. The local authority had applied for care orders in respect of four
young children on the grounds of inadequate parenting by their mother,
who was said to be suffering from a profoundly disordered personality. The
children were living in a foster home under interim care orders but the
mother was seeking rehabilitation. The voluntary agency carrying out an
assessment of the family reached the conclusion that a lengthy residential
assessment at a specialist hospital might offer a chance of rehabilitation and
it received an assurance from the local authority that funding for this would
be forthcoming. The court made an order for an exploratory interview with
the family at the hospital and this proved positive, but at a further hearing
(delayed on account of a listing error at the court) the local authority
announced that it was withdrawing its offer of funding. An explanation was
sought from the authority and when the court reconvened three months
later the authority announced restoration of the funding. By that time,
however, the hospital unit was full and a residential assessment could not be
offered for another four months. The High Court, recognizing that the
children had been in 'forensic limbo' for far too long, reluctantly dismissed

the mother's application for a six-week residential assessment of herself and her children. This decision virtually destroyed the mother's hopes of recovering her children and the judge expressed the view that she had been victimized by the local authority's conduct of the case: 'it seems to me absolutely tragic that a mother who in recent contact has been able to demonstrate a warmer relationship with her children should be denied the opportunity to explore further the viability of a residential assessment with a view to long-term psychotherapeutic treatment for the family'. Cases like this reflect little credit on the family justice system and have led some to question whether there is a better way of dealing with problems of child maltreatment, but as long as the litigation process is central to child protection practitioners will need to acquire a good understanding of procedural matters.

Like the previous legislation, the Children Act does not attempt to lay down a comprehensive procedural code for compulsory intervention proceedings. While some procedural rules are in the Act, most were made during 1991 by specially appointed committees of lawyers in the form of rules of court. Under the Act, it is possible for care order applications to be dealt with by the magistrates' court or by the county court or by the Family Division of the High Court (this 'concurrent jurisdiction' is discussed in Chapter 12) and such an arrangement explains why there is more than one set of rules. There are, in fact, two sets: the Family Proceedings Courts (Children Act 1989) Rules 1991 covering applications made to the magistrates' court, and the Family Proceedings Rules 1991 covering applications made to the superior courts. As with the rules governing section 8 order applications, the care order rules in these two documents have been drafted in largely the same terms, so that cross-reference between them is a fairly straightforward matter. Various amendments to the rules have been effected since 1991 in order to deal with difficulties exposed during the initial implementation period. Set out below are the main features of care order procedure.

The prescribed form

The applicant is required to file with the court an application in the form set out in Schedule 1 to the rules. The one prescribed for care order (and supervision order) cases is Form C1 (the basic Children Act application form) supplemented by Form C13. Form C1 is divided into 13 sections with headings such as 'The child(ren) and the order(s) you are applying for' and 'The parents of the child(ren)'. Supplementary Form C13 is divided into four sections whose headings are: The grounds for the application, The reason(s) for the application, Your plan(s) for the child(ren) and The direction(s) sought. Whereas Form C1 is designed to elicit basic factual information concerning the parties, the supplementary form requires the local authority or the NSPCC to say something about its case against the care-giver(s) and what it proposes to do in the future if its arguments are accepted. As a result, the child's family will come to appreciate the general nature of the issues in the case (if for some reason they did not know them before) right at the beginning of the proceedings. So will the guardian ad litem. This ties in with the overall thrust of Children Act procedure, which is to encourage advance disclosure of evidence to the court and the other parties, and to reduce the element of forensic surprise.

Which court?

Although the Children Act itself appears to give an applicant for a care order a free choice between the magistrates' court, the county court and the High Court, a government Order made in 1991 had the effect of imposing restrictions. These restrictions, contained in the Children (Allocation of Proceedings) Order, are discussed in more detail in Chapter 12 of this book but for present purposes it may be noted that their general effect is to require applications to be made to a magistrates' court. Not only are there exceptions to this rule, however, there is also an important power to transfer a care case upwards from the magistrates in appropriate circumstances.

Participation in the proceedings

In all proceedings under the Act, there is a distinction between those persons who are full parties ('respondents' to an application) and those persons who are not parties but to whom notice of the proceedings must nevertheless be given. Respondents, being parties, are entitled to call evidence in the case, cross-examine witnesses and appoint an advocate; they can also exercise the right of appeal. Those to whom notice must be given do not possess these rights but they can acquire them by becoming parties, and the rules of court enable them to apply for such status. Indeed, the court can confer party status itself, without a specific application having to be made.

In care order cases the initial respondents are: every person whom the applicant believes to have parental responsibility for the child; and the child himself (who will often participate through a guardian ad litem). Those to whom notice of the proceedings must be given are: persons who are caring for the child at the time when the proceedings are commenced; every person whom the applicant believes to be a party to pending Children Act proceedings in respect of the same child; and every person whom the applicant believes to be a parent without parental responsibility for the child. The inclusion of this last category means that an unmarried father will normally be either a respondent or a person to be notified, depending on whether he has acquired parental responsibility (on which see Chapter 2). In the case of *Re X* (1995) the High Court ruled that the obligation to notify the unmarried father without parental responsibility is not an absolute one. There, the court decided that the Muslim father of a child should not be told about a care order application because of the damage it could cause both parents within their community (the father was the mother's brother-in-law). The validity of the ruling in this case is questionable but even if it stands, it will apply only in the most exceptional circumstances.

The appointment of a guardian ad litem

This matter is dealt with in Chapter 13. In summary, though, it may be noted that section 41 of the Children Act requires the court to appoint a GAL for the child in every care order case unless it is satisfied that it is not necessary to do so in order to safeguard his interests. The precise functions of the guardian are spelt out in the rules of court and it is quite obvious from what is stated there that the guardian occupies a pivotal role in the handling of the application.

Directions appointments

Rule 14(2) of the magistrates' courts rules reads as follows:

In any relevant proceedings the justices' clerk or the court may give, vary or revoke directions for the conduct of the proceedings, including –
(a) the timetable for the proceedings;
(b) varying the time within which or by which an act is required, by these rules, to be done;
(c) the attendance of the child;
(d) the appointment of a guardian ad litem;
(e) the service of documents;
(f) the submission of evidence including experts' reports;
(g) the preparation of welfare reports;
(h) the transfer of the proceedings to another court;
(i) consolidation with other proceedings.

The rules for the superior courts are similarly worded. The directions appointment, which the parties or their representatives are expected to attend, was one of the principal innovations introduced by the Children Act rules of court. Its object is to advance the interests of the child by facilitating the smooth running of the final hearing of the application by the magistrates or the judge. Its effect is (or should be) to put the court in firm control of the course of the proceedings, as opposed to leaving it to the parties and their lawyers as used to happen, often to the great detriment of the child. Though not mandatory, these preliminary hearings have become standard in care order cases. How many there are in a case, and what precise form they take, depends on the particular circumstances.

Both the senior judiciary and the Children Act Advisory Committee have sought to emphasize the critical role of the directions appointment. According to Mr Justice Wall: 'A summons for directions is not a formality. It is a vital part of the judicial process. Not only is it an essential cog in the machine which prepares a case for trial, but it is also a forum for the parties to exchange information, and agree on progress' (*Re M* (1993)). In its Annual Report 1993/94 the Advisory Committee recommended that there should always be a final directions appointment approximately two weeks before the final hearing of an application. This should be conducted by the judge or justices' clerk who will preside at the final hearing. The guardian ad litem's report, the case chronology and the bundles of relevant documents should be available at this appointment. The Committee published a Best Practice Form of Directions which it recommended for general use (Annex 2 to Chapter 2) but observed that its suggestions would not be employed to best advantage unless courts were prepared to adopt an interventionist role during the interim stages of cases. This is a message which has been repeated many times by the senior judiciary.

Timetables and the avoidance of delay

Reference was made in Chapter 3 to the provisions in the Act which concern delays in private law proceedings. There are equivalent provisions for public law proceedings. Section 1(2) applies, so that a court hearing an application for a care order must have regard to the general principle that any delay in disposing of the application is likely to prejudice the welfare of the child. In addition, the court is required by section 32 to draw up a timetable 'with a view to disposing of the application without delay' and to give 'such directions as it considers appropriate for the purpose of ensuring, so far as is reasonably practicable, that that timetable is adhered to'.

Section 32 has been supplemented by the rules of court, especially by the provisions concerning directions appointments noted above. Significantly, the rules require the court to fix a return date whenever proceedings are postponed or adjourned. Directions appointments are absolutely crucial for the purpose of achieving an effective and speedy (but not rushed) disposal of a case and practitioners representing or assisting parties have found the courts far less pliant on the question of timing than they used to be. Thus in *H v Cambridgeshire County Council* (1996) the High Court upheld decisions of magistrates refusing a mother permission to show the papers in pending care proceedings to a psychiatrist and refusing to postpone the final hearing of the local authority's application. The mother had been given such permission once already but she had chosen not to avail herself of that opportunity, resulting in the permission being withdrawn. Her second application for leave was made only a few weeks before the date fixed for the final hearing and came too late, since the children's welfare would be adversely affected by the consequential delay.

Despite the express provisions of the legislation – provisions which were not to be found in the old law – care order proceedings since 1991 have been blighted by long delays. Indeed, delay in public law litigation has become one of the biggest problems arising out of the implementation of the Children Act. It received very considerable attention from the Children Act Advisory Committee and was the subject of a special report compiled by Dame Margaret Booth. Commentators seem to agree that the reasons for delay are not always the same but that they can include the following:

• failure by courts to play a sufficiently active role in controlling the timetable
• poor communication between tiers of court
• poor listing practice within courts
• lack of court time
• a proliferation of parties to proceedings (this has been made easier by the more liberal rules on participation, noted earlier)
• a proliferation of experts
• the need to undertake thorough assessments
• failure by lawyers to provide realistic time estimates for cases
• sloppy preparation of document bundles by lawyers
• lack of expertise in child law on the part of lawyers.

The multiplicity of factors at work here makes it difficult to produce a tidy solution to the problem of delay. However, there is no doubt that the role of the courts in assuming firm control of care order applications has emerged as especially important. This key function has been emphasized time and again. Unfortunately, the retention of arrangements under which children's proceedings are handled by three separately organized courts, and the consequent failure to establish a proper family court, has hindered progress in carrying it out (see further, Chapter 12 below).

Evidence

The way in which a local authority seeks to prove the prescribed conditions for a care order has traditionally been a matter for its judgment, and the Children Act and the secondary legislation did not attempt to change this.

What they do aim to do, however, is provide some special ground rules which will ensure fair play, both for the child (who may need protection) and for his family (who may need the same). The interests of the child can be seen to be reflected particularly in three rules. The first is concerned with hearsay evidence (e.g. a statement about abuse made by the child to a teacher or a foster carer who is giving evidence). Cases decided under the old law threw into question the validity of such evidence in care proceedings and as a result a section was inserted in the Children Act (section 96) enabling the Government to regulate the matter. From 14 October 1991, the Children (Admissibility of Hearsay Evidence) Order has had effect. This lays down a simple rule: 'In civil proceedings before the High Court or a county court and in family proceedings in a magistrates' court, evidence given in connection with the upbringing, maintenance or welfare of a child shall be admissible notwithstanding any rule of law relating to hearsay'. This relaxation in the evidential position has been helpful to care agencies, although it should be borne in mind that the weight that will be attached to hearsay by the courts may not be as great as the weight given to evidence produced directly in the courtroom.

The second rule applies where a guardian ad litem for the child has been appointed. In these circumstances, section 41(11) of the Children Act permits the court to take account of (a) any statement contained in the GAL's report and (b) any evidence given in respect of the matters referred to in the report 'in so far as the statement or evidence is, in the opinion of the court, relevant'. For good measure, section 42(2) of the Act confirms that any official records which are examined by the GAL can be used as evidence in the proceedings. To the extent that these provisions enable hearsay evidence to be brought forward, they overlap with the Order described above.

The third child-centred rule is concerned with examinations. In many cases, a medical or other assessment of the child is needed in order to produce the sort of evidence which will either substantiate a claim or refute one. Since the Cleveland affair in 1987, practitioners have been alive to the dangers of uncontrolled and/or repeated examinations and this awareness is reflected in the Children Act procedures. We saw, for example, in Chapter 8 how the court can impose restrictions on examinations when making emergency protection orders and child assessment orders. The same applies in care order cases because the court can set conditions when making interim orders (see page •• below). In addition, however, the rules of court clearly state that no person may cause the child to be medically or psychiatrically examined or otherwise assessed, for the preparation of expert evidence for use in the proceedings, without the leave of the court. If this prohibition is infringed, any resulting evidence may be excluded at the hearing.

As far as protecting the interests of all parties is concerned, it is important to note the emphasis in the rules of court on advance disclosure of evidence.

In too many cases in the past, evidence was brought forward at a very late stage, thereby creating a sense of injustice. Each of the parties is now required to file with the court, and serve on the other parties, (a) written statements of the substance of the oral evidence which he intends to place before the court and (b) copies of any documents upon which he intends to rely (this includes experts' reports). Sorting out this evidence and attempting to bring the parties together on as many issues as possible is a central function of the directions appointment. What happens if at the hearing the applicant agency or the respondent parent wishes to call a witness or produce a document whose existence has not previously been mentioned? The rules do not prohibit this, for such a prohibition could run contrary to the child's interests, but they do require the court's permission to be obtained. Such permission cannot always be taken for granted.

The objective of ensuring fair play for the child's family means that social workers compiling statements of evidence for the proceedings need to strive for balance at all times. This applies particularly to their accounts of dealings with the people whose parenting capacity is in issue. In *Re JC* (1995) the High Court found reason to criticize statements submitted by three social workers because they failed to refer to the positive aspects of parental contact episodes and concentrated exclusively on the negative ones. Mr Justice Wall said:

> All parties have a duty in family proceedings not to be tendentious in the presentation of their evidence. That duty is, however, particularly acute in relation to local authority evidence, and never more so than when the local authority are advising the court of their view of the outcome of an assessment of parental capacity or otherwise setting out their recommendations and plans. The duty of local authorities to be objective, fair and balanced cannot be over-emphasized.

The proliferation of expert witnesses in the period following implementation of the Children Act has already been noted. This development may be seen as beneficial in so far as the involvement of appropriately qualified experts is, in principle, bound to enhance the quality of decision-making within the courtroom. The drawbacks relate to the additional expense and delay generated, and because these can be so substantial the judges – backed up by the Children Act Advisory Committee – have issued guidelines on expert evidence in a series of cases. The first of these was *Re M* (1993), in which three days of court time were taken up by paediatric evidence given by three doctors. In his oral evidence one of the doctors offered an opinion which was at variance with the written report he had compiled (this report having been the basis of the report of one of the other experts). Furthermore, during his cross-examination the existence of crucial photographs taken during a medical examination was revealed for the first time. Mr Justice Wall stated that the value of expert evidence in children's cases could not be overestimated. 'In the instant case,' he said, 'the paediatric evidence of sexual assault ... transformed the case. The pity was that the evidence only emerged more than halfway through the case. In an ideal world it would have been established between the experts well before the trial began.' He noted that the result of this had been that the parents in the case had suddenly to face the medically established fact halfway through the trial that one of their children had been sexually abused whilst in care by a member of the family. The judge went on to lay down ten guidelines. They emphasize the importance of experts being given proper instructions, of their being kept up to date with case developments, of their being invited to meet with each other before trial to agree issues, and of their delivery of oral evidence being properly planned by the parties' legal teams, acting in a non-adversarial spirit. Further guidelines were laid down by the same judge in the later case of *Re G* (1994), in which lawyers acting for the child's mother had instructed a total of six experts who produced their reports only two days before the final hearing. He sought to emphasize the critical role of the court in controlling the appointment of experts (this control arises from the provisions in the rules of court which require the leave of the court to be obtained before case papers are disclosed to non-parties) and said that the court must be fully involved in the process of defining and limiting the scope of expert evidence. The parties 'must come to court prepared to demonstrate the area of expertise for which leave is sought and to justify the grant of leave by reference to the specific facts of the case and the relevance of expert evidence to those facts'. These guidelines were subsequently endorsed by the Children Act Advisory Committee, which published a Draft Letter for Joint Instruction of an Expert in Children Act cases (Annual Report 1994/95, Annex to Chapter 2). Best Practice Guidance on experts in Children Act proceedings was published by the Committee in June 1997 in its *Handbook of Best Practice in Children Act Cases.*

The local authority's plans for the child

During the passage of the Children Act, the Government announced that it intended the rules of court to require a local authority to provide the court with details of its proposals for the child should the care order be granted. Such a requirement was seen as meshing in with the duty of the court to ensure that making an order would be better than not making one. To decide this matter, the court will need to know what the local authority expects to do with the child, and a plan will convey this information. The Government's intention was partially implemented via the official form prescribed for care order applications: as noted earlier, Form C13 contains a section headed 'Your plans for the child(ren)'. The DH Guidance of 1991 offers the following advice in relation to plans:

> The level of details given will be determined to some extent by the stage reached in the investigation of the child's circumstances. Any plan should be able to address the checklist of factors identified in section 1(3) of the Act and will need to be more than embryonic given the presumption of no order in section 1(5).

One specific aspect of the local authority's plans is regulated by the Act itself: parental contact. Section 34 contains an elaborate series of provisions on this difficult subject and these are considered below. At this stage, however, it is worth noting section 34(11). This states that before making a care order, the court must (a) consider the arrangements which the local authority has made, or proposes to make, with regard to contact and (b) invite the parties to comment on those arrangements. The singling out of this issue was a clear reflection of the importance which was attached to it.

While some proposals from the local authority have to be included in the original application form, the circumstances of many cases are such that a detailed plan for the child can emerge only during the course of the proceedings (it should not be forgotten, for example, that the emergency protection order provides a relatively short period within which a case for a long-term order can be prepared). The timing of this event falls within the scope of directions appointments. In the case of *Re R* (1993) the High Court stated that the care plan is an extremely important document which should be rigorously scrutinized by the court. The importance of this exercise has been heightened by the abolition of the court's power to monitor the actions of a local authority once a care order has been made (on which see page 190 below). It was further stated in *Re R* that the plan delivered by the local authority should accord, so far as possible, with the requirements listed in Volume 3 of the DH Guidance concerning children being looked after (even though these requirements were not drawn up with care order proceedings in mind) and that if the court is not satisfied about material aspects of the plan it may decline to make a care order, although this is unlikely to occur if the effect would be to expose the child to danger. That does not mean that in all cases every aspect and consequence of the plan must be known at the time of the final hearing: as was said in *Re R*, 'there are cases in which the action which requires to be taken in the interests of children necessarily involves steps into the unknown and provided the court is satisfied that the local authority is alert to the difficulties which may arise in the execution of the care plan, the function of the court is not to seek to oversee the plan but to entrust its execution to the local authority'. It is fair to say that other judicial decisions have suggested a rather tighter approach to cases in which the care plan is inchoate, and it is therefore not surprising to find the Children Act Advisory Committee reporting that 'there is a wide disparity throughout the country as to how detailed the care plan should be and what form it should take' (Annual Report 1994/95).

Before we leave this subject, the point should be made that, while plans and proposals have to be produced to the court, there is no question of the local authority being forever tied to them. It is a cardinal principle of the public law framework that case management is principally a matter for the social services department rather than the court. Once the child is in care the department's overriding duty is to promote his welfare; if that demands a deviation from the arrangements previously indicated to the court, then the department should not feel inhibited about following this course. The Committee of Inquiry into the Tyra Henry case (*Whose Child?*, 1987) recommended that the means by which a department proposed to implement a care order should be annexed to the order and that if any 'significant change' was proposed the court's consent should be obtained. This was an interesting recommendation (and one which, judging by the post-Children Act case law, might command considerable support in some quarters) but it ran directly counter to the Department of Health's views on the allocation of functions in children's cases, so it is not surprising that it was rejected.

When criminal proceedings are pending

Reference has already been made to some of the issues arising out of contemporaneous child protection and criminal investigations. It has also been noted that courts hearing care proceedings are in principle prepared to release case documents to the police in order to facilitate the prosecution of an offender (see page 150 above). There are, however, other aspects of the so-called interface between civil and criminal proceedings. One issue that often needs to be addressed is the sequencing of proceedings. If a parent is being prosecuted for a criminal offence arising out of the same facts which have generated the local authority's intervention, should the care application be held over until the criminal proceedings have ended? Such a postponement will by definition cause delay in settling the future arrangements of the child and the delay may well be substantial and damaging. The civil courts have accepted that they are not in a position to dictate the pace of criminal proceedings, which are governed by a completely separate legal regime. They have, on the other hand, emphasized the desirability of being kept informed of the state of the prosecution process. Where issues cannot be resolved before a criminal trial has been heard, the court should gear its directions and timetabling to the care application being dealt with as soon as possible after the criminal trial has ended (*Re A and B* (1994)).

As for the need for postponement, the leading case is now *Re TB* (1995) in which Lady Justice Butler-Sloss stressed the importance of the 'no delay' principle contained in section 1(2) of the Children Act and ruled that 'criminal proceedings of themselves are not a reason to adjourn the care proceedings. There must be some detriment to the children in the broadest terms for not bringing on the care proceedings because delay is detrimental generally to the children ... I think we do have to hold the line that in the majority of cases, unless there are circumstances which warrant taking a different course, the care proceedings should come on, even if they are to be heard before the criminal proceedings'.

Although it lies outside the scope of this book, it may be noted that discontent about the way in which child witnesses and victims are treated within the criminal justice system remains widespread (see, for example, Chapter 4 of the Children Act Advisory Committee's Annual Report 1994/95).

The role of the court

The function of the court at the final hearing of a care order application is two-fold:

1 To consider whether the threshold criteria contained in section 31(2) of the Act are satisfied.
2 If the criteria are satisfied, to consider what order, or combination of orders, to make.

The first exercise requires the court to address questions of fact (e.g. what harm has been suffered by the child?) and also questions of law (the correct legal meaning of the words of section 31(2)) and has already been considered (see page 155 above). The second exercise is essentially discretionary, although in carrying it out the court is necessarily obliged to weigh various facts in the balance (e.g. how capable are the child's parents of meeting his needs?). When exercising its discretion the court must adhere to the provisions of section 1 of the Children Act. According to section 1(1), the child's welfare is the court's paramount consideration. Section 1(3) contains the welfare checklist which is a mandatory consideration in care order cases. It was described in Chapter 3 (see page 35). Finally, section 1(5) states that the court is not to make an order unless it considers that doing so would be better for the child than making no order at all. This particular rule was suggested by the Law Commission in the context of its study of private child law but the Government decided that it could usefully be employed in the public law field as well, so as to implement the recommendation of the Child Care Law Review that the legislation should require the court to be satisfied that the order contemplated is the most effective means available to it of safeguarding and promoting the child's welfare.

The provisions of section 1 do not reveal any bias in favour of any type of order in a section 31 application. Nor do the provisions of Part IV of the Act. The judges for their part, while indicating the advantages and disadvantages of particular orders, have emphasized the need to consider each case on its individual merits and have tended to avoid precepts of general application. One of the exceptions is the case of *Re H* (1994), in which Mr Justice Hollis expressed the view that in the child protection context, adoption should be a course of last resort: 'Sometimes it has to be done ... but if there is a reasonable alternative within the family it should be taken'. A further, and possibly more significant, exception is the case of *Re O* (1996) in which Mrs Justice Hale stated that in a section 31 case 'the court should begin with a preference for the less interventionist rather than the more interventionist approach'. Whether this incipient presumption against making a care order develops remains to be seen. The range of options – other than a care order – available to courts in section 31 cases is discussed at page 195 below.

In some cases, all of the parties are agreed at the outset that the threshold criteria are met and here most, if not all, of the arguments will relate to the type of order to be made. Similarly, there are cases where the appropriateness of a care order is accepted by all parties. In this latter situation, the court retains its duty under section 31(2) to satisfy itself that the threshold criteria are met as well as its discretion to select the most suitable order. If there remain areas of disagreement between the parties which relate to the facts (e.g. the cause of the significant harm) the court will confine its investigation to those parts of the evidence which are directly relevant to the issue of harm and findings which are necessary for the proper disposal of the case (*Hackney London Borough Council v G* (1993); Children Act Advisory Committee Annual Report 1993/94, Chapter 3).

The legal effect of a care order

The legal consequences of compulsory care under the previous statutory framework were not easy to describe in straightforward terms. There were two main reasons for this. The first was the existence of three, completely separate, compulsory procedures whose respective effects were stated in different terms. The second lay in the very obscurity of the effects as stated. As we have seen, the aim of the Children Act was to construct a single compulsory care procedure. This effectively eliminated the first cause of the previous confusion. As for the second, it may be thought that the Act achieves as much certainty as can reasonably be expected from a piece of legislation.

Parental responsibility

In *Re O* (1996) Mrs Justice Hale described the care order as 'the most Draconian order which is permitted under the 1989 Act'. The principal effects of the order are set out in section 33 of the Act. Under section 33(1) it is the duty of the local authority to receive the child into its care and to keep him there while the order remains in force. Under section 33(3) the local authority 'shall have parental responsibility for the child'. This brings us back to the introductory part of the Act, where the concept of parental responsibility is defined as: 'all the rights, duties, powers, responsibilities and authority which by law a parent of a child has in relation to the child and his property' (section 3(1)). In principle, therefore, the social services department acquires through a care order the complete range of parental 'rights' recognized by English law (on which see Chapter 2). First and foremost amongst these, and a driving force behind many care order applications, is the right to decide where the child is to live. Other rights are also obtained. This is why, in the case of *Re B* (1996), the High Court declared that a local authority can provide legal authorization for a doctor to use reasonable force on a child in care for the purpose of imposing necessary medical treatment. Not every parental right, however, is acquired, because section 33 excepts certain specific matters from the general rule:

1 The local authority shall not cause the child to be brought up in any religious creed other than that in which he would have been brought up if the order had not been made. This repeats the previous law. There was some misunderstanding of this provision during the passage of the Act and it should be emphasized that the section does not prevent a change of religion if the child wishes this to occur. All it does is to prevent the social services department taking the initiative and imposing an alteration on the child.
2 The local authority does not acquire rights in relation to adoption. Here, too, the previous law has been preserved. While the birth parents retain the right to veto an adoption, this is subject to the power of the adoption court to dispense with their consent.
3 The local authority does not acquire the right to appoint a guardian for the child. If a guardian is appointed by the birth parents (on which see Chapter 2) and he assumes parental responsibility on their death, the local authority's position is not prejudiced in any way because the care order will remain in force during these events. The guardian's 'rights' will be subject to those of the authority. As will be seen, however, the guardian will fall within the contact provisions of the Act and he cannot therefore be ignored. He will, moreover, be in a position to apply for the discharge of the care order.

4 The local authority does not acquire the right to effect a change of surname. Section 33(7) states that while a care order is in force nobody may change the child's surname without either the written consent of every person who has parental responsibility or the leave of the court. Whilst the local authority gains parental responsibility under a care order, the parents retain it, and so if they (or either of them) object to a change in the name of the child, the local authority must obtain permission from the court.

5 Although parental responsibility gives the local authority the right to decide where the child is to reside, if it (or anybody else) wishes to remove him from the UK, the same requirements apply as for a change of name, i.e. written consent or the leave of the court (the UK, incidentally, means England, Wales, Scotland and Northern Ireland – it does not include the Channel Islands or the Isle of Man). The only exception is where the authority plans to remove the child for less than a month: this facilitates holidays abroad with schools and foster carers etc. There are special arrangements for the permanent emigration of care order children and these are dealt with below (see page 190).

Subject to the above-mentioned exceptions, then, the general effect of a care order is to deprive the parents of decision-making power in relation to the upbringing of their child. They do not lose parental responsibility – this happens only on adoption – but their ability to exercise it as they think fit is caught by the provision in section 2(8) which states that the fact that a person has parental responsibility shall not entitle him to act in any way which would be incompatible with any order made with respect to the child under the Act. Just to put beyond doubt the ascendancy of the local authority, the Government put into the Act a provision (section 33(3)) which states that the authority shall have the power to determine the extent to which a parent or guardian of the child may meet his parental responsibility for him. It is only to exercise this power where it is satisfied that it is necessary to do so in order to safeguard or promote the child's welfare and, as the DH Guidance points out, where restrictions are being considered the authority should discuss them first with the parents and take steps to incorporate them in its plan so that they will be periodically reviewed.

Of course, when a care order is made, the court is not always starting with a blank sheet of paper. What is the position when orders have already been made in respect of the child? The orders most relevant here are the section 8 orders described in Chapters 3 and 4, especially those concerning residence and contact. There may, for example, be a complex network of such orders in force made in a succession of matrimonial hearings. Section 91 of the Children Act imposes a simple result: the making of a care order discharges any section 8 order automatically. It also brings wardship to an end. Past orders can therefore be ignored.

Contact

The former law relating to contact with children in compulsory care afforded a classic illustration of the complicated and confused way in which
our public child care regime developed over the years. For a long time there
was no legislation directly on the subject at all, which meant that, certainly
for care order children, the social services department had virtually a free
hand in the matter of regulating contact. Some parents who were denied
contact attempted to deal with the problem by making their children wards
of court in the hope of persuading the High Court to impose a contact
requirement on the department. However, in a series of controversial cases
the judges declined to allow the wardship jurisdiction to be used by parents
(or relatives) in this way. Eventually, specific legislation was enacted: the
Health and Social Services and Social Security Adjudications Act 1983
(HASSASSA). The 1983 Act enabled applications to be made to the court
for 'access orders' in relation to children in compulsory care and it directed
the DH to issue a Code of Practice. But this legislation was quickly exposed
as unsatisfactory in a number of respects. For example, it was concerned
only with cases in which contact was completely terminated or refused; it
was useless in cases (and there were many of them) where it was the *amount*
of contact which was being questioned. Relatives were excluded from the
scope of the Act. In addition, the drafting was in many respects defective,
which caused problems of interpretation.

HASSASSA and the Code of Practice were swept away by the Children
Act and replaced by a completely fresh set of provisions, modelled on the
carefully considered proposals of the Child Care Law Review. The approach of the Act could be said to be two-pronged. On the one hand, there
are provisions of a general variety, applicable to all children who are being
looked after by a local authority, which are designed to encourage family
contacts. On the other hand, there are the very specific provisions geared to
care order children. These provisions have transformed the climate of
compulsory care, so much so that the old law, and the practice it fostered,
now seem truly primitive.

The general provisions

Some of these have already been mentioned in Chapter 6 in relation to
children who are accommodated on a voluntary basis under section 20 of
the 1989 Act. It will be recalled that Schedule 2 to the Act requires the local
authority to endeavour to promote contact between the child and his parents, any non-parent having parental responsibility, any relative or friend,
and 'any other person connected with him', unless it is not reasonably
practicable or consistent with his welfare. The location of the child's residence is obviously a vital factor in the contact context, and section 23(7) of

the Act requires that the accommodation provided shall be 'near his home', subject to the usual considerations of practicability and welfare. Schedule 2 pushes this theme a stage further by requiring the local authority to take reasonable steps to keep the child's parents (and any non-parent with parental responsibility) informed of his present address. Again, though, this is qualified: if the authority has reasonable cause to believe that informing them would prejudice the child's welfare, the duty does not apply. Finally, there is provision made in Schedule 2 for the payment by the local authority of travel expenses etc. incurred by parents and others in visiting the child (and vice versa).

All these provisions are important and helpful, particularly the first one, but they only go so far. Without more, the position of parents, relatives and other interested parties in the matter of contact would be wholly dependent upon the view of the case taken by the social services department. There are social services professionals who would be inclined to support a drawing of the line at that point but the view of the Government, as expressed in the 1991 DH Guidance, was that contact 'is too important to be regarded as simply a matter of management within the sole control of the local authority'. Consequently, we must now turn to the specific, rights-oriented, contact provisions in the Children Act.

The specific provisions

Section 34 contains the specific provisions (the contact order provisions in Part II of the Act, described in Chapters 3 and 4, are not available for care order children). It was designed to encapsulate and extend the previous provisions and it does this by imposing a duty on the local authority to allow reasonable contact, by giving interested parties the opportunity to test the authority's plans and decisions in court, and by giving the court ample powers, both at the time of the making of the care order and subsequently. Looking at this matter from a temporal angle, the question of future contact should first arise for discussion during the care order proceedings themselves. Section 34(11) is quite explicit on this point:

Before making a care order with respect to any child the court shall –
(a) consider the arrangements which the authority have made, or propose to make, for affording any person contact with a child to whom this section applies; and (b) invite the parties to the proceedings to comment on those arrangements.

So the local authority is expected to arrive at the final hearing with proposals relating to contact, and the prescribed application form for a care order ensures that the matter is directly addressed in the run-up to the case. How detailed the proposals can be must, of course, be dependent upon the particular facts, but the authority should be prepared for rigorous questioning from all sides on the extent to which it plans to provide contact arrangements for the child. In deciding whether or not to make an order, the court will take these proposals into account.

The Act goes further than this, however, by enabling the court to attach to a care order specific contact conditions. This was a significant departure from the previous law, which permitted court control of contact only after an order had been made and after contact had been refused or terminated by the local authority. Section 34 enables the court to make 'such order as it considers appropriate with respect to the contact which is to be allowed' with the child (this means allowed by the local authority: if an order is made, the authority must not erect obstacles to contact). Conditions can be imposed if the court thinks they are warranted (section 34(7)), so that for example the start of contact can be delayed for a period, or the court can stipulate that a certain individual must, or must not, be present during contact periods. Maximum flexibility is achieved through this simple device.

However, there are restrictions on the circumstances in which a contact order can be made. The court is given the power to make an order of its own motion, i.e. without anybody formally applying for one (section 34(5)). Such an order can be in favour of any named person. Short of this, though, a contact order needs to be applied for. If the local authority or the child makes an application, the court may order contact in favour of any named person, whether related to the child or not (section 34(2)). What of applications from other parties? On this, the Act draws a distinction between those who are entitled to apply and those who can apply only with the leave of the court. Those entitled to apply are the child's parents (this includes the unmarried father), any guardian, any non-parent who holds a residence order in respect of the child and any non-parent who has been given care and control in wardship proceedings (section 34(3)). Relatives, therefore, are required to obtain the leave of the court before applying for contact, unless they hold a residence order or have care and control through wardship. This requirement was not uncontroversial but the Government held to the view that it was necessary to prevent unwarranted interference.

In addition to making an order *for* contact, the court can make one *against* it. It has the power to make an order authorizing the local authority to refuse to allow contact between the child and his parent(s), guardian or any non-parent who holds a residence order or has care and control through wardship (section 34(4)). This power is necessary because, as will be seen shortly, there is a general obligation on the part of the local authority to allow these persons reasonable contact once a care order has been made. It can be exercised on an application made by the authority or the child himself; alternatively, the court may make a refusal order of its own motion. Again, conditions can be attached by the court as appropriate, so that for example a limited time-scale can be built in, or the court can give the local authority the power to deny contact in specified circumstances.

What is the position regarding contact, then, when a care order has been made? The answer to this depends on whether or not the court has attached any specific provision to the care order. If it has not done this, section 34(1) applies. This states that, following the making of a care order, the local authority shall allow the child 'reasonable contact' with his parents (including the unmarried father), any guardian, anybody who held a residence order immediately prior to the care order (the word is 'held' rather than 'holds' because the effect of a care order is to discharge a residence order) and anybody who had care and control through wardship. So we have here a statutory presumption in favour of reasonable contact – confined, though, to the categories mentioned. The Act recognizes, however, that contact may sometimes have to be curtailed, and it therefore permits the local authority to refuse contact if it is satisfied that it is necessary to do so in order to safeguard or promote the child's welfare *and* the refusal is decided upon as a matter of urgency and does not last for more than seven days (section 34(6)). The Contact with Children Regulations 1991 provide for formal notification of a decision to use this suspensory power to the appropriate persons (including the child himself if he is of sufficient understanding). The time restriction puts the onus on the local authority to apply to the court for an order authorizing continued refusal of contact with the person or persons concerned. Such an order may also be sought by the child.

If the parents (or guardian etc.) feel that the local authority is not providing reasonable contact, they can apply to the court for a specific order; so can the child himself. Indeed, others can do this – relatives, for example – although they first have to get the leave of the court to intervene. An alternative – and opinions may differ as to how attractive an option this is – is for the aggrieved person to utilize the authority's complaints procedure established under section 26.

If specific contact arrangements *have* been ordered by the court as part of the care order package, then the position is that the duty to provide reasonable contact to those in the specified categories remains, but it is subject to the arrangements made by the court. So if, for example, the court when making the care order authorized the local authority to refuse contact with the child's father, the authority will still have the duty to allow the child reasonable contact with his mother, subject, though, to its power to refuse contact for up to seven days and its power to go to court and ask for an order authorizing continued refusal. If the court has made an order *for* contact, the same power to suspend the arrangements for up to seven days is given to the local authority. This power is useful in those cases where the court has been persuaded to make a contact order but the working of it in practice proves disastrous so that urgent action is called for. Several other features of section 34 deserve a mention. First, all orders of the court regarding contact can be varied or discharged. Sensibly, the Contact with Children Regulations allow the local authority to depart from the terms of an order without a formal variation provided the person concerned and the child (assuming he is of sufficient understanding) agree. Written notification must be sent to appropriate parties. Secondly, where an application to court has been refused (including an application for variation or discharge), another application cannot be made by the unsuccessful party within six months without the leave of the court (section 91(17)). Thirdly, while the Code of Practice issued under the 1983 legislation has disappeared, much of the advice contained within it has reappeared as DH Children Act Guidance (Volume 3). As one would expect, this seeks to drive home the message about the importance of partnership, consultation and good communication on contact issues.

Section 34 in practice

Given the radical change in the legal framework effected by these contact provisions, and the general perception of family contact as being central to the philosophy of the Children Act, it is hardly surprising that they have received close attention from both researchers and practitioners. In 1994 the SSI produced the *Contact Orders Study*, a document based on the experiences with section 34 of SSD managers, social work staff and guardians ad litem in four local authority areas. This study confirmed that contact issues in compulsory care cases under the 1989 Act are often extraordinarily complex and demanding. Practitioners were said to be fully alive to the increased requirements imposed by section 34, particularly in relation to the preparation and scrutiny of care plans, and they reported that the arguments in court surrounding these plans were 'often exhaustive and quite challenging'. Many plans were proving very expensive to operate, both in terms of money (e.g. to provide travel costs or a suitable location for contact) and staff time. Section 34 litigation was also costly and plagued by delays.

As far as the judiciary's approach to section 34 is concerned, there is no doubt that the case of *Re B* (1992) was a landmark development. Indeed, the decision in this case stands in many ways as a beacon for the general reforming effect of the Children Act. The case was concerned with two children aged 2 and 4 who had been in care for two years following neglect by the mother (who had herself been in care as a child). The mother had for a long time enjoyed only sporadic contact with the children and had told their foster carer that she did not want any further contact for their sake ('she was pregnant at the time, unsettled in her plans and remorseful about her treatment of the children'). The local authority accordingly made plans for their adoption. Following the birth of her third child, however, the mother's parenting skills improved and she started seeing the older two again on a regular basis. She was said to have shown determination and commitment to these contact visits, which went well for all concerned. In spite of this, the local authority proceeded with its adoption plans (albeit at a rather leisurely pace) and it applied to the county court for an order under section 34(4) authorizing it to refuse contact. This application was contested by the mother who was now hoping for a complete rehabilitation, an outcome which the authority regarded as unrealistic in view of the demands being made by the mother's youngest child. The authority already had prospective adopters for the children lined up. The guardian ad litem was impressed by the mother's increased maturity and parenting ability and came to revise her original opinion as to the merits of the adoption plan. Reversing the decision of the county court judge, the Court of Appeal dismissed the local authority's application. Lady Justice Butler-Sloss observed that the Children Act was a major piece of reforming legislation which marked a fresh start in the area of child law. Narrowing the focus, she said that section 34 and other contact provisions in the Act reflected 'a dramatic shift in the philosophy of the legislation'. Whereas the general effect of a care order was to exclude the possibility of judicial monitoring of the local authority, this was not the position with regard to contact because section 34 expressly gave the court a continuing jurisdiction. Furthermore, the child's welfare was the court's paramount consideration in section 34 applications. It followed from all this that the court, in section 34 proceedings, was in a position to query the local authority's long-term plan for the child to the extent that the plan excluded or restricted parental contact. This included plans for adoption.

The judgment in *Re B* had the effect of changing the law because in cases decided under previous legislation the courts had treated local authority plans as sacrosanct. The extent of the change was confirmed in the subsequent case of *Re E* (1993). There, agreed care orders were made in respect of two boys aged 3 and 5 on grounds of inadequate parenting. In contrast to *Re B*, it was accepted that the prospects of rehabilitation were nil. The local authority formulated a plan which involved closed adoption for both children since it took the view that continuing contact would not be beneficial. This view, however, was strongly disputed by the guardian ad litem and a clinical psychologist. The Court of Appeal ordered a rehearing of the local authority's application for an order authorizing it to refuse contact and stated that the possibility of an open adoption should be investigated. It was not sufficient for the local authority to dismiss the likelihood of obtaining suitable adopters prepared to entertain face-to-face contact upon the basis that there were none on its books at that time. Lord Justice Simon Brown said that the effect of *Re B* was as follows:

> If on a section 34(4) application the judge concludes that the benefits of contact outweigh the disadvantages of disrupting any of the local

authority's long-term plans which are inconsistent with such contact, then, slow and reluctant though no doubt the judge would be to reach that conclusion, he must give effect to it by refusing the local authority's application to terminate the contact.

Judging by the evidence contained in the SSI's *Contact Orders Study*, these cases have had a significant impact across the country. The SSI found that local authority managers were questioning whether the balance between court and social services department was correct:

> They drew attention to cases where evidence of very serious harm to children was established and where there seemed very little prospect of the parents ever being able to offer effective parenting. Such children, they argued, needed long-term substitute families urgently. They posed the question whether the courts now went 'beyond the extra mile' in allowing parents opportunities to prove their suitability through extensive contact arrangements. Was the exercise of exhaustive justice for the parents operating to the disadvantage of their children?

The proper approach to contact order applications made by relatives was considered in the case of *Re M* (1995). It will be recalled that relatives normally require leave from the court in order to proceed. The Court of Appeal observed that, while the Children Act prescribes specific criteria (in section 10(9) – see page 50 above) to be taken into account in applications for leave to apply for section 8 orders, there are no equivalent criteria for section 34 cases. Nevertheless it ruled that the same approach should be applied, with necessary modifications. This means that the court should be particularly concerned with the nature of the contact being sought, the connection of the applicant to the child, the risk of the proceedings disrupting the child's life ('the factor of crucial significance') and the views of the parents and the local authority. The onus is on the applicant to satisfy the court that there is a serious issue to try, and it must be shown that there is a 'good arguable case'.

The treatment of the child in care

In Chapter 6 we saw how children who are provided with accommodation by a local authority under section 20 arrangements become subject to the code of treatment contained in sections 20–29 and Schedule 2 of the Children Act. This code is also applicable to children 'in care', i.e. those who are the subject of a care order. As was mentioned in Chapter 6, this arrangement is no different in principle from the previous law. It is not proposed to rehearse all the contents of this code in the present chapter. The reader is referred to Chapter 6 for a description and commentary. It is important to note, however, that the two groups of children – accommodated children and care order children – are not treated by the Act in exactly the same way in every single respect. Differences exist in certain key areas. Such differences as there are have come about for a variety of reasons, but one of them is fairly obvious: in a care order case, it will necessarily have been shown to the satisfaction of a court that the child was suffering, or was likely to suffer, significant harm attributable either to a shortfall in parenting standards or to the child's being beyond parental control. With that as a backcloth, special safeguarding provisions are clearly necessary. The features of the code of treatment which bear especially on care order children are described below.

The individual plan

While the Arrangements for Placement of Children Regulations 1991 apply to care order children, the SSD's obligations are not exactly the same as they are when accommodation under section 20 is being provided. In the first place, there is no duty to agree the child's plan with those having parental responsibility. This is realistic, given the compulsory nature of care order proceedings. Secondly, the nine matters listed in Schedule 4 of the Regulations (these were set out at page 94) are inapplicable, being geared towards voluntary arrangements. These modifications are not intended to detract from the partnership approach. Indeed, the DH Guidance (Volume 3) urges authorities to reach agreement with parents wherever possible: 'a child's interests are likely to be served best if the parents are encouraged to keep in touch and take an active role in planning for the child. This will be the case even where the long-term plan for the child is that he remains in care.'

The plan for the child will usually reflect the plan presented to the court during the care order proceedings, but this is not mandatory (see page 173 above).

Selecting the child's placement

The selection of an appropriate placement for the child is a matter wholly within the local authority's discretion. As Mrs Justice Hale said in *Berkshire County Council v B* (1996):

> The court cannot impose its own conditions upon a care order or direct the local authority how to look after a child in their care. The court cannot direct a particular type of placement, whether it be at home or in foster care or in a residential home or anywhere else. The court cannot direct that particular services be provided for a child.

Even if a care order is made by the court on the understanding that the child will go to live with a certain person, this does not in any way prevent the authority from pursuing other arrangements.

Notification of child's address

The local authority's duty to keep the parents notified of the child's residence is qualified. This provision, described earlier (see page 181), is required for those cases where a persistent parent, for whatever reason, needs to be kept well away from the child.

Placing the child at home

Although the local authority has considerable freedom in selecting a placement, there are special provisions in section 23(5) concerning the release of the child back into the care of his parents: the authority may only allow him to live with a parent (or a non-parent with parental responsibility or the former holder of a residence order) in accordance with regulations made by the DH. A child is 'living with' a parent for these purposes if he stays with him for a continuous period of more than 24 hours. These provisions are based on the previous law, which was largely contained in the so-called charge and control regulations of 1988. The 1988 regulations were essentially a well-intentioned response to the Jasmine Beckford tragedy, but their conception and implementation were fraught with difficulties and many practitioners were glad to see the back of them.

The regulations made under section 23(5) are the Placement of Children with Parents etc. Regulations 1991. They state that before a placement is made, the local authority must make all necessary enquiries in respect of (a) the health of the child, (b) the suitability of the person with whom it is proposed the child should be placed, (c) the suitability of the proposed accommodation, (d) the educational and social needs of the child, and (e) the suitability of all other members of the household, aged 16 and over, in which it is proposed the child will live. Schedule 1 of the regulations lists particulars which are to be taken into account when considering a person's suitability. Further safeguards prescribed include the reservation of a placement decision to the Director of Social Services or the Director's nominee, the making of a written agreement on the placement arrangements with the parent (based on the authority's plan for the child), the notification of the placement decision to appropriate persons and the support and supervision of the placement once it takes effect. There are special rules covering the over-16s, immediate placements and series of short-term placements.

While the child is with the parent under these regulations, decision-making must necessarily be shared between the parent and the SSD. Ultimately, though, it is for the department to decide how much freedom to grant the parent, and the regulations partly reflect this, for according to them the placement agreement ought at the very least to deal with consents for medical treatment and consent to the child staying with third parties. The department's autonomy will, of course, be restricted if there is a section 34 contact order in force. In these circumstances, both the department and the parent with whom the child is placed will be obliged to facilitate the contact which the court has directed. The Act's provisions on contact generally will also need to be borne in mind.

The regulations are the subject of extended comment in Volume 3 of the DH Guidance. The Guidance notes that they apply to the placement of children who have entered care for a variety of reasons, and it invites local authorities to 'consider carefully whether a placement under the regulations is the only way to achieve placing the child with a parent. Where it is decided that a child's best interests will be met by such a placement the authority should look again at why it is considered that the care order is still required. It may be that an arrangement can be negotiated between the parent and the authority that would enable the authority to agree that application to discharge the care order is appropriate'.

Additional guidance on placements with parents can be found in the case law. In *Re T* (1993) the Court of Appeal observed that there will be cases (and this was one) where it is appropriate to make a care order even though the child has remained at home throughout the proceedings and may continue to do so afterwards. Such an arrangement can provide a number of benefits not obtainable under a supervision order (see further, page 196 below). In *Re S and D* (1994) the trial judge agreed that the threshold criteria for a care order were satisfied but he refused to make the order because he strongly disagreed with the local authority's proposal to attempt a rehabilitation. He took the view that this plan was too dangerous for the children on account of their mother's shortcomings. On appeal, the Court of Appeal stated that in such a situation, the court is obliged to choose the lesser of two evils: either it makes a care order, in which case the authority will be free to implement its plan, or it makes no care order, with the result that the child can immediately be taken home by his parent. One of the judges expressed regret that the Children Act does not permit the court, when making a care order, to prohibit a placement with parents.

Reviews

The Review of Children's Cases Regulations 1991, described at page 95, make special provision for children in care. First, the responsible authority is required to consider as part of a review whether an application should be made to discharge the order. Secondly, it is required to explain to the child 'any steps which he may take under the Act'. Where the child is in care, this will include his right to apply for the discharge of the order under section 39 (on which see page 193 below).

Secure accommodation

Parents have no entitlement to remove the child from secure accommodation (as do the parents of accommodated children). This is simply a consequence of the central thrust of the care order, which is to vest the right to decide the child's residence in the local authority. The provision of secure accommodation remains subject to stringent criteria (see page 88).

Emigration

There are special rules concerning emigration (Schedule 2, paragraph 19). The local authority can arrange this but the arrangement can go ahead only with the approval of the court. The Government could give approval under the previous legislation but the view now is that the court should be involved on account of the gravity of the matter. Schedule 2 lists a number of conditions on which the court must be satisfied, one of these being the consent of those with parental responsibility. This consent, however, can be dispensed with by the court on three grounds (taken from adoption law): the person cannot be found, or is incapable of consenting or is withholding consent unreasonably. If the child is going to live in Northern Ireland, the Channel Islands or the Isle of Man, regulations made under section 101 of the Act enable the care order to be transferred to an authority in the new area.

Volume 8 of the DH Guidance contains useful commentary and advice on the emigration provisions. They are also considered in the guidance concerning family placements (Volume 3).

Case management: who is in charge?

In the light of the preceding discussion, this may be an appropriate point to take an overall look at the position of the social services department in relation to the child in care and consider the extent to which it, rather than the court, is in control of his case management. This is a fundamental issue which was keenly debated prior to the Children Act and which has continued to generate controversy.

One of the main reasons for the start of the debate was the growth during the 1970s in the use of wardship by local authorities. Wardship was invoked in many cases as a result of the unsatisfactory features of care proceedings under the Children and Young Persons Act 1969, a state of affairs which the Children Act attempted to rectify, of course. A by-product of this, whether intended by the local authorities or not, was that they became, in respect of the children concerned, subject to the general wardship rule that no important step can be taken in relation to the ward without the court's consent. Furthermore, the wardship court had explicit statutory powers to issue directions to the local authority as to the exercise of its responsibilities to him. This continuing court involvement in child care cases was not always popular with social services departments but it nevertheless attracted considerable support, with the result that there was pressure from some quarters to extend the principle into care proceedings generally.

Both the House of Commons Social Services Committee (1984) and the Child Care Law Review (1985) came out against the idea of general judicial supervision of children in care. According to the latter:

> the court should be able to determine major issues such as the transfer of parental rights and duties where there is or may be a dispute between parents and local authorities, while the management of the case should be the responsibility of the local authority ... it is necessary that the body with day to day responsibility for the child should have a positive duty to 'take a grip on' the case and make firm and early decisions without the temptation to pass responsibility to another body.

The House of Commons Committee took an even stronger line. It felt that SSDs cannot be viewed simply as agents of the court. A mandatory requirement of regular court supervision would, in its view, paralyse local authorities and lead to a reduction of staff morale, quite apart from dividing the care of children between yet more adults in different organizations.

In the event, and perhaps inevitably, the Children Act reveals some ambivalence on this question. Once a care order is made, decision-making is handed over to the social services department. In relation to all types of decision, the department is obliged to ascertain the wishes and feelings of the child and his parents (and others – see page 82 above), so far as is reasonably practicable, and give due consideration to them. In relation to some types of decision, however, the department is subject to direct court control. These have been mentioned in the preceding pages of this chapter, but to summarize, they are:

1 Decisions on contact.
2 Decisions on secure accommodation.
3 Decisions on change of surname.
4 Decisions on removal of the child from the UK for longer than one month.
5 Decisions on emigration.

It is not being suggested here that the intervention of the courts in these matters is unjustified. Each of the decisions in the list is important. What may be difficult to sustain, however – certainly as a matter of logic – is the drawing of the line at these particular points. If a local authority needs the

consent of the court before arranging a six-week trip overseas for the child,
why is no consent needed before moving him to long-term foster carers at
the other end of the county? If the court can impose conditions regarding
contact, or secure accommodation, why should it not be able to regulate
medical treatment? There is no completely satisfactory answer to such
questions. The effect of the Children Act, like the previous legislation, is to
leave both the court and the local authority with hands on the steering
wheel, although at certain stages in the journey one of them must relinquish
control to the other. In some cases, e.g. those involving decisions on contact,
the authority may not welcome the prospect of court interference. Conversely in others, e.g. where it wishes to see rehabilitation being pursued
vigorously, the court may regret not having the ability to issue directions, as
opposed to exhortations. Opinions will obviously differ as to whether the
balance of power created by the Act is an acceptable one.

The problematic nature of this issue has inevitably arisen for discussion
in the courts. It has been discussed in a variety of contexts and has generated a variety of views. One of the first cases to emerge was *Kent County
Council v C* (1992), in which a magistrates' court made a care order and
then directed that the child's guardian ad litem should remain involved
in the case for a further three months in order to monitor the proposed
rehabilitation of the child with her mother (a rehabilitation regarded by
the guardian as doomed to fail). On appeal, the High Court confirmed
that such a direction is not permitted by the legislation. Even though the
court might have misgivings about the local authority's plan, its implementation is a matter for the authority. In *Re R* (1993) the High Court expressly
acknowledged the abolition of the rules under the previous law concerning
the monitoring of care orders, and disapproved the practice of making
a succession of interim care orders simply as a device to ensure the continuing involvement of the court. It sanctioned the making of full care
orders even in cases where the local authority's plan is still incomplete (see
page 174 above). Although this case was subsequently approved by the
Court of Appeal in *Re L* (1995), other reported decisions concerning
interim care orders reveal a rather different emphasis, one which is
more distrustful of local authority autonomy (see page 206 below). We may
also note the anxious tones of the Court of Appeal's judgment in *Nottinghamshire County Council v P* (1993) to the effect that local authorities
cannot be compelled to apply for a care order (see page 164 above), as well
as the expression of regret in *Re S and D* (1994) concerning the court's
inability to prohibit a placement with parents (see page 189 above). It was
said in *Re L* (above) that the interchange between the judicial control
of children and the local authority responsibility for children placed in care
is a difficult and sensitive area. These cases confirm this opinion. It is
therefore in no way surprising to find an absence of consensus within the
judiciary.

The duration of a care order

Unless it is brought to an end earlier, a care order will continue in force until the child reaches the age of 18 (section 91(12)). There are a number of methods by which the order can be terminated prior to this statutory expiry date. These are as follows:

1 The court discharges the order following an application by the local authority, the child or any person having parental responsibility.
2 A residence order is made by the court under section 10 of the Act.
3 The child is adopted.
4 The child is freed for adoption.

The first two methods call for comment.

Applications to discharge a care order

These are governed by section 39 of the Children Act. The persons having parental responsibility (apart from the local authority itself, of course) will normally be the parents of the child, or the mother if the parents are unmarried and no steps have been taken to vest responsibility in the father. The child does not require leave to make an application (in contrast to the position when a child seeks a section 8 order). Section 39(4) gives the court power to substitute a supervision order for the care order as an alternative to simply discharging the care order. The court also has the power to make a section 8 order (e.g. a contact order in favour of a foster carer, or a residence order in favour of an unmarried father or a grandparent). This is a good example of the way in which the Act usefully merges the private law orders with the public law ones, a matter discussed in the next section.

Under section 91(15), once an application is made, whether for simple discharge or for the substitution of a supervision order, no further application may be made for another six months without the leave of the court. As the Child Care Law Review observed: 'a balance has to be struck between fairness to applicants, the freedom of social workers to manage the case with foresight and the interests of the child in not being unnecessarily disturbed'. Needless to say, applications for discharge of a care order are governed by the welfare principle in section 1 of the Act and the checklist of factors also applies. The procedure is set out in the 1991 rules of court. While each application necessarily turns on its own particular facts, the courts are naturally cautious about the idea of removing the protection and professional control afforded by a care order. Unmeritorious applications are certainly not unknown, as Mr Justice Thorpe made clear in *Re O* (1994):

> Those who sit in this building know how repeatedly, how vainly, how without any seeming justification, how without any seeming change of circumstances parents apply for discharge of care orders.

Sustained efforts were made during the passage of the Children Act to incorporate a provision giving the court power to order the discharge of a care order while postponing its implementation. The object was to enable the court to direct a phased rehabilitation of the child with a view to reducing the adverse effects on the child of a sudden removal from care. Under the previous law, the High Court was able to achieve this sort of result, thanks to its flexible wardship jurisdiction. The Government resisted this proposal, even though it had received support from the Child Care Law Review, on the grounds that it would interfere excessively with the case management functions of the social services department. Its view was that, where phased rehabilitation was desirable, it could be achieved by the department through the exercise of its powers in relation to the child (e.g. generous contact coupled with home-on-trial arrangements). When everything was in place ready for the child's permanent residence at home, an application for discharge could, and should, be made. The point was reiterated in the DH Guidance on placements with parents, issued in 1991. Opinions will differ as to whether the Act draws the line between court control and local authority control at the right place in this matter. It is worth remembering, however, that parents looking for a discharge order in the future may be in a position to work towards that goal with the court's help, by making use of the contact provisions in section 34 of the Act. In other words, while the court is unable to direct a phased rehabilitation, it *is* able to order increasing contact vis-à-vis the child, the effect of which may be to enhance the prospects of an ultimate application for discharge of the care order being successful. This can be done whether the SSD agrees or not.

Finally, it should be noted that the facility of applying for a discharge order makes a specific appearance in the 1991 review regulations (see page 189 above).

Residence orders

Residence orders may be sought by either parents or non-parents (see Chapters 3 and 4). In the latter category, foster carers and relatives spring to mind as potential applicants where the child is in care. However, as we saw in Chapter 4, the Children Act imposes various restrictions on non-parental applications; in particular, the leave of the court or the consent of the local authority may have to be obtained first, depending on the circumstances of the case. Parents, on the other hand, are entitled to apply for residence orders and, in view of the effect of such orders, there is no real difference from their point of view between applying for the discharge of the care order and seeking a residence order in respect of the child. There is one important exception to this, however. While the unmarried father without parental responsibility may not apply for discharge of a care order, he *does* have the right to apply for a residence order which, if granted, will supersede the care order. In this way, unmarried fathers have been given the chance to win the control of their children who have been taken into care.

An interesting example of the interaction between the residence order and the care order was provided by the case of *Re C* (1993). Here, the child was 14 years old and living in a children's home. She wanted to leave care and live with a woman friend. The local authority's attitude to this proposal was neutral but the child's mother was completely opposed. The child's friend was happy to assume responsibility for her. The child applied for, and was granted, leave to apply for a residence order. Although she could have made an application to discharge the care order under section 39 (an application for which leave would not have been required), a residence order application was felt to be more appropriate: the effect of a successful section 39 application would have been to restore exclusive parental responsibility to the child's mother, a result not desired by the child. As the High Court observed, the direct approach being pursued by the child informed the court and all of the other parties precisely what outcome was sought and directed the evidence to the issues involved. Of course, because the applicant was a child the court could only grant leave upon being satisfied that she had sufficient understanding (section 10(8) of the Act – see page 55 above) but in this case the condition was fulfilled.

The making of other orders on a care order application

When the court is invited to make a care order by a local authority, it has a discretion in the matter even though the threshold criteria are satisfied. Section 1(3)(g) of the Children Act – part of the welfare checklist which must be considered in care order proceedings – requires the court as part of the balancing exercise to have regard to 'the range of powers available to the court under this Act'. The range of orders available extends beyond simply the one being sought. The Act, repeating the previous law, enables the court to make a supervision order instead of a care order (section 31(5)), but it also enables the court to make one or more of the section 8 orders. This latter power (derived from section 10(1)) has been made possible by the manner in which the Act integrates the public and private law frameworks, something which was sadly lacking in the old legislation.

What this means is that the court is in a position to refuse, or adjourn, an application for a care order but at the same time make, say, a residence order in favour of a relative who has intervened in the proceedings on hearing about them (the 1991 rules of court allow for this). Alternatively, it can refuse a care order but combine a supervision order with a section 8 order. Under previous law, separate legal proceedings had to be started to achieve results like these, an absurd waste of time and money. If the care order application is a many-sided contest, it makes sense for the one court to be given all the tools it needs to reach a result which is both practicable and in the child's best interests. The Act made a welcome breakthrough in this respect.

The discretion of the court is not entirely unfettered, however, when it comes to the question of making section 8 orders in care order proceedings. Under section 38(3), where the court makes a residence order in such proceedings, it must also make an interim supervision order unless it is satisfied that the child's welfare will be satisfactorily safeguarded without one. The assumption being made here is that even if the child is not going into care, some sort of social work support and supervision will be called for, in view of the fact that the local authority must have felt, when starting the proceedings, that compulsory intervention was necessary. The interim supervision order will enable social workers to keep an eye on the child's circumstances and perhaps return to the court for further measures if the residence arrangements do not work out.

The importance of this marriage of section 8 orders and care order proceedings should not be underestimated. The DH Guidance on compulsory intervention (Volume 1) states that before proceeding with an application, the SSD should always seek legal advice on (among other things) the implications of another party to the proceedings opposing the application and applying for a section 8 order instead; the department should also consider whether use of a residence order linked with a supervision order would be an appropriate alternative to a care order. In addition, it is relevant to point out that under the rules of court, one of the functions of the guardian ad litem is to advise the court on 'the options available to it in respect of the child and the suitability of each such option'. Practitioners should accordingly expect child protection conference discussions to embrace such matters.

Care order or supervision order?

Making a supervision order is always an option for the court once the threshold criteria have been satisfied. This is the case even where both the applicant local authority and the guardian ad litem are adamant that only a care order will fully meet the child's needs. Deciding the most suitable outcome requires an assessment of many factors, but throughout the decision-making process the court will need to bear in mind the essential features of what are two very different orders, and in particular the fact that a care order gives the local authority prime responsibility for the child (including the right to dictate the child's placement). As is explained in the next chapter, a supervision order does not have this effect. The difficulty in deciding between the two orders may be at its most acute when it is agreed by all of the parties that the child should remain at home with his parents. Care orders can of course be made in such circumstances (see page 188 above). Although each case must depend on its own facts the reported decisions contain useful illustrations of the way in which judges attempt to resolve the problem, and a selection of these appear below.

Re G (1992)

In upholding a decision of magistrates to make a care order in respect of a 13-year-old girl, Mr Justice Waite referred to 'the very limited range for vigilance that is in practice afforded by a supervision order'. This was a case where the child desperately wanted to remain at home with her father but the local authority argued that she needed to be removed from a damaging environment.

Re D (1993)

The High Court made a care order in respect of a child of 13 months contrary to the wishes of the local authority, which thought a supervision order would suffice. The child's father had a history of cruelty and was considered to have been responsible for the death of a previous child, although he denied it. The local authority feared that a care order might undermine the co-operation it was getting from the parents but the judge said that the protection of the child was the most important aspect of the case: 'the decisive point in coming to a decision whether there should be a supervision order or a care order is that if there is to be a lifting of the safeguards surrounding this child that lifting ought to be done by the court on consideration of the evidence and the lifting of the safeguards ought not to be left to the responsibility of individuals'.

Re T (1993)

The Court of Appeal upheld the decision of a county court judge to make a care order in respect of a child of 6 months. The parents' four older children had all been removed and placed for adoption following massive neglect. No harm had yet befallen the child but the evidence suggested that the standard of parenting continued to be inadequate. Although the child

was still living at home, a supervision order was considered an inappropriate response. A care order would 'concentrate the minds of the parents on
their responsibilities' and would place on the local authority a positive duty
to ensure the welfare of the child.

Re V (1994)

The child in this case was 16 years old and severely disabled. He attended
a special school as a weekly boarder. His mother came to regard his attendance at the school as damaging, a view contradicted by all the professionals.
Fearing that the child was regressing under the influence of the mother's
care at home, the local authority applied for a care order in order to ensure
his continued attendance at the school. The trial judge accepted that the
threshold criteria were satisfied but declined to make a care order on the
grounds that it would run too grave a risk of destroying the parents' marriage and therefore the child's future home. A supervision order was
granted instead. The Court of Appeal reversed this decision and made a
care order. It was felt that the risk of a care order undermining the parents'
relationship was outweighed by the risk of serious harm which the child
stood to suffer if he were to be deprived of the opportunities at the school
during the last 12 months of his minority. A supervision order would not
ensure the child's attendance at the school.

Re FS (1995)

The Court of Appeal upheld the decision of a county court judge to make
a supervision order in respect of a child of 6 following a finding of serious
sexual abuse committed by the child's father. The local authority and the
guardian ad litem had argued for care orders in respect of the child and her
two siblings so as to enable social workers to control the reintroduction of
the father into the family home. The judges were satisfied that sufficient
protection would be afforded by the mother (even though she had never
fully accepted that sexual abuse had occurred) against the background of a
supervision order.

Re B (1996)

In making supervision orders in respect of three children who were going to
remain at home, the High Court acknowledged the importance of the
impact that care orders would have on the children and their parent. Specifically, there was a high risk of the mother's co-operation being lost and of
the children's trust in the SSD being damaged. The children were 8, 9 and
11 years old and were capable of understanding what a care order meant,
especially as two older children were living away under care orders.

Re O (1996)

As mentioned earlier (see page 177), this is the case in which Mrs Justice Hale said that the court should begin with a preference for the less interventionist rather than the more interventionist approach. It was a case in which the children were going to remain at home with their parents and the judge stated that the nub of the choice in such a situation 'comes down to what is best going to persuade the parents to co-operate with the authorities in their concerns for the children's welfare; and . . . what is best going to persuade the local authority to take their responsibilities towards these children seriously'.

Care order or residence order?

Each of these orders confers parental responsibility on the holder and each of them enables the holder to decide on the child's placement (the residence order envisages, of course, that the child will actually have his home with the holder but this is not essential). A care order can be made only in favour of a local authority; a residence order can be made in favour of any individual, including a birth parent. In the context of a section 31 application brought by a local authority, the making of a residence order will result in a denial to the authority of effective control over the child's upbringing. It is true that a supervision order can be made to run alongside the residence order, but this will make possible only a measure of social work monitoring (see Chapter 11). As with the care order/supervision order question, the reported case law since 1991 has shown the courts considering the merits of a private law outcome in diverse situations.

Newham London Borough Council v AG (1992)

A care order was made in respect of a child of 2. The local authority's plan was for adoption outside the family with no contact between the child and his mother, who was suffering from mental illness. The maternal grandmother was fiercely opposed to this plan and offered herself as a carer for the child but the local authority and the court felt unable to accept her offer, even though she was a loving and caring person, because she was considered to have no real insight into the nature of the mother's illness and the consequent risks to the child. The mother had been described as unstable and unpredictably violent and the child needed protection of a type which the grandmother could not provide.

Re B (1993)

The mother in this case was diagnosed as suffering from Munchausen Syndrome by Proxy. Her two children were removed from her care and were the subject of care order applications. The local authority intended to work towards the early placement of the children with their respective fathers, who had new partners. The court granted the care orders and expressed the hope that they would eventually be replaced by residence orders in favour of each father. One of the fathers wanted a residence order immediately so as to be 'in charge' but the judge said that it was too early for this. The case was a complex one which might need the fuller resources available to the local authority; care orders would give moral support to the fathers and would give a signal to the mother (who remained a threat) not to interfere.

Re M (1994)

A care order was confirmed by the House of Lords following the murder of the child's mother by his father (see page 157 above). By the time of the appeal, the child had been living with a relative for seven months and it was agreed that his future lay with her. A residence order in favour of the relative could, of course, have been made – and in fact had been made by the Court of Appeal – but the House of Lords preferred a care order on the grounds that it would enable the local authority to monitor the progress of the child and control the exercise by the father (who was in prison) of his parental responsibility: 'having regard to M's history and circumstances it is highly desirable that the local authority shall exercise a watching brief on his behalf'. Far from simply giving the local authority a watching brief, this arrangement had the effect of handing full control of the child's upbringing to the authority. The relative's position as long-term carer of the child was wholly dependent upon the authority's consent.

Re H (1994)

This was the case in which it was stated that adoption should be a course of last resort in child protection situations (see page 177 above). The High Court set aside a care order made by magistrates and granted a residence order in favour of the child's grandmother. The guardian ad litem had criticized the local authority for having over-reacted to the threatening behaviour of the child's mother and having 'rushed into decisions about adoption without giving proper consideration to restraints inherent in the extended family'. The grandmother seems to have been rejected as carer by the local authority on insufficient grounds.

Re K (1994)

This case concerned two children aged 5 and 6 who had suffered harm at the hands of their mother, a woman suffering from paranoid schizophrenia. The local authority applied for care orders and in the meantime placed the children with the maternal grandparents. By the time of the final hearing, it was agreed that the children would be staying with the grandparents and the local authority therefore proposed that residence orders be made in their favour along with supervision orders. The grandparents, however, did not want residence orders because, they said, they would feel uneasy having prime parental responsibility for the children. They felt that care orders would give them greater support from the local authority, bearing in mind the fact that both children had been diagnosed as suffering from muscular dystrophy. The High Court made care orders. It stated that whereas a residence order should not normally be made in favour of a non-parent who does not want one, a care order may properly be imposed upon an unwilling local authority where – as was the case here – the child's welfare dictates it. The failure to make care orders in this case would have left the children insecure and unprotected.

Re B (1995)

This was a non-accidental injury case in which the child had been removed into foster care under interim care orders. The outcome of the case – which ended in the Court of Appeal – was that the mother was exonerated from all blame for the child's injuries and was given a residence order. The noteworthy feature, however, was that there needed to be a phased rehabilitation and the Court of Appeal dealt with this by stating that the residence order was being made 'upon a basis that the child will remain accommodated for so long as it takes (and in our judgment, it must be sooner rather than later and must be a period measured in weeks and certainly not in months) for the mother to build up her contact with her daughter to ease the transfer into her care'. As a matter of law, the making of the residence order gave the mother the right to immediate possession of the child but this strict legal position was in practice qualified by the understanding relating to the delayed transfer. The judges were confident that both parties would respect the understanding and this was clearly a crucial factor in leaving things on such an informal and flexible basis.

In 1995 over 1000 residence orders were made by the courts in public law proceedings.

Interim care orders

When an order can be made

Section 38 of the Children Act empowers the court to make an interim care order in two situations. The first is where an application has been made for a care order or a supervision order and that application is adjourned by the court. The second situation is where there are family proceedings (e.g.

divorce) before a court and the court decides under section 37 to order the local authority to investigate the possibility of applying for compulsory powers.

The court has complete discretion whether or not to grant an interim order but it can only do so if it is satisfied 'that there are reasonable grounds for believing that the circumstances with respect to the child are as mentioned in section 31(2)'. In other words, the court has to be satisfied that there is reason to believe that the threshold criteria pertaining to a full care order are present. It may turn out in the end that the harm grounds are not actually satisfied but if at the interim stage there are reasonable grounds to believe this, the court has power to make the order (as the DH Guidance points out, it would not be realistic to require proof of the condition for a full order at the interim stage when the guardian's final report will probably not have been submitted and all evidence heard). In exercising its discretion, the court should be guided by the same principles, set out in section 1 of the Act, as apply to the making of a full order, i.e. the welfare principle (including the checklist of relevant factors) and the principle that an order should be made only if it will produce positive benefits for the child.

The temporary nature of the order

Interim orders, by definition, are only short-term measures: they are designed to be not an end in themselves but simply a stop-gap. It was said in the case of *Re G* (1993) that the making of an interim care order is an essentially impartial step, favouring neither one side nor the other, and affording no one, least of all the local authority in whose favour it is made, an opportunity for tactical advantage. At the same time, however, they can have a critical effect on the family concerned, as the case of *Avon County Council v N* (1995) amply demonstrates (see page 165 above). To prevent their abuse, time limits are necessary, and the Children Act constructs these by using the device of listing a number of events and stating that an interim order will cease to have effect when any of these events first occurs. The starting point is that an interim order will last for as long as the court says, but it cannot in any circumstances last for more than eight weeks. If the application for a full order is disposed of within that time, the interim order will lapse at that earlier time. If the interim order is a second or subsequent such order, it can last only for four weeks, unless it was made less than four weeks after the first order, in which case it can last until eight weeks from the first order.

The normal pattern, therefore, where successive interim care orders are made, is for an initial eight-week limit to apply, followed by limits of four weeks. It can be seen that the eight-week initial period links in with the time which is normally to be given to a local authority under a section 37 investigation order. Where the court reduces the investigation time-scale, however, the maximum duration of any interim order it makes is reduced too. So if the court in family proceedings orders a local authority investigation to be completed within, say, 14 days, an interim order made can last only for that time (further interim orders can, however, be made if the local authority, having carried out its enquiries, decides to apply for compulsory powers).

Using private law orders in the interim period

The integration of public and private law procedures in the Children Act, noted earlier, has a significant bearing on interim, as well as long-term, compulsory intervention. The DH in its Guidance has been anxious to emphasize this:

> where a suitable relative or other person connected with the child is prepared to look after him and is likely to be able to meet his needs at least for a trial period, the residence order – supported where necessary by an interim supervision order – offers an attractive alternative to the interim care order. The local authority should always weigh carefully the pros and cons of such an arrangement.

The legal effect of an interim care order

The legal consequences of an interim care order are similar to those of a full care order, except for the limited duration factor. The reason for this is that section 31(11) of the Children Act defines 'care order' so as to include an interim order, so that the provisions in the Act which spell out the effects of a 'care order' automatically extend to interim measures unless there is any express provision to the contrary. The important and crucial effect of an interim care order is therefore to vest prime parental responsibility in the local authority, with the result that it is in a position to exercise parental powers in relation to the child (subject to the specified exceptions). In exercising these powers it is subject to the code of treatment for children in care (on which see page 186 above), so that the rules and guidance relating to plans, reviews, placement with parents, complaints procedures and so on have effect as appropriate. The DH Guidance states that while the temporary nature of the interim order should be allowed for in the discharge of the authority's responsibilities 'it is not a reason for not taking them seriously'.

It is important to bear in mind that although the interim care order gives prime parental responsibility to the local authority, the authority is not entirely free from court control. Indeed, since by definition there are legal proceedings pending in a section 38 case, the local authority will be only too aware that its actions throughout the interim period will be open to scrutiny by both the court and the guardian ad litem at later hearings. The significance of these figures in the background should not be underestimated. In *Re G* (above) it was said that 'Parliament intended the regime of an interim care order to operate as a tightly run procedure closely monitored by the court and affording to all parties an opportunity of frequent review as events unfold during the currency of the order'. This is very different from the position when a full care order is in force. On three matters, the Children Act expressly provides for direct court control of local authority behaviour. The first matter is contact. The contact provisions in section 34, described earlier, are fully applicable to interim orders and aim to secure the protection of parents' and other parties' interests. The DH Guidance (Volume 3) stresses that the first weeks in care 'are likely to be particularly crucial to the success of the relationship between the parent, the social worker and the child's carers and to the level of future contact between parent and child'.

The second matter is the medical and psychiatric examination of the child. According to section 38(6), on making an interim care order, or subsequently, the court may give such directions as it considers appropriate with regard to such examinations or other assessment; and the direction may be to the effect that there is to be no examination or no examination unless the court directs otherwise. A direction can be varied at any time. This provision has generated significant case law. In *Re L* (1995) the Court of Appeal ruled that section 38(6) does not give the court power to direct that a child is to live at a specified place during the assessment. The decision as to the child's placement under an interim care order was one wholly within the local authority's discretion, just like such a decision under a full care order. The Court of Appeal took matters a stage further in the case of *Re M* (1996). A county court judge had made a direction under section 38(6) that there should be a residential assessment of the mother and her baby at a specified mother and child unit. On appeal, the Court of Appeal ruled that such a direction was outside the scope of the subsection. For one thing, there was power to direct an assessment only of the child, not of the parents or the family as a whole; for another, the court had already ruled in *Re L* that there was no power to specify the child's placement during an assessment. The Court of Appeal made it clear that the Act did not empower the court to compel a local authority to spend substantial sums of money by placing a family in a particular unit for a lengthy period. The decisions in *Re L* and *Re M* were reviewed by the House of Lords in *Re C* (1996), a case in which the local authority was unwilling (not simply for financial reasons) to fund a residential assessment of a child and his parents. In a problematic ruling, the House of Lords rejected the approach taken in the earlier cases and stated that section 38(6) enables the court to order 'any assessment which involves the participation of the child', including an assessment of the parent/child relationship. In exercising its discretion whether to order any particular assessment, the court should take into account the cost of the proposed assessment and the fact that local authorities' resources are notoriously limited. The House of Lords stated that section 38(6) was ambiguously worded. The crucial argument which pointed towards a broad interpretation was that in a section 31 application the court needs extensive information and assessments in order to decide whether a full care order can, and should, be made. As for the argument that section 38(6) covers only assessments of children, it was said that 'it is impossible to assess a young child divorced from his environment. The interaction between the child and his parents . . . is an essential element in making any assessment of the child'. This reasoning, it is suggested, is unconvincing. It would have been very easy for the draftsman of the Children Act to refer to an assessment of persons other than the child, but this course was not taken. The effect of the case is that during the interim care period, the court is in a position to dictate the child's placement as long as some element of assessment is involved. How this can be reconciled with the local authority's duties and discretions under the code of treatment contained in Part III of the Act and the various regulations made under it is a mystery (the House of Lords suggested that a placement arranged under a section 38(6) direction is not a 'placement' under Part III at all, a proposition which flies in the face of the statutory framework).

If the child is of sufficient understanding to make an informed decision, he may refuse to submit to an assessment. This is identical to the rule applicable to emergency protection orders, discussed in Chapter 8. In the controversial case of *South Glamorgan County Council v W* (1993) the High Court ruled that an assessment can be imposed upon a competent child, despite the clear wording of section 38, if its inherent jurisdiction is invoked. This very difficult issue is considered in Chapter 14 below.

The final matter on which there is court control is secure accommodation. As with the contact provisions, those in section 25 concerning secure accommodation are equally applicable to interim orders.

Exclusion requirements

Section 38A of the Children Act was inserted by the Family Law Act 1996 and was brought into force during the autumn of 1997. It enables the court to include an exclusion requirement in an interim care order. The conditions which need to be fulfilled, and the effect of such a requirement, are similar to those pertaining to requirements attached to emergency protection orders, and these have already been considered (see page 137 above). It is important to note that an exclusion requirement can last only for the duration of an interim care order: it cannot survive the making of a full care order. It is also important to realize that the exclusion requirement is not free-standing – it is attached to an interim care order. This means that, although the child can safely be left at home (the suspected abuser having been expelled), the local authority will have prime parental responsibility and the child's arrangements will be covered by the Placement with Parents etc. Regulations 1991. If the local authority does not want prime parental responsibility, some other mechanism will have to be employed in order to eject the relevant adult (e.g. the inherent jurisdiction of the High Court, described in Chapter 14 below). Having an interim care order will enable the local authority to remove the child from the family home at any time. By the same token, however, the authority will have obligations relating to contact between the child and both parents (under section 34).

Discharge of interim care orders

The rules here are the same as for full care orders, so that an application for discharge can be made by the local authority, the child or any person having parental responsibility. If an application fails, the six-month rule relating to full orders (see page 193 above) does not apply, so further applications may be made freely.

When to terminate the interim care period

The rules described earlier make it clear that the court has a greater degree of control and influence over the local authority under an interim care order than it has under a full care order. The effect of the decision of the House of Lords in *Re C* (1996) has been to strengthen even further the court's position during the interim period. This being the case, there will inevitably arise in many situations the question of deciding the right time for bringing a sequence of interim orders to an end and replacing it with a full care order arrangement. This is a question which only the court can resolve. Common sense suggests that an interim care order regime should be brought to an end when all the relevant facts have been established by evidence. 'Relevant' in this context means relevant to the allegation of significant harm and relevant to the matters referred to in the welfare checklist contained in section 1(3) of the 1989 Act. This approach works reasonably well in cases where the evidence establishes beyond any doubt that the child's parents will never be in a position to offer him proper care. Much more difficult are those cases in which it is argued that the parent(s) *might* be able to provide proper care at some point in the future, depending on the sort of treatment they receive, how they respond to it, and so on. In such cases, will 'the facts' ever become clear? At what point should the court stop waiting for a distinct picture to emerge and, trusting to the local authority's discretion, hand over long-term responsibility for the child under a full care order? Also difficult are those cases in which a parent is undergoing assessment of their parenting capacity. Should the court always wait until the assessment is complete?

A variety of views have been expressed by the judges on this issue. An influential early case was *Re C* (1992), in which the parents were being assessed to see whether it would be safe to return their children to them. The judge was very clear that the court should wait for the assessment before making a full order:

> We have heard much, as we prepared for the implementation of the Children Act, about partnership. One of those partnerships is the very important one between the court and the local authority where the part played by the court is to consider all the facts presented to it by the local authority and to make a decision finally disposing of the case when all of those facts are as clearly known to the court as can be hoped. That stage has not been reached in this case. The court does not know what the result of the assessment would be ... The court should be slow to abdicate its responsibility until all the facts are known ... delay is ordinarily inimical to the welfare of the child but ... planned and purposeful delay may well be beneficial. A delay of a final decision for the purpose of ascertaining the result of an assessment is proper delay and is to be encouraged.

A rather different emphasis may be seen in the case of *Re L* (1995). This was a sexual abuse case in which there were doubts about the mother's ability to protect the children from the father and the extended family. The local authority's care plan contained a proposal for adoption but a social worker told the judge that the authority would reconsider the plan in the light of the expert evidence advocating an attempt at rehabilitation. The judge said: 'there is a fair chance here on the evidence that I have heard that these children could be rehabilitated with their mother if the work is successfully carried out as proposed by Dr R and with luck and good circumstances, and if everything goes smoothly'. He proceeded to make a full care order, but the mother appealed on the ground that this was premature. The Court of Appeal dismissed her appeal, ruling that the point at which the court withdraws from continuing control over a child and passes responsibility to the local authority is a matter of the exercise of discretion by the court and will vary with each set of circumstances. Here, there had been a 17-day hearing intended to provide a conclusion to what was already prolonged litigation and there was no prospect of the children leaving foster care for many months. In these circumstances, the making of a series of further interim orders for an indefinite period was felt to be an artificial use of the legislation. The Court of Appeal regarded the decision in *Re C* (above) as turning on its own facts but in truth it reflected a different approach. Different judges seem to have different views about the correct balance of power between the courts and local authorities and section 38 of the Children Act, like other provisions, allows them to implement their views at their discretion.

Best Practice Guidance

Best Practice Guidance on the renewal of interim care orders was published by the Children Act Advisory Committee in June 1997 in its *Handbook of Best Practice in Children Act Cases*.

Aftercare

The aftercare provisions of the Act, contained in section 24, apply to children in care in the same way as they apply to accommodated children. They are described in Chapter 6.

11

Supervision orders

Introduction

The term 'supervision order' had many connotations under the previous law and it continues to have many under the Children Act. The Children and Young Persons Act 1969 provided for the making of supervision orders both in criminal proceedings against a young offender and in care proceedings in respect of children at risk. Matrimonial and other 'family' legislation also provided for the making of supervision orders but the legal effects of these differed from the effects of orders made under the 1969 Act. Even within the 1969 Act there were differences, since supervision orders made in criminal proceedings could contain special conditions which were not available in care proceedings.

The effect of the Children Act has been to replace the rules relating to supervision orders made in care proceedings and family proceedings. Criminal supervision orders remain governed by the Children and Young Persons Act 1969, a result consistent with the policy of hiving off the law relating to young offenders into a completely separate and self-contained code.

In Chapters 3 and 4 it was seen how the 1989 Act enables a family assistance order to be made in family proceedings. This type of order can be made only with the consent of the parties concerned, and its main object is to facilitate the provision of fairly short-term social work support to the family following marital breakdown. A supervision order, on the other hand, is a form of compulsory intervention – albeit less drastic in its effects than a care order – which is designed for cases with a child protection element where a wider range of supervisor's powers may be needed. Nor should the supervision order be confused with the education supervision order created by the Act. That order is designed for truancy cases only and is governed by a separate set of rules. To summarize, the following forms of supervision have been available through a court order since the passage of the 1989 Act:

1 A supervision order made under the 1989 Act.
2 A supervision order made in criminal proceedings under the 1969 Act.
3 An education supervision order.
4 A family assistance order.

The present chapter is devoted to the first type of order: a supervision order made by the court on grounds of harm, or likely harm, to the child.

During the passage of the 1989 Act, there was comparatively little discussion or debate on the question of supervision orders in care proceedings. The general impression conveyed was that the subject is uncontroversial. If this is indeed the case, one of the reasons is no doubt the limited amount of intervention which the making of such an order involves. As the Children Act Advisory Committee put it (Annual Report 1993/94):

> The essence of a supervision order is to help and assist a child where the parents have full responsibility for the child's upbringing. It does not involve any statutory level of monitoring, does not create sanctions, and does not give the local authority parental responsibility.

The provisions of the Children Act concerning these orders reflect the recommendations of the Child Care Law Review, which drew attention to a number of defects in the previous law, particularly the absence of any power to impose requirements directly on the child's carer (as distinct from the child himself).

Matters on which the rules coincide with those governing care orders

In a number of respects the Children Act treats supervision orders and care orders in an identical fashion. These are listed below. Each of the matters in the list is discussed in the previous chapter.

- Applicants for an order
- The children concerned
- The grounds for an order
- When an application can be made
- The discretion to apply for an order
- The processing of an application
- When criminal proceedings are pending
- The role of the court
- The making of other orders on a supervision order application.

The effect of the last point is that a care order can be made instead of a supervision order. A section 8 order can also be made, either instead of or alongside a supervision order (but the Act does not allow a residence order or a contact order to be made in favour of a local authority). A section 8 order and a care order cannot be made together.

The legal effect of a supervision order

According to section 31(1) a supervision order is an order putting the child under the supervision of a designated local authority or a probation officer. The legal framework of this 'supervision' is set out partly in section 35 and partly in Schedule 3 at the back of the Act. This arrangement was simply the draftsman's way of making the provisions more digestible: the idea was to put the more basic rules in the section, with the detail being relegated to the Schedule.

The basic duty of the supervisor

Section 35 states that while a supervision order is in force it shall be the duty of the supervisor to advise, assist and befriend the supervised child. In carrying out this duty, the social worker has almost unlimited discretion in the sense that the terms used – 'advise' etc. – are not defined or regulated in any way. Probation officers, however, should take into account the National Standards published by the Home Office in 1995 (see page 214 below).

Other duties of the supervisor

Section 35 imposes two other duties on the supervisor. The first is to take such steps as are reasonably necessary to give effect to the order. The second duty arises where the order is not completely complied with or may no longer, in the supervisor's opinion, be necessary. In these circumstances, the supervisor is required to consider whether or not to apply to the court for a variation or discharge of the order.

Selection of the supervisor

The supervisor will be the local authority, unless the authority requests the appointment of a probation officer and an officer is already working (or has worked) with another member of the child's household.

Requirements which may be included in an order

Schedule 3 to the Children Act specifies various types of requirement which the court may insert into a supervision order. The possibilities are as follows:

- The child is to live at a place or places as directed by the supervisor for a specified period or periods.
- The child is to present himself to a person as directed by the supervisor at specified places on specified days.
- The child is to participate in activities as directed by the supervisor on specified days.
- The 'responsible person' – this is any person having parental responsibility for the child or any other person with whom the child is living (e.g. relatives or private foster carers) – is to take all reasonable steps to ensure that the child complies with any direction given by the supervisor. The responsible person has to consent to this requirement: the Government's view was that the effectiveness of supervision orders would depend upon co-operation between the supervisor and the family ('there would be little purpose in imposing a requirement that a person should seek to ensure that a child complies with directions unless that person consented').
- The responsible person is to comply with any directions given by the supervisor requiring him to attend, with or without the child, at a specified place for the purpose of taking part in specified activities (the responsible person has to consent to this requirement). The Child Care Law Review mentioned child care classes and mother and toddler groups as examples of 'specified activities'.
- The responsible person is to take all reasonable steps to ensure that the child complies with any requirement relating to medical examinations or treatment (again, consent is needed).
- The responsible person is to keep the supervisor informed of his address if it differs from the child's.
- The child is to keep the supervisor informed of any change in his address.
- The child is to allow the supervisor to visit him at his place of residence.

The hallmark of these requirements is flexibility: none of them has to be included in a supervision order and many of them lend themselves to being specially adapted to fit the features of the case. Some are applicable to children of all ages, others are useful only where the child is reasonably mature. Where the supervisor is authorized to issue directions, there is discretion both in the issuing of the directions and in defining their precise content. This is the social worker's discretion, not the court's. The original text of the Children Act provided that the total number of days in respect of which the child or the responsible person could be required to comply with directions could not exceed 90. The Government evidently had second thoughts about this because in 1990 the 90-day limit was taken out (by the Courts and Legal Services Act). It was felt that such a limit, which applies to criminal supervision orders, was inappropriate for civil orders made on grounds of significant harm.

The DH Guidance (Volume 1) urges supervisors to review the need for, and reasonableness of, any directions given under an order, the arrangements made for carrying them out, and whether it would be in the interests of the child to change them.

Duties of the responsible person

Whatever the requirements built into the order, Schedule 3 enables the supervisor to demand details of the child's address from the responsible person (assuming it is known) and requires that person to allow the supervisor reasonable contact with the child.

Psychiatric and medical examinations and treatment

Given that supervision orders are made only in cases involving actual or anticipated harm, the question of health examinations and health treatment assumes considerable importance. Schedule 3 contains special rules on these matters.

As far as *examinations* are concerned, the Act enables the court to incorporate in the order a requirement that the child is to submit to a medical or psychiatric examination or a requirement that the child is to submit to any such examination 'from time to time as directed by the supervisor'. Any examination is to be conducted – and the order must specify this – by a named medical practitioner, or at a named establishment at which the child is to attend as a non-resident patient, or at a health service hospital (or, in the case of a psychiatric examination, a hospital or mental nursing home) at which the child is to attend as a resident patient. This last option is available only in cases where the court is satisfied on expert evidence that the child may be suffering from a physical or mental condition that requires, and may be susceptible to, treatment, and that a period as a resident patient is necessary if the examination is to be carried out properly.

Two general restrictions are imposed on the making of medical examination requirements. First, the court must be satisfied that satisfactory arrangements have been, or can be, made for the examination. Second, where the child has sufficient understanding to make an informed decision, the court must be satisfied that he consents to the inclusion of the requirement. This was another concession to the self-determination ideas discussed in the *Gillick* case in 1985.

Turning to *treatment*, the Act draws a distinction between psychiatric and medical cases. In both cases, the court is enabled to include in the supervision order a requirement that the child shall submit to such treatment as is specified for such period as is specified (it is the court which orders the treatment, not the supervising social worker). The treatment must be given by a named practitioner, or else received by the child as a non-resident patient at a specified place, or as a resident patient in a health service hospital (or, in psychiatric cases, in a hospital or mental nursing home). The common condition which must be met for a treatment requirement is that the court is satisfied on expert evidence that the condition of the child is such as requires, and may be susceptible to, treatment. In psychiatric cases, the court must also be satisfied that the child's mental condition is not such as to warrant his detention in pursuance of a hospital order under the Mental Health Act 1983.

The same general restrictions as apply to examination requirements apply to treatment: satisfactory arrangements for the treatment must be in hand and a child who has sufficient understanding must consent to the inclusion of the requirement.

Once treatment gets under way, circumstances may change. New facts may come to light, for example. The Act caters for this by providing for a written report to be sent by the medical practitioner in charge of the child's treatment to the supervisor if he becomes unwilling to continue to treat the child, or if he forms the opinion that the treatment should be continued beyond the specified period, or that the child needs different treatment, or that the child is not susceptible to treatment, or that the child does not require further treatment. If such a report is sent, the supervisor must refer it to the court, which may then cancel or vary the requirement (e.g. by extending the period of treatment) depending on the circumstances.

The National Standards

The Home Office document *National Standards for Probation Service Family Court Welfare Work* (1995) contains a chapter devoted to supervision orders under which the supervisor is a probation officer. It states that contact should be made with the child and his carer(s) within five working days of receipt of the case papers from the court. A written supervision plan should be drawn up, indicating how the overall objectives of the supervision order are to be met. Progress against the objectives should be reviewed quarterly with the child and the family and any amendment to the plan recorded in writing. A record should be kept of contact with the family, including any failure to attend meetings or comply with directions or obligations.

Matters which may not be regulated by an order

Cases decided since 1991 have highlighted a number of issues relating to the scope of Schedule 3 requirements:

- A condition of 'no contact' cannot be attached to a supervision order. If the court wishes to prohibit a person from contacting the child, it should make a prohibited steps order (*Re H* (1995)).
- There is no provision in Schedule 3 for the giving by the responsible person of formal undertakings as part of a supervision order (i.e. undertakings which, if broken, can lead to contempt of court proceedings). However, it is possible for agreements to be recorded in a preamble to an order so that any shortcomings can be brought to the court's attention in subsequent proceedings (*Re B* (1995)).

The duration of a supervision order

According to Schedule 3, paragraph 6, a supervision order shall cease to have effect at the end of the period of one year beginning with the date on which it was made. This represented a change in the law, since under the Children and Young Persons Act 1969 a supervision order could be made for up to three years. The Government's view was that the shorter duration would 'make orders more effective, induce a greater sense of purpose and reduce the risk of undermining parents' confidence in relation to their children'. The supervisor can, however, apply to the court for one or more extensions up to a three-year period. In *M v Warwickshire County Council* (1994) the High Court ruled that the wording of Schedule 3 permits the court to make a supervision order which runs initially for less than a year, and in *Re A* (1994) the Court of Appeal confirmed that it is not necessary for the local authority to prove again the section 31(2) threshold criteria when it applies for an extension of an order. On such an application, the court should be guided simply by the welfare provisions contained in section 1 of the Act.

If the child reaches the age of 18 before the statutory expiry date, the order automatically lapses (section 91(13)). Similarly, a supervision order can be discharged in advance of the expiry date by the court on the application of the supervisor, the child or any person having parental responsibility (section 39(2)). To deter groundless applications for discharge, section 91(15) provides that at least six months must elapse between such applications unless the leave of the court is obtained. If a care order is made in respect of a supervised child, the supervision order is automatically discharged (section 91(3)). On this point, it needs to be borne in mind that if a care order is to be made, the threshold criteria do have to be proved once again.

Variation of the supervision order

Care orders cannot be varied but supervision orders can be (section 39(2) and (3)). This can be done so as to alter the requirements which have been included in the order, e.g. by inserting a requirement authorizing directions to be given by the supervisor, or inserting a requirement concerning medical examinations or treatment. Such variation can be sought by the same persons who can apply for discharge (see above). In addition, a variation can be sought by a person with whom the child is living, even if that person cannot apply for discharge. This enables somebody such as a relative who is caring for the child to apply for a variation of any require-ment which has been imposed on him as a 'responsible person'.

Interim supervision orders

The interim supervision order was a novelty in 1989 since it did not fea-ture in the previous legislation. Section 38 is the governing provision and the rules it prescribes are essentially the same as the ones pertaining to interim care orders – on which see Chapter 10. One difference is worth noting, however: although the court generally has a discretion whether or not to make an order, section 38(3) states that where, on an applica-tion for a care order or supervision order, the court makes a residence order, it shall also make an interim supervision order, unless satisfied that the child's welfare will be satisfactorily safeguarded without an interim order being made. The reasoning behind this was described earlier (see page 196).

It is also worth noting that none of the special provisions relating to psychiatric and medical examinations and treatment in Schedule 3 applies to interim supervision orders. Instead, section 38 itself contains rules (de-scribed in Chapter 10). The DH Guidance suggests that medical and other assessment directions may be necessary where a child assessment order reveals only a partial picture of harm or failure to thrive, the SSD's con-cerns are not dispelled and further investigation is called for.

The provisions relating to exclusion requirements, inserted into the Children Act by the Family Law Act 1996 (see page 205 above), do not apply where an interim supervision order is made. They are restricted to interim care order and emergency protection order cases. This restriction – which not surprisingly has been questioned by some organizations – was defended by Mrs Justice Hale (a former Law Commissioner) during the Parliamentary proceedings on the legislation in the following way:

> One can see more to be said for attaching the requirement to an interim supervision order . . . but this would contravene the principle that the local authority must have the power to remove the child if need be, and it would not allow them to do that and so, therefore, they would have no immediate recourse if the person excluded did in fact return to the home.

Obstruction of the social worker

The effect of the supervision order provisions has been to involve parents and other carers much more directly: not only can requirements now be imposed on them by the court (with their consent), the Act itself imposes obligations – to inform the supervisor, on demand, of the child's address and also to allow the supervisor reasonable contact with the child. Where the supervising social worker meets with obstruction, the legal sanctions which can ultimately be applied need to be fully understood. The legal position in this respect was spelled out by the Court of Appeal in the case of *Re V* (1994):

> ... a supervision order rests primarily upon the consent of the parent affected by it. Any provisions incorporated into a supervision order, either by direction of the supervisor or by requirements directly stated by the judge, are incapable of being enforced directly through any of the ordinary processes by which courts of law enforce obedience to their directions. The only sanction, when any infringement of the terms of a supervision order, or of directions given under it, occurs is a return by the supervisor to court. There the ultimate sanction will be the making of a care order under which the local authority will be given the necessary legal powers to enforce its will.

If action has to be taken in an emergency, then the fact that a supervision order has been made will not prevent the supervisor, the NSPCC, the police or others from utilizing the various intervention procedures established by the Act. The use of these procedures will be necessary to effect a forcible removal of the child, since a supervision order does not give this power. In this connection, mention should be made of the provision in the Act which is specifically geared to the obstruction of a social worker acting under a supervision order. This is section 102 (also discussed in Chapter 9) which enables the court to issue a warrant authorizing any constable to assist a person in the exercise of certain specified functions. One of these functions is the entitlement of a supervisor to have reasonable contact with the child, laid down by Schedule 3. So if entry to the child's residence, or access to the child within his residence, is denied, it is possible for the supervisor, via a court order, to call upon the police for assistance.

Supervision order or care order?

In the last chapter there was noted the difficulty, which is often presented to the court, of choosing between a supervision order and a care order once the threshold criteria have been satisfied. Summaries of some of the reported cases on the point were given (see page 196) and it is not proposed to rehearse them here. What may be noted, however, are some of the factors pertaining to supervision orders which, in those cases at any rate, appear to have been especially influential:

- The limited duration of the order
- The absolute discretion of the supervisor to seek an extension
- The limited range of requirements
- The absence of sanctions for breach of directions
- The retention by the parents of exclusive parental responsibility and the absence of a power immediately to remove the child from the family home
- The relatively low level of monitoring associated with the order.

12

Courts and appeals against court decisions

The preceding chapters have explained how the Children Act created a substantial number of legal procedures under which applications can be made to 'the court' for a variety of orders. As we have seen, these procedures have come to be categorized as either 'public' or 'private'. The primary purpose of the present chapter is to describe those provisions of the legislation which are concerned with the courts having jurisdiction (i.e. power) to deal with these applications.

The concurrent jurisdiction principle

As it happens, the provisions of the Act dealing with the courts are reasonably straightforward, for this is yet another subject where the really detailed rules were left to be formulated by the Government. According to section 92(7), for the purposes of the Act 'the court' means the High Court, a county court or a magistrates' court. This definition will normally apply wherever the Act refers to a 'court' and, on the face of it, it means that all the procedures described in this book can be initiated in any of the three courts mentioned, the applicant having a choice in the matter.

This sort of arrangement is certainly not new: custody applications, for example, could be made to all three courts under the previous legislation. In the public law field, however, probably the most significant consequence of section 92(7) has been that it has opened up the possibility of local authorities applying for care orders and supervision orders in the county court and the High Court. It has also made it possible for disputes concerning contact with children in care to be taken to these courts. Under the Children and Young Persons Act 1969 and the Child Care Act 1980, only juvenile courts (i.e. magistrates' courts) had the power to make orders. One of the beneficial consequences of the jurisdiction rules under the 1989 Act is to render it more likely that all the issues in any particular case can be resolved in one court. The former concentration of local authority applications in the juvenile court was an obstacle to this.

The subordinate provisions

Section 92(7) tells only half the story, however. As indicated above, it was always the Government's intention to supplement this provision by detailed subordinate measures, and these measures duly appeared in 1991. Authorized by Schedule 11 to the Act, they have the effect of depriving the applicant of complete freedom of choice of court in certain situations. Under the Schedule, orders can be made requiring specified classes of proceedings to be initiated in specified courts and orders may prescribe the circumstances in which proceedings are to be transferred from one court to another. These powers have been used to the full.

The Children (Allocation of Proceedings) Order 1991

This order was the main device whereby the Government's views on case allocation were implemented. The text of the order, together with a circular issued jointly by the Lord Chancellor's Department and the Home Office, was included in Volume 7 of the DH Children Act Guidance. Although the wording of the order is at times rather dense and technical, the overall messages are clear enough. First, proceedings of a 'public law' nature should normally be started and heard in a magistrates' court (which for Children Act purposes has been renamed the family proceedings court). Secondly, such proceedings can be transferred to other courts if the circumstances are appropriate. Thirdly, proceedings of a 'private law' nature may normally be started in the court of the applicant's choice, but they may be transferred before being completed. Fourthly, all courts in all proceedings must use their transfer powers in conformity with the fundamental principle set out in section 1(2) of the Act: any delay in determining issues is likely to prejudice the welfare of the child.

With regard to the first objective, the order does not actually use the expression 'public law' (as was explained in Chapter 1, this is a loose non-statutory shorthand term). Instead, it simply lists specific types of proceedings. Eighteen types of case are in the list, the most important of which are as follows:

1 Applications for emergency protection orders.
2 Applications for child assessment orders.
3 Applications for care orders and supervision orders.
4 Applications concerning contact with a child in care.

5 Applications for secure accommodation orders.
6 Applications for police assistance warrants.

These, and the other listed proceedings, must normally be commenced in a magistrates' court. There are exceptions, however, designed to keep all relevant proceedings concerning a family under the same roof. If the High Court or the county court during family proceedings directs a local authority investigation (see page 163 above) and the authority decides as a result to apply for a care order, a supervision order, an education supervision order, a child assessment order or an emergency protection order, then it should return to the court which issued the direction. Similarly, if for some reason public law proceedings in respect of the child are pending in the High Court or a county court, further public law proceedings should be instituted in that court rather than the magistrates' court.

The provisions in the order governing transfer draw a distinction between public law and private law cases. As regards the former, although as a rule the magistrates' court will be the forum, a case can be transferred up to the county court where the magistrates or their clerk consider it in the interests of the child to do so. They are instructed by the order to have regard to the 'no delay' principle contained in section 1(2) of the Act and the following questions:

1 Whether the proceedings are exceptionally grave, important or complex, in particular (i) because of complicated or conflicting evidence about the risks involved to the child's physical or moral well-being or about other matters relating to the welfare of the child; (ii) because of the number of parties; (iii) because of a conflict with the law of another jurisdiction; (iv) because of some novel and difficult point of law; or (v) because of some question of general public interest;
2 Whether it would be appropriate for those proceedings to be heard together with other family proceedings which are pending in another court; and
3 Whether transfer is likely significantly to accelerate the determination of the proceedings, where (i) no other method of doing so, including transfer to another magistrates' court, is appropriate, and (ii) delay would seriously prejudice the interests of the child who is the subject of the proceedings.

Not surprisingly, EPO applications cannot be transferred: the delay would be unacceptable. The power of transfer can be exercised after an application by a party or of the magistrates' court's own motion, although one would expect the views of the child's guardian ad litem to be canvassed before a decision is made (indeed, the rules relating to the guardian's functions expressly mention this). If a transfer request is turned down, the applicant can apply to the county court for a reconsideration of the matter, a procedure which is regulated partly by the Allocation Order and partly by the rules of court. Finally, it should be noted that public law cases can be transferred on to the High Court where the county court considers that the proceedings are 'appropriate for determination in the High Court' and that such determination would be in the child's interests; they can also be transferred back to the magistrates' court in certain circumstances. In the period immediately following implementation of the Children Act, there arose a number of cases in which the senior judiciary considered the correct general approach to the transfer of public law proceedings. The following guidelines were laid down:

- Magistrates should not ordinarily undertake cases where the estimated duration exceeds three days (it should be noted, however, that in its Annual Report 1993/94, the Children Act Advisory Committee expressed the view that magistrates are capable of hearing straightforward cases lasting up to five days provided they are able to sit on consecutive days and there are no complex issues involved).
- Magistrates should not deal with cases which involve decisions both serious and difficult about which experts are in disagreement, and difficult decisions concerning the evaluation of future risk.
- Applications under section 38(6) – this relates to interim care and supervision orders – for an order directing a child to be tested for HIV should be heard by the High Court.

As for the transfer of private law cases, the provisions are less complicated on account of the free choice of initial forum offered by the order. All such proceedings are liable to be transferred upwards or downwards (or, indeed, sideways to another magistrates' court or county court) on a criterion of the 'interests of the child'. Such a move might be effected because of the importance of the case or because of the need to consolidate several sets of proceedings which have been initiated by different persons. As always, the 'no delay' principle should be borne in mind. It was noted in Chapter 4 how the courts have directed that applications by children for section 8 orders be dealt with by the High Court. That court has also been stated to be the preferred forum for applications concerning the sterilization or emergency medical treatment of a child, applications concerning the removal of a child from the UK, and applications made by birth parents following adoption proceedings. Furthermore, it has been directed that applications by local authorities for prohibited steps orders should not be made to the magistrates' court.

An additional complication introduced by the Allocation Order concerns county courts. In order to improve efficiency and develop expertise, the Government designated selected county courts for the disposal of certain types of case. The result is that for the purposes of case allocation under the Children Act, there are three types of county court: divorce centres, family hearing centres (which deal with, among other things, contested section 8 order cases) and care centres (which deal with public law proceedings under Parts III, IV and V of the Act). Those county courts which fall into the last two categories are listed at the back of the order, and in the case of care centres, the magistrates' areas which act as 'feeders' under the transfer provisions are also set out. Special provision has been made for London, where the Principal Registry of the Family Division is treated as an all-purpose county court.

The terms of the Allocation Order, though bristling with discretion, are not uncontroversial. During the passage of the Children Act, there was a sustained attempt to curtail the jurisdiction of magistrates' courts over public law matters on the grounds that the issues at stake were simply too important and complex to be left to a lay tribunal. Such objections were brushed aside by the Government, which subsequently reaffirmed its confidence in the members of the family panels. In 1995 the proportion of public law cases transferred by magistrates to the county court was estimated to be approximately 25 per cent. This figure, however, disguised massive variations in practice across the country. The Children Act Advisory Committee expressed concern that some magistrates might be losing expertise on account of an insufficient workload (Annual Report 1994/95).

The Family Proceedings (Allocation to Judiciary) Directions

These directions build upon the Allocation Order. Just as the order designates certain county courts for specified purposes, so the directions designate certain county court judges for specified purposes, notably the hearing of applications in that court under the Children Act. The point here is that a wide variety of judges can in principle sit in the county court (circuit judge, deputy circuit judge, recorder, assistant recorder, district judge, assistant district judge, deputy district judge). To permit all these people to preside in Children Act proceedings would have been inconsistent with the declared aim of the Government that 'children's cases in the higher courts should be heard by judiciary who, by reason of their experience and training, are specialists in family work'. Consequently, the directions stipulate which types of judge can hear which types of case. In effect, a Family Division of the county court has been created and has taken its place alongside the Family Division of the High Court and the family panels of the magistrates' courts.

A family court?

The effect of section 92 of the Children Act has been to retain the previous system whereby children's cases are spread across the magistrates' courts, the county courts and the High Court. Quite apart from the difficult question of case allocation between these courts, the inclusion of section 92 was bound to stir up the still deeper issue of the need for a proper unified family court. Attempts to amend the Children Bill so as to facilitate the creation of such a court were duly made, but they were resisted by the Government on the grounds that this was the wrong piece of legislation for the job, since it was concerned only with children, not families in general. What the Government did suggest was that the provisions creating concurrent jurisdiction between the three courts could be seen as a preliminary step towards the development of a more radical court structure, should the adoption of such a structure ever be deemed appropriate. By 1995, the Government's perception of its achievements had evidently changed because in a Parliamentary debate in that year the then Lord Chancellor said:

> The Children Act – particularly with its jurisdictional provisions – in effect set up a family court, because it allowed these proceedings to be taken either in the family proceedings court at the magistrates' level or in the county court, presided over by judges who have made special studies, and, finally, the Family Division. The result is that at every level one gets the necessary family jurisdiction.

This statement was, at best, misleading. By no stretch of the imagination can we be said to have a family court of the type for which campaigners have been so vigorously pressing for the past 20 years. The fact is that, while we may have concurrent jurisdiction, it is a jurisdiction that is shared by three completely different organizations, with different personnel, different processes and different traditions. As long as these different power structures endure, there will be problems for the family justice system in this country. The type of problem that can arise out of the present fragmented arrangements was well illustrated by the research study carried out by Dame Margaret Booth and published in 1996 (*Avoiding Delay in Children Act Cases*). She reported that 'in the majority of courts visited there was a marked lack of liaison between district judges and justices' clerks'. She also reported that 'many magistrates expressed disappointment that they had relatively little, if any, personal contact with the full-time judiciary'. The creation of a proper family court would not, of course, resolve all liaison and contact difficulties overnight. What it would do, however, is provide a more rational system for handling children's proceedings than the present fudge.

Appeals against court decisions

In the private area of child law, rights of appeal have always been available fairly extensively, and this position was preserved by the Children Act. In public law cases, however, there used to be major problems, caused mainly by defects in the Children and Young Persons Act 1969: local authorities, for example, lacked a right of appeal on the facts against the refusal by a juvenile court of a care order. Such problems were resolved by the 1989 Act in two ways. The first way arises out of the concurrent jurisdiction provisions of the Act, noted above. Care cases which are taken to the county court or the High Court automatically attract appeal procedures under the general courts legislation: an appeal can be made to the Court of Appeal. The second way has been to provide expressly for wide rights of appeal against any decision made by magistrates, including a decision to refuse an order. This is done by section 94 of the Act and the appeal will go to the High Court. The Children Act Advisory Committee's *Handbook of Best Practice in Children Act Cases* (1997) contains a section devoted to appeals from magistrates' courts (see section 6).

The right to appeal has for many years been regarded as one of the cornerstones of British justice and it is undoubtedly the case that the more extensive provisions of the Children Act on this matter have brought about an improvement in the overall situation. However, appealing a decision in a child's case may have the effect of inflicting further damage on him and his family. While litigation subsists, polarized positions are likely to persist. Making plans for the future may prove impossible. In addition, the child may well be subjected to further intrusive questioning and examination at the hands of well meaning professionals. The courts are alive to these difficulties and have laid down guidelines on appeals with the intention of discouraging unmeritorious (and expensive) applications. The guidelines are widely referred to as the '*G v G* guidelines' since it was in the 1985 case of that title that the House of Lords produced them. According to *G v G*, where the party appealing is questioning the exercise of discretion by the trial judge (or magistrates), the appeal court can intervene only if it is satisfied, not merely that the judge made a decision with which the court might reasonably disagree, but that his decision was so plainly wrong that the only legitimate conclusion is that he erred in the exercise of his discretion. Many children's cases turn on the exercise of discretion and the *G v G* test has been used on dozens of occasions over the years to reject appeals brought by discontented parties. A typical example is the case of *Re D* (1994), in which a county court judge had made residence orders in respect of three young girls in favour of their father. Dismissing the mother's appeal, Lady Justice Butler-Sloss acknowledged that it was a very difficult decision which might have gone either way. However:

> The judge took a considerable degree of care over it, and she has given valid reasons for the decision to which she came. Not only was she not plainly wrong, she was probably right. It is not for this court to say what we would have done had we been trying the case, but I think

it is probably what I would have done, but I do not know because, unlike the judge, I did not see and hear the witnesses and I do not have, as she had, the proper feel of the case of the judge at first instance. That is why the appellate court should not intervene unless it is obvious that the judge is wrong.

No appeal is possible from the making or refusal of an emergency protection order or any direction given under one (or an order extending or discharging an EPO). This is slightly misleading, however, because as we saw in Chapter 8, applications for discharge of an EPO are possible at the 72-hour point.

Protecting the child pending an appeal

As explained above, local authorities are able to appeal against a decision of a court refusing to sanction compulsory intervention. In some cases, the child concerned will already be subject to an interim order of some sort and therefore under the authority's wing. Section 40 of the Act allows the court to preserve this position pending an appeal by the authority. This power is exercisable where the court dismisses an application for a care order or a supervision order. The section also extends to cases where the court grants an application to discharge a care order or supervision order. It may order that its decision is not to have effect pending an appeal. When continuing the status quo, the court can attach conditions, so that in this respect it has a role in case management.

As is pointed out in Volume 1 of the DH Guidance, the continuation of proceedings by an appeal can be unsettling for the child: 'the court must continue to have regard to the presumption against making an order in section 1(5) and will need persuading that a pending-appeal order is required.'

13

Welfare reports and guardians ad litem

The development of the law concerning welfare reports in children's cases and the related matter of the appointment of guardians ad litem for children reveal many of the problems which have beset child law generally in modern times. The legislation in place before the Children Act was complicated and it arrived in a piecemeal and uncoordinated fashion. Underlying the haphazard advance of the law was the perennial problem of resources and the resulting need to prioritize issues in relation to the allocation of hard-pressed social work and legal personnel. From the social worker's point of view, the differences between providing a welfare report and acting as a guardian ad litem may often be ones of form only, rather than substance. In both situations, the social worker temporarily becomes an officer of the court, and the purpose of the appointment is the provision of an independent, objective and detailed analysis of the child's situation and prospects, judged by reference to the proposals being put before the court by the parties. Despite the similarity of function, however, it is necessary for present purposes to maintain a distinction between the two areas, because the applicable rules are different.

Welfare reports

The subject of welfare reports is governed by section 7 of the Children Act. This is a very simple provision. It enables a court which is considering 'any question with respect to a child under this Act' to ask for a report on such matters relating to the welfare of the child as are required to be dealt with. The request – which must, of course, be complied with – can be made either to a probation officer or to a local authority and an authority can arrange for any report to be compiled either by one of its social workers or else by a third party. A total of 35 400 reports were prepared during 1995.

The court's discretion

It can be seen that under this provision, the court has a discretion, not a duty, to order a welfare report. This is for the most part a repetition of the previous law.

When a report can be ordered

It can also be seen that the court is given the power to order a report in a wide range of situations: whenever it is considering a 'question with respect to a child under this Act'. In practice, it is used most frequently in 'private law' applications concerning section 8 orders and applications by unmarried fathers for parental responsibility. This is because the various 'public law' proceedings – applications for care orders, supervision orders, emergency protection orders, and so on – are subject to the separate guardian ad litem provisions of the Act (discussed below). The Court of Appeal has ruled that only in exceptional circumstances should a welfare officer be asked to assist once a guardian ad litem is involved in a case, because of the probable duplication of work (*Re S* (1992)).

The delivery of the report

Section 7(3) states that a welfare report may be made in writing or orally, as the court requires. Section 7(4) states that the court may take account of any statement contained in the report in so far as it is, in the court's opinion, relevant to the question which it is considering, whether or not it is consist-ent with the strict rules of evidence. According to the Law Commission, this emphasizes the fact that 'these are reports for the court and not evidence presented by one or other of the parties to the case'. Some concern was expressed in Parliament about the use of hearsay in welfare reports, and it was suggested that special safeguards should be built in, in fairness to the parties. In the event, the weight to be attached to such material was left to the court exercising its discretion.

The 1991 rules of court contain three specific provisions on reports. Under the first (rule 13(1)) the welfare officer is not obliged to attend a hearing at which the report is to be considered unless the court so directs. If the officer does attend, any party to the proceedings may question the officer about the report. Under the second (rule 13(2)) the welfare officer is to file a copy of any written report at or by such time as the court directs or, in the absence of a direction, at least 14 days before the relevant hearing; and the court should serve a copy of the report on the parties 'as soon as practicable'. This deadline will take its place in the timetable fixed by the court in accordance with section 11 of the Act.

The third relevant provision in the rules of court is designed to maintain the confidentiality of the report. Rule 23(1) states that no document (other than a record of an order) held by the court and relating to Children Act proceedings shall be disclosed other than to a party, the legal representative of a party, the guardian ad litem, the Legal Aid Board or a welfare officer, without the leave of the court. Welfare reports clearly fall within this rule, so that sanctions can be imposed if they are wrongfully disclosed.

When the court disagrees with the report

If the court reaches a decision which differs from that recommended by the welfare officer, reasons for the departure from the report should be given. This long-standing rule has been reaffirmed in the post-Children Act case law.

The limits of the welfare officer's function

The function of the court welfare officer is to advise the court as to the child welfare aspects of the case. The nature of this advice will, of course, be in part dependent upon the facts but where the facts are unclear – because, for example, they are contested by the parties – caution needs to be exercised. It is not the function of the officer to resolve disputed questions of fact. An example of the dangers lurking in this area was provided by the case of *Re T* (1994), a contested contact application in which the mother alleged sexual abuse on the part of the applicant father. The court welfare officer conducted separate interviews with the parents and proceeded to make specific findings as to their respective credibility. The judge commented:

> In a stark case where the fundamental issue is has the father sexually abused his son, I believe that welfare officers are wise to step back from the investigation and pre-determination of what is the fundamental issue for the judge. Of course it is helpful if they visit each parent, record their respective positions, make some assessment of the home, make an assessment of the relationship between the primary carer and the child, and assess the quality of care that the child is receiving, but it is not for welfare officers to assess adult credibility and conclude that the mother's allegations are well-founded and that the only effective issue is whether or not contact should be allowed.

Withholding information from the parties

The parties and their lawyers are normally entitled to see a welfare report, it being a fundamental principle of English law that the administration of justice should be open. However, case law has sanctioned the use of the court's discretion to admit material from a welfare officer in private, i.e. without disclosure to the parties or their lawyers. But the Court of Appeal has emphasized that admitting secret information in this way should be done only in the most exceptional circumstances, when the information appears reliable and withholding it is considered necessary to prevent real harm to the child whose welfare is in issue (*Re G* (1993)). The decision whether or not to disclose 'confidential' information emanating from a welfare officer belongs to the court. Welfare officers should not, therefore, give guarantees of confidentiality to persons who provide information to them during their enquiries.

The National Standards

The *National Standards for Probation Service Family Court Welfare Work* were issued by the Home Office in 1994. This document sets out 'basic standards of good practice which the Home Office expects of the family court welfare service'. It prescribes guidelines on matters such as directions appointments, mediation and the compilation of welfare reports. It states that reports should normally be filed with the court within ten weeks of the receipt of the case papers by the court welfare service.

Best Practice Guidance

In its Annual Report 1993/94 the Children Act Advisory Committee published a Best Practice Note for the judiciary and magistrates' courts when ordering a report under section 7. For convenience, this has been republished in the Committee's *Handbook of Best Practice in Children Act Cases* (1997). Further guidance was issued in the Committee's Annual Report 1994/95 on the question of the disclosure of medical experts' reports to a child's GP at the conclusion of a case.

Guardians ad litem

> Child: Remind me what you are called again. You are my . . . ?
> Guardian: Your guardian ad litem.
> Child: I thought you were my bodyguard.
> Guardian: Why do you think that?
> Child: Because you need a bodyguard in times of war!
> (Conversation with a child of 6 recorded in *The GALRO Service Annual Reports 1994–1995* (DH, 1995))

Background

Although the drafting of the Children Act met with general approbation, at least one distinguished Parliamentarian viewed the retention of the expression 'guardian ad litem' as regrettable, in that it is technical and legalistic and liable to be misunderstood by those members of the public not versed in Latin. The use of Latin terms is indeed a pernicious feature of the English legal system but it is probably the case that this particular term has become so firmly entrenched as to be irremovable.

The former GAL provisions of the Children Act 1975 (fully implemented only in 1984) represented a classic irrational fudge between the need to introduce second opinions in care and related proceedings and the need to go easy on scarce resources. Under these provisions, the appointment of a GAL was made possible but it was limited to cases in which there was or might be a conflict of interest, and even then it was left to the discretion of the court; the exercise of discretion, however, was weighted in the case of an unopposed application to discharge a care order or supervision order. GAL appointments were, in addition, linked in a complicated fashion to the questions of separate legal representation and legal aid provision for the child's parents.

When a guardian is appointed

Section 41 of the Children Act introduced a framework at once simpler and stronger than the previous one, the sort of framework which many wished to see on the statute book in the 1970s. The appointment of a GAL is mandatory in 'specified proceedings' unless the court is satisfied that an appointment is not necessary in order to safeguard the child's interests. The expression 'specified proceedings' is defined (partly by section 41 and partly by the 1991 rules of court) so as to cover the following:

(a) applications for a care order or supervision order
(b) family cases where the court has ordered (under section 37) the local authority to investigate the child's circumstances and has made, or is considering whether to make, an interim care order
(c) applications for the discharge of a care order or the variation or discharge of a supervision order
(d) applications by supervisors to extend a supervision order
(e) cases where the court is considering whether to make a residence order in respect of a child in care
(f) cases involving contact with a child in care
(g) applications under Part V of the Act (emergency protection orders and child assessment orders)

(h) appeals against decisions involving care orders or supervision orders and related decisions, and decisions involving child assessment orders
(i) applications for secure accommodation orders
(j) applications for leave to cause a child in care to be known by a new surname and applications for leave to remove such a child from the UK
(k) applications by local authorities to arrange for a child in care to live outside England and Wales
(l) appeals arising out of the applications mentioned in paragraphs (i), (j) and (k).

As a result of these provisions there has been a considerable increase in the number of GAL appointments. Although section 41 retains an element of discretion as to appointment, the emphasis is firmly directed towards GAL involvement. The Government's view, as expressed during the Parliamentary debates, was that 'the courts are unlikely to find many cases in which it would not be appropriate to appoint a guardian' (it thought that 'a straightforward case involving an older child who has already instructed his own solicitor' might not require a GAL). In the year ending 31 July 1996 about 8300 requests for a guardian were made by courts in England in specified proceedings.

There is no provision in the Children Act for panel guardians to be appointed in purely private law proceedings. In exceptional circumstances the county court or the High Court can order that the child be separately represented by the Official Solicitor (see page 241 below) or 'some other proper person', and the appointee will be known as the child's guardian ad litem, but the arrangements are completely different from those operative under section 41. However, as is indicated in paragraph (b) in the above-mentioned list, there is provision for a section 41 appointment in a hybrid private law/public law case where a court in family proceedings directs a local authority child protection investigation under section 37 of the Act. The special features of this type of appointment were considered by the High Court in the case of *Re CE* (1994). It was stated that when exercising the power to appoint a guardian under this particular provision the court should act cautiously. Careful consideration should be given both to the guardian's likely role and to the information which the court requires the guardian to provide. Appointment, it was said, should in no sense be automatic in cases where a section 37 investigation is directed: because the local authority's involvement in the family may only just have started, the guardian may have no real role to play. The court also considered the question of the duration of an appointment once made. It ruled that the proceedings cease to be 'specified proceedings' within the meaning of section 41 if the local authority, as a result of its investigation, decides not to apply for a care order or a supervision order and so informs the court. At this point, the guardian's role normally comes to an end.

The appointment process

The appointment of a GAL is governed by rule 10 of the 1991 rules of court. This provides that as soon as practicable after the commencement of 'specified proceedings' or the transfer of such proceedings to the court, the court is to appoint a guardian unless (a) such an appointment has already been made by the court which made the transfer or (b) the court considers that such an appointment is not necessary to safeguard the interests of the child. If an appointment is not made at the outset, it can be made at a later stage in the proceedings if considered appropriate.

Rule 10 goes on to prescribe classes of person who cannot act as guardian. This is an attempt to ensure the guardian's independence of the local authority. A GAL shall not (a) be a member, officer or employee of a local authority which is a party to the proceedings unless he or she is employed by the authority solely as a member of a GALRO panel; (b) be, or have been, a member, officer or employee of a local authority or voluntary organization who has been directly concerned in that capacity in arrangements relating to the care, accommodation or welfare of the child during the five years prior to the commencement of the proceedings; or (c) be a serving probation officer, except that a probation officer who has not in that capacity been previously concerned with the child or his family and who is employed part-time may act. Figures for the year ending 31 March 1995 indicated that of the 914 guardians then operating in England, about 6 per cent worked for a voluntary organization, 5 per cent were probation officers, 20 per cent were employed by a local authority and 70 per cent were fee-attracting sessional workers.

The powers and duties of a guardian

Section 41(2) of the Act states that the guardian shall be under a duty to 'safeguard the interests of the child'. This obligation is filled out by rule 11 of the 1991 rules of court. The functions listed in this rule, when considered alongside the range of 'specified proceedings', show very clearly how the role of the guardian under the Children Act is pivotal. The functions are as follows:

1 The GAL must appoint and instruct a solicitor to represent the child. This is dealt with separately below.
2 The child must be given such advice as is appropriate having regard to his understanding on all matters relevant to his interests which arise in the course of the proceedings.
3 The GAL is to attend all directions appointments and hearings, unless excused by the court.
4 The GAL is to advise the court on the following matters:

(a) whether the child is of sufficient understanding for any purpose, including the child's refusal to submit to a medical or psychiatric examination or other assessment that the court has power to order
(b) the wishes of the child in respect of any matter relevant to the proceedings, including his attendance at court
(c) the appropriate forum for the proceedings
(d) the appropriate timing of the proceedings
(e) the options available to the court in respect of the child and the suitability of each such option including what order should be made in determining the application
(f) any other matter concerning which the court seeks the GAL's advice or concerning which the GAL considers the court should be informed.

This advice can be given orally or in writing, subject to any order of the court, and any party may question the guardian about it.

5 The GAL shall, where practicable, notify any person whose participation as a party to the proceedings would be likely to safeguard the child's interests, of that person's right to apply to be joined. The court should be notified of the guardian's actions in this regard.

6 Not less than seven days before the date fixed for the final hearing of the proceedings, the GAL is to file a written report advising on the interests of the child (this obligation is subject to any contrary direction from the court). When a report is filed, the court is required to serve copies on the parties as soon as practicable.

7 In a case where no solicitor has been appointed, the GAL is to serve and accept documents in the proceedings on behalf of the child and, where the child has sufficient understanding, advise him of their contents.

8 The GAL is to make 'such investigations as may be necessary for him to carry out his duties'. In particular, the guardian must (a) contact or seek to interview such persons as he or she thinks appropriate or as the court directs; (b) if records are inspected under section 42 (see below) bring to the court's attention all such records and documents which may, in his or her opinion, assist in the proper determination of the proceedings; and (c) obtain such professional assistance as is available which is thought appropriate or which the court has directed.

9 The GAL is to provide to the court such other assistance as may be required.

In addition, it should be noted that rule 5 allocates a role to the guardian where an applicant wishes to withdraw an application. Under this rule, the court's permission is required before a withdrawal and such permission can be granted only after the guardian has been given an opportunity to make representations. Rule 11 states that in discharging all these functions, the guardian is to have regard to the 'no delay' principle contained in section

1(2) of the Act and also to the first six matters in the welfare checklist contained in section 1(3) (on which see page 35 above). In *Re M* (1994) the Court of Appeal observed that a guardian appointed in a secure accommodation case 'has to adapt his general duties to the specific requirements of the application before the court'. The court noted that there will inevitably be cases (and this was one) where the judge or magistrates consider that a final order has to be made without waiting for input from the guardian.

The appointment of a solicitor

As stated earlier, the rules of court require the GAL to appoint and instruct a solicitor to represent the child. This is not the only way in which a solicitor can be appointed, however. Section 41(3) of the Act contains express provisions enabling the court to do this if for some reason no guardian has been appointed, or if the child has sufficient understanding and expresses a wish to instruct a solicitor, or if it appears to the court that legal representation would be in the child's best interests. A solicitor can also be appointed by a child directly. The result, therefore, is that in 'specified proceedings' a solicitor may be drawn in to act for the child either on the initiative of the guardian, or on the initiative of the court, or on the initiative of the child himself.

Rule 12 of the rules of court is concerned with solicitors who are appointed by the GAL or by the court. Such a solicitor is to represent the child in accordance with instructions received from the GAL, except that if the solicitor considers that the child wishes to give instructions which conflict with those of the guardian and considers that he is able to give such instructions on his own behalf, the proceedings are to be conducted in accordance with them. In this type of situation, the role of the guardian must necessarily alter and rule 11 so provides: where it appears that the child is instructing his solicitor direct, the guardian should inform the court and thereafter is subject to its directions regarding the performance of the usual duties and participation in the proceedings. The rule enables the court to authorize legal representation – to be paid for by the local authority in charge of the GAL panel – for the guardian. (These provisions also apply in the exceptional case where the child intends to conduct the proceedings in person.) In the case of *Re M* (1993) the High Court stated that guardians must be alert from the outset to the possibility of a conflict between the guardian's recommendations and the views of the child. Should this situation arise, the guardian is advised to take an early opportunity to discuss the likely difficulties with the child's solicitor and bring the matter to the attention of the court and the other parties via a directions appointment. The court acknowledged that the circumstances in which it would either wish or be able to interfere with the decision of a child and his solicitor to seek separate representation from the guardian will be limited. If the court has appointed a solicitor but decided against a GAL, rule 12 requires the solicitor to represent the child in accordance with instructions received from him. If no instructions are forthcoming, the solicitor is to act 'in furtherance of the best interests of the child'.

The Final Report of the Children Act Advisory Committee (1997) disclosed that the Lord Chancellor's Department was conducting a review of the rule which requires the instruction of a solicitor by the GAL in every case. Official concern was said to centre not so much on the expenditure involved (though this is considerable) but on the increased delay generated by a surfeit of lawyers. The Committee suggested that a distinction might be made between the need for legal representation of the GAL at the trial of specified proceedings and such a need during an appeal. It pointed out that it is often possible for appeals to be conducted satisfactorily by joint counsel.

Termination of appointments

The termination of an appointment as GAL or solicitor before the end of a case may be necessary for one of a number of reasons (e.g. illness or conflict of interest), and rules 10 and 12 contain express provisions concerning both guardians and solicitors. Under rule 10, the appointment of a GAL is to continue for such time as is specified by the court or until terminated by it; under rule 12, solicitors appointed by a GAL or the court can have their appointment brought to an end by the court. In each case the person concerned must be given reasons for the decision. If the solicitor has been instructed by the child direct, the child can terminate the arrangement in the same way as any other private client.

Access to records and evidence

Section 42 of the Act was designed to remove doubts about the right to inspect local authority records. It authorizes a GAL to examine and take copies of all relevant material relating to the child held by a local authority (this does not mean just the authority involved in the GAL's case). An amendment to the Act by the Courts and Legal Services Act 1990 extended this power so that it covers records held by the NSPCC, and the Children's Homes Regulations 1991 make similar provision regarding records held by voluntary homes and private children's homes.

Section 42 goes on to state that any records copied by the GAL will be admissible as evidence in the proceedings. This relaxation of the normal evidential rules, which is encountered in other parts of the legislation, shows how the need to protect the interests of the child has been given primacy. It should be read alongside the provisions of section 41(11), which allow the court to take account of any statement contained in a guardian's report and any evidence given in respect of the matters referred to in it, in so far as the statement or evidence is in the court's opinion relevant. It can be seen that this last rule is identical to the one pertaining to welfare reports, noted earlier in this chapter.

Disclosing and withholding information

The issue of confidentiality has featured prominently in the post-Children Act case law, and the position of GALs, like that of other professionals, has come under scrutiny. A significant ruling was delivered in the case of *Oxfordshire County Council v P* (1995). There, care proceedings were commenced by a local authority following a diagnosis of non-accidental injury to a baby. The guardian interviewed the parents and in the course of the interview the mother confided to the guardian that she had become distraught by the baby's constant crying after he had been immunized the previous day and had thrown him repeatedly onto a bed and possibly onto the wooden edge of a changing unit. The guardian immediately informed the local authority as well as the child's solicitor. The local authority was working on the case with the police and it informed the police of the mother's admission to the guardian. The police then interviewed the guardian and obtained a witness statement from her. Criminal proceedings were instituted against the mother. The mother made an application in the care proceedings for the removal of the guardian, claiming that she had lost confidence in her following the guardian's dealings with the police. In granting this application, the High Court ruled as follows:

1 Under the 1991 rules of court, a guardian's report is confidential and must not be disclosed to third parties without the leave of the court. If such a report attracts confidentiality, it must be a necessary inference that the information collected by the guardian for the purpose of preparing the report must equally enjoy confidentiality. It would be absurd to rule that information coming to the guardian's knowledge could be freely and widely published outside the proceedings before it had been committed to writing and made a document in the proceedings.
2 Consequently, the guardian acted incorrectly in making a witness statement to the police without having first obtained the leave of the court.
3 However, the guardian was not at fault in disclosing the mother's admission to the local authority: 'the cloak of confidentiality is not lifted when there is an exchange of information relating to the proceedings passing between the parties in the proceedings if the information remained confidential'. In other words, since the local authority was a party to the care proceedings, disclosure of the information to it was permitted by the 1991 rules of court.

In the later case of *Re C* (1995) the High Court considered the position concerning non-disclosure of information to a party more – specifically, the making of a confidential report to the court. The general rule, of course, is that GAL reports are to be made available to all of the parties. In that case, the guardian received information from the child (who was 16 and very disturbed) which the child did not want passed on to her mother. The guardian sought directions from the court which ruled as follows:

1 It can never be proper for a GAL to promise a child that information disclosed by the child will not be communicated to the court. A guardian cannot make promises of complete confidentiality.
2 The court may in its discretion restrict disclosure of information to the relevant party's lawyer.
3 In any event, it is essential that any party to whom information is not to be revealed should have the opportunity of making representations to the court.
4 In deciding whether or not to authorize secrecy, the court will act cautiously, starting from a presumption in favour of disclosure; but it will attach importance to the likelihood of harm resulting from disclosure.
5 The question of non-disclosure should be dealt with in the High Court.
6 On the facts, it was of vital importance that the child maintain links with, and faith in, the GAL and the local authority's social workers. The court was satisfied that disclosure would most probably result in harm to the child and therefore the GAL would be given permission to deal with the information in question in a confidential supplementary report.

The limits of the guardian's function

In *B v B* (1993) the High Court criticized a GAL who had ventured an opinion on the likelihood of sexual abuse having occurred. It stated that in a case where whether or not abuse has occurred is in issue, the issue itself is for the court, not the GAL, to decide: 'the guardian should present to the court a fair and balanced assessment of the factors which seem material and point in either direction, and base his or her recommendations on alternative premises, namely whether a finding of abuse is to be made or not'. The same approach has been adopted in relation to reports by welfare officers in private law proceedings (see page 229 above).

GAL panels

Section 41(7) of the Act enables the DH to issue regulations providing for 'the establishment of panels of persons from whom guardians ad litem must be selected' and this power was exercised by the making of the Guardians ad Litem and Reporting Officers (Panels) Regulations 1991. These regulations were supplemented by Volume 7 of the DH Children Act Guidance. It is not proposed to set out here the detailed provisions of the panels regulations. Their main thrust, however, can be appreciated by referring to the explanatory note which was appended to them:

> These regulations make provision for the establishment of panels of guardians ad litem and reporting officers by local authorities; complaints boards and panel committees; appointments to panels; termination of panel membership; complaints about the operation of the panels and members of the panels; administration of panels; panel committee functions; expenses, fees and allowances of panel members; monitoring the work of guardians; training.

The DH Guidance is concerned with the management of panels. Issues addressed include the following:

1 The role of the panel manager.
2 Panel committees, whose general functions are to assist with liaison between the local authority and the courts and to give advice on specific matters.
3 Expenses, fees and allowances of GALs. On this, the Guidance states that guardians need to judge the extent of enquiries necessary in each individual case to which they are appointed: 'if there is uncertainty as to whether the work proposed by the GAL is appropriate and necessary, then the proper channel for this to be clarified is likely to be through the directions hearing'.
4 Appointment, reappointment and termination of appointment of panel members.
5 Case allocation. The Guidance recommends that where possible, the initial selection of a GAL should be undertaken by the manager on the grounds that this will allow the most effective deployment of panel resources and will facilitate improved matching between the needs of the case and the skills or other attributes (e.g. race and gender) of particular GALs.
6 Monitoring, review of guardians' work, training and complaints. The complaints board which has to be maintained under the regulations is quite separate from the 'representations' machinery regulated by section 26 of the Act. The remit of the board is confined to complaints arising out of the operation of the GALRO service.

Emergency protection order cases

The DH Guidance contains a discrete section on arrangements in emergency protection order cases. The extension of the GAL system to EPOs was recognized as a potentially troublesome feature of the Children Act, so this special treatment was fully justified. The Guidance reminds authorities that it is necessary to have in place arrangements to ensure the immediate appointment of a guardian where an EPO has been applied for. However, 'the court's expectations of the GAL service where the initial application is being dealt with are likely to be limited'. On appointment, the guardian will be required to undertake whatever duties are practicable in the time available, and the Guidance invites panel managers and justices' clerks to 'clarify expectations' of guardians, should a challenge to an order be made at the 72-hour point. As late as 1995, there was evidence of continuing difficulties surrounding the appointment of guardians in EPO cases (*The GALRO Service Annual Reports 1994/1995* (DH, 1995)).

Attendance at child protection conferences and reviews

While it can readily be appreciated how the status and experience of a guardian can enhance the quality of discussion at a child protection conference, there is an obvious danger of the guardian placing in jeopardy his or her independence. The matter is the subject of explicit DH guidance, contained in *Working Together* (1991):

> Since their duty is to represent the interests of the child in court proceedings, it should be exceptional for GALs to take part in child protection except in the case of a child protection conference following an application for an EPO or interim care order, when it might be helpful for them to be present as part of the process of gathering information for the court. The GAL would be present as an observer, not a participant, given his/her position as an officer of the court.

Further guidance, this time from the judiciary, has emerged in the case of *Re M* (1995). Mr Justice Wall stated:

> In my judgment this case demonstrates the need in public law cases for the local authority to keep the guardian ad litem fully informed of its actions. This means that the guardian should be notified of all important case conferences and given the option to attend. Whether or not guardians attend such conferences must be a matter for their professional judgment and discretion. There may, for example, be occasions when the guardian feels that to attend a case conference may compromise his or her independent status in the eyes of the parents. There are also other occasions when the decision-making process of the local authority is in operation and it would be inappropriate for the guardian to attend its deliberations, even as an observer.

But guardians ad litem are enjoined by the rules to safeguard and promote the welfare of the child: they are the child's protection against bad or inappropriate social work practice. It is therefore vital that the local authority keeps them fully informed of its actions, and gives them the opportunity to attend statutory reviews and important case conferences.

The National Standards

In 1995 the DH issued a 21-page document entitled *National Standards for the Guardian ad Litem and Reporting Officer Service*. It stated that the standards 'build on existing statutory requirements, guidance and good professional practice'. Fourteen separate standards were published, covering the responsibilities of local authorities, panel managers, panel committees and individual guardians. Like other national standards (e.g. those relating to court welfare officers), the language employed is often less than precise and as the document itself acknowledges, it has no legal force.

The Official Solicitor

According to section 41(8) of the Children Act, the provisions of the section concerning panels 'shall not be taken to prejudice the power of the Lord Chancellor to confer or impose duties on the Official Solicitor'. The effect of this rather terse statement was to retain the Official Solicitor as a player in public law proceedings under the Act. The Official Solicitor (OS) – part civil servant, part judicial officer – and his staff occupy an anomalous but well established position in our family justice system. Their involvement has been felt most keenly in wardship cases, although the expansive nature of their functions has been such as to make their appearance possible in many other types of High Court litigation.

One week before the Children Act was implemented, the Lord Chancellor issued a practice direction setting out the role of the Official Solicitor in proceedings instituted under it. The main thrust of the direction is that in 'specified proceedings' in the High Court, the OS can be appointed guardian ad litem if the following conditions are satisfied:

(a) the child concerned does not have a GAL in the proceedings; and
(b) there are exceptional circumstances which make it desirable in the interests of the welfare of the child concerned that the OS, rather than a member of a panel, should be appointed having regard to (i) any foreign elements in the case which would be likely to require the GAL to make enquiries, or take other action, outside the jurisdiction of the court; (ii) the likely burden on the GAL where several children are to

be represented; (iii) the existence of proceedings relating to the child in any other Division of the High Court in which the OS is representing the child; and (iv) any other relevant circumstances.

If the appointment is made, then the usual GAL functions (as set out in the Act and the rules of court) apply, with the exception of the duty to appoint a solicitor.

Further guidance issued after the implementation of the Act clarified the exceptional circumstances in which the OS will agree to act on behalf of a child in non-specified (i.e. private law) Children Act proceedings in the county court or the High Court:

- there is conflicting or controversial medical evidence
- the child is ignorant of the truth as to his parentage, or is refusing contact with a parent in circumstances which point to the need for psychiatric assessment
- the case involves a substantial foreign element
- the case involves difficult or exceptional points of law
- the OS is already representing the child in other current proceedings
- there are unusual or complicating features, such as where one parent has killed the other, or is a transsexual.

A practice note issued in 1995 summarizes the various functions of the OS in relation to children's cases and includes a questionnaire to be completed prior to his inquiries. The text of this note has been published in the Children Act Advisory Committee's *Handbook of Best Practice in Children Act Cases* (1997). Volume 7 of the DH Children Act Guidance refers briefly to the functions of the Official Solicitor. It states that the frequent use of experts such as paediatricians and child psychiatrists in High Court proceedings has afforded the OS an opportunity to have access to such specialists nationwide, and their knowledge will be of value to panel GALs. Panel managers are invited to establish liaison links between their panel and the OS, so that panel guardians may have access to such specialists if the need arises in a particular case.

Beyond the Children Act: the future of child welfare reporting

The need for an independent source of advice and assistance for the courts in children's proceedings has been clearly established over recent years. This need has been accepted even in relation to cases brought by local authorities, where an intelligent onlooker might be forgiven for thinking that, since such authorities are charged by statute with acting in the best interests of the children concerned, no further 'independent' advice could possibly be required. The aftermath of the Maria Colwell tragedy in 1973 put paid to such thinking.

But if the need for child welfare reports is beyond argument, how satisfactory are the present arrangements for their delivery? How easy would it be to explain to our intelligent onlooker that, depending on the circumstances, a court will receive its advice and assistance from a probation officer, a social worker employed by a local authority social services department or a voluntary organization, a self-employed social worker, or a London-based civil servant? In many ways, the present chaotic arrangements mirror the fragmented nature of the court system itself. If, as many believe, a unified family court would be a way of making the Children Act even more successful, a unified court welfare service would be a natural complement to such a development. Pressure for change along these lines has been maintained ever since the Children Act was passed, not least from the panel GAL sector, where the close financial and organizational links with social services departments are understandably regarded as a drag on guardians' sense of independence. This issue, like the family court question, will not go away. The next opportunity for prolonged official scrutiny will probably occur when the keenly awaited Adoption Bill is presented to Parliament, and it may be that in the wake of those reforms the courts' welfare services will finally receive the shake-up they require.

14

Wardship and the inherent jurisdiction of the High Court

Introduction

The existence and modern development of the High Court's wardship jurisdiction made life difficult for those seeking a full understanding of English child law because it always added an extra dimension to whatever legislative activity was taking place. The boundaries of wardship were fixed for the most part by the judges, and the unhappy result was development of the law along two distinct channels: one in Parliament (legislation) and one in the courts (wardship). The benefits of wardship are well known. The case is handled by a senior professional judge and its outcome will be dictated, not by the application of rigid statutory criteria but simply by what is in the child's best interests. In addition, the range of orders available to the judge is virtually limitless. During the 1970s and 1980s, local authorities – urged on by the judges – became increasingly aware of these attractive features and it is hardly surprising that many of them turned to wardship in preference to the widely criticized care jurisdiction of the juvenile courts. By 1989 local authorities were involved in 62 per cent of wardship cases, in contrast to the 1971 figure of 3 per cent. The principal object of the Children Act was to replace the numerous and chaotic statutory jurisdictions concerning children with a coherent and properly integrated framework, both in the private law and the public law spheres. In these circumstances, the question inevitably arose: what should be done with wardship? One answer would have been to abolish it completely, leaving litigants to obtain what they could from the statute. Parliament, following the advice of the Law Commission, did not go this far. The argument seemed to be that, while the Children Act was indeed bringing in a completely new set of procedures and orders, not every contingency might have been foreseen. Wardship should therefore be retained for those exceptional cases which slipped through the statutory net.

However, what the Act did do was to impose restrictions on the use of wardship by or in favour of local authorities (as opposed to private individuals). This was done because the Government believed that the new public law framework concerning care and supervision orders was sufficiently comprehensive, and that in any event State intervention should be strictly controlled by express statutory provisions. These restrictions are contained in section 100 of the Act, whose overall thrust is clear: where a statutory procedure is available to a local authority, that procedure, rather than wardship, must be used. This underlying notion of wardship as a fallback device has been adopted by the judiciary in the private law field.

The inherent jurisdiction of the High Court

The provisions of the Children Act tend to refer, not to wardship, but to 'the inherent jurisdiction of the High Court'. This continues to be a source of considerable confusion. Before the Act, practitioners – both legal and non-legal – had seldom, if ever, used this expression, nor had Parliament when enacting children's legislation. Indeed, many lawyers were unaware of the existence of an inherent jurisdiction. The reason for the change in terminology was as follows. The team of government lawyers which drew up the 1989 Act was of the opinion that wardship was simply a part, albeit a major part, of the High Court's ancient non-statutory (i.e. inherent) jurisdiction over children. On this view of the law, a child can be the subject of High Court intervention without actually being warded. The unique effect of wardship is that no important step affecting the child can be taken without the court's consent. This element of continuing court supervision does not apply in cases where the inherent jurisdiction is exercised without the child being warded. It follows that the High Court's inherent jurisdiction can be invoked *either* by making a child a ward of court *or* by making an application to the High Court outside the wardship procedure. The wording of the Children Act reflects this view of the law.

Public law cases: the effect of section 100

The restrictions imposed on local authorities by section 100 are twofold. The first is that the High Court is not able to use its inherent jurisdiction (this includes wardship, of course) to place a child in local authority care, or to put a child under local authority supervision, or to confer on any local authority the power to decide any issue concerning an aspect of parental responsibility for a child (section 100(2)). What this means is that if a local authority wishes to take over or retain the care of a child, or wants a supervision order, or wishes to assume some aspect of parental authority, it is obliged to use the compulsory intervention procedures established by

Parts IV and V of the Act (described in Chapters 7–11). This, of course, involves the local authority in proving grounds for an order. Furthermore, if a care order is made, the local authority assumes general control of the management of the case in accordance with the provisions of Part IV. The power of the wardship court to give directions simply does not arise. The Act reinforces this point by stating that no child in care may be made a ward of court (section 100(2)(c)).

The second restriction is that in any event a local authority is unable to apply for any exercise of the inherent jurisdiction without the leave of the court (section 100(3)). Leave may be granted only if the court is satisfied that there is no statutory procedure available to the authority to achieve its objective and that there is reasonable cause to believe that if the jurisdiction is not exercised the child concerned is likely to suffer significant harm (section 100(4)). This restriction has kept the door slightly ajar for local authority cases but stringent conditions have been imposed. The significant harm criterion harks back to Part IV of the Act and reflects the need to control State intervention. Applications for care orders and supervision orders obviously do not fall within this gap because of the first restriction noted above; nor do orders which give the local authority power to decide some issue of parental responsibility, for the same reason.

What, then, is left? There is in fact no fixed list of situations in which local authorities are free to use the inherent jurisdiction (subject to leave). Indeed, the open-ended nature of the jurisdiction precludes this. The first reported case in which section 100 featured was *In re W*, decided by the Court of Appeal in July 1992. This was in many ways an appropriate debut for the new provisions because the exceptional nature of the facts of the case chimed with the residual role carved out for the inherent jurisdiction. The child involved was 15 years old (16 by the time of the appeal), in local authority care under a care order, and suffering from anorexia nervosa. The local authority, having realized that it might become necessary to arrange for medical treatment against the child's wishes, applied under section 100 for leave to move her to a named health establishment without her consent and leave to administer medical treatment without her consent. In its judgment, the Court of Appeal confirmed that the powers of the High Court under its inherent jurisdiction are 'theoretically limitless'; more specifically, it confirmed that the High Court has power to override the refusal of a child – of any age – to undergo medical treatment. It agreed with the High Court that on the facts of this case, it was in the child's best interests for the local authority to be given the authorizations it was seeking. The reasons why the local authority decided to invoke the inherent jurisdiction in W's case were probably twofold: first, there were at that time doubts about an authority's power to provide a valid medical consent in respect of a child in care who was objecting (case law has since resolved these doubts – see page 178 above); second, a specific issue order under the Children Act cannot be made in respect of a child in care (section 9(1) of the Act) and so that Act did not seem to provide a way out of the problem. On the evidence, there was reasonable cause to believe that if the court's inherent jurisdiction was not exercised, W was likely to suffer significant harm. Accordingly, the conditions prescribed by section 100(4) were satisfied.

In the wake of *In re W* came the High Court's decision in *South Glamorgan County Council v W* (1992). Here, a disturbed child of 15 was the subject of an interim care order. The court had given directions under section 38(6) of the Children Act for the child to be assessed at a psychiatric unit but the child refused to comply with the directions. The court was then invited by the local authority to exercise its inherent jurisdiction by making an order authorizing the forcible removal of the child from her father's house to the unit in question. The court granted this order, even though the child was considered to have sufficient understanding and even though section 38(6) appears to give such a child an absolute veto. As in all cases under the inherent jurisdiction, the judge acted in what he thought was the child's best interests (though not surprisingly his decision attracted criticism from the children's rights lobby). Other section 100 applications brought before the courts since 1991 have ranged well beyond the field of medical treatment. They include the following:

Re DB and CB (1993)

A local authority commenced care order proceedings in respect of a child of 16 months. On the same day, but before the papers had been served on the parents, the child was taken abroad by a relative and handed over to her grandparents. The High Court nevertheless made an interim care order and under the inherent jurisdiction made an order directing the parents to bring about the return of the child to the UK.

Re O (1993)

Following the contested adoption of two of their children, the birth parents camped outside the home of the adopters and took photographs and video recordings. On the application of the local authority which had acted as an adoption agency, the High Court granted injunctions against the birth parents ordering them to keep away from the children. (The adopters themselves could have invoked the inherent jurisdiction on these facts but they were reluctant to become directly involved in litigation.)

Re S (1993)

The High Court granted an injunction excluding the father of four children from the family home. He had been found to have sexually abused his step-child and he was considered to pose an unacceptably high risk to the children as long as he lived with them. It should be noted that under sections 38A and 44A of the Children Act (brought into force in 1997), it is now possible for the courts to achieve this sort of result by attaching an exclusion requirement to an emergency protection order or an interim care order. Those sections, however, contain fairly tight requirements which will not be satisfied in all cases. In *Re S*, for example, the ouster order was opposed by both parents, a factor which would probably rule out an exclusion requirement. See further, pages 137 and 205 above.

Re X (1994)

This case concerned a child who had been adopted. The Court of Appeal made an order that during the minority of the child the Registrar General should not disclose to any person without the leave of the court the details of the adoption entered in the Adopted Children Register. The application to court was made by the local authority which had acted as an adoption agency, following the receipt of information suggesting that the child's birth mother might seek to trace the child and disrupt the placement.

Private law cases

The provisions of section 100 are concerned only with cases in which a local authority is involved. It follows that, as far as the Children Act is concerned, private individuals (e.g. parents) are free to use the inherent jurisdiction to resolve their disputes as and when they please. Proceedings under this jurisdiction are classified as 'family proceedings' for the purposes of the Act, which means that section 8 orders can be made by the court at its discretion (under section 10) and that the court can direct the relevant local authority to undertake a child protection investigation (under section 37) if it appears that it may be appropriate for a care or supervision order to be made with respect to the child. A family assistance order can also be made (under section 16).

Although the 1989 Act has certainly not prohibited the use of the inherent jurisdiction in private law situations, the existence of the carefully crafted provisions contained in Part II of the Act relating to section 8 orders (see Chapters 3 and 4) does at the very least suggest that private individuals should think twice before calling upon the scarce resources of the Family Division of the High Court. This is clearly the view of the judiciary, which has emphasized the need to look to the Children Act first whenever litigation is being considered. In the important case of *Re T* (1993) – discussed on page 56 above – the Court of Appeal stated:

> The courts' undoubted discretion to allow wardship proceedings to go forward in a suitable case is subject to their clear duty, in loyalty to the

scheme and purpose of the Children Act legislation, to permit recourse to wardship only when it becomes apparent to the judge in any particular case that the question which the court is determining in regard to the minor's upbringing or property cannot be resolved under the statutory procedures in Part II of the Act in a way which secures the best interests of the child; or where the minor's person is in a state of jeopardy from which he can only be protected by giving him the status of a ward of court; or where the court's functions need to be secured from the effects, potentially injurious to the child, of external influences (intrusive publicity for example) and it is decided that conferring on the child the status of a ward will prove a more effective deterrent than the ordinary sanctions of contempt of court which already protect all family proceedings.

The effect of this ruling was to reserve the inherent jurisdiction for exceptional situations. An example of such a situation is provided by the case of *Re W* (1995), in which the father of four boys had made them wards of court in the course of an acrimonious dispute with their mother. After a long series of court hearings and provocative actions (including the publication of an article in a national newspaper) the father applied for the wardship to be brought to an end. The Court of Appeal rejected his application. It acknowledged that the wardship should be continued only if it offered advantages to the children which could not be secured by use of the orders available under the Children Act but it found such advantages here: first, the 'important steps' rule (see page 245 above) would ensure continuing court supervision of the children's upbringing by the father, and second, the Official Solicitor as continuing guardian ad litem for the children (see page 241 above) would be in a position to act as a buffer between the parents. He would also be in a position to take action to protect the children if this became necessary. The court went on to issue an injunction against the father restricting his ability to give interviews and information about the proceedings to the press and broadcasting media.

The decline of the inherent jurisdiction

The dramatic effect of the Children Act, particularly section 100, on the inherent jurisdiction was evidenced by judicial statistics assembled by the Children Act Advisory Committee in its Annual Report 1992/93. These revealed that the number of wardship applications made over the period 1988–1992 was as follows: 1988: 3704; 1989: 4327; 1990: 4721; 1991: 4961; 1992: 492.

15

Care outside the local authority sector

Anyone casting an eye over the Children Act will notice that a substantial proportion of it is concerned with care outside the local authority sector. To be specific, there are sections or groups of sections (together with supplementary Schedules) covering the following matters:

1 Voluntary homes (Part VII of the Act).
2 Private children's homes (Part VIII).
3 Private fostering (Part IX).
4 Child minding and day care for the under-eights (Part X).
5 Independent boarding schools (section 87).

These provisions superseded the rules previously contained in the Nurseries and Child-Minders Regulation Act 1948, the Foster Children Act 1980, the Child Care Act 1980 and the Children's Homes Act 1982. It is not proposed to analyse here the rules concerning these subjects. This is partly for reasons of space and partly because many of the provisions are technical and uncontroversial and to an extent a repeat performance of the previous law. What can be said about the provisions by way of general commentary, however, is that a number of themes clearly bind them together. There will be found in most, though not all, of the sections covering the above topics rules relating to:

1 Relevant definitions (e.g. 'voluntary home', 'privately fostered child', 'child minder').
2 The requirement to register or notify.
3 The power of the registering authority to impose requirements.
4 The cancellation of registration or the imposition of a prohibition.
5 The local authority's duty to satisfy itself that the child's welfare is being satisfactorily safeguarded and promoted.
6 The local authority's power to enter and inspect the premises.
7 Restrictions on who may be involved in the care of children.

8 The criminal liability of those who fail to register, breach requirements or prohibitions, or obstruct inspections.
9 Appeals against adverse decisions.

In each case, the rules in the Act have been supplemented by regulations and DH guidance. Although local authority involvement is to a large extent of a regulatory nature, two provisions in the Act require the authority to go further. The first is section 19. This imposes a duty on every authority to review periodically child minding and day care provision for the under-eights in its area. This complements the authority's duty to review its own day care facilities provided under section 18 (see page 73 above). The second provision is section 24, which is concerned with aftercare. The contents of this section are discussed in Chapter 6 from the perspective of children accommodated by local authorities. The important point for present purposes, however, is that the 'target group' also comprises those people under 21 who after the age of 16 spent time in voluntary sector accommodation, in a private children's home, or in a private foster home. The local authority's function of advising, befriending, etc. extends to members of these groups, although there is a duty (as opposed to a discretion) only in relation to those leaving voluntary sector accommodation. Furthermore, an extra condition is inserted to the effect that the authority must be satisfied that the person or organization which provided the accommodation does not have the necessary facilities for advising or befriending. To facilitate the provision of aftercare there is an obligation on the part of voluntary organizations and private homes to inform the local authority when a child over 16 leaves their care (this will be the authority within whose area the child proposes to live).

Children accommodated in hospitals, nursing homes and schools

In its White Paper which preceded the Children Act, the DH expressed concern about the welfare of children accommodated for long spells in hospitals or nursing homes and children placed in residential schools by education departments. There was evidence that significant numbers of such children were losing contact with their families. To meet this concern, sections 85 and 86 were included in the Act. They require the relevant social services department to be notified of the child's situation by any health authority, NHS trust, education department, residential care home, nursing home or mental nursing home which is providing him with accommodation for a consecutive period of three months or more. Upon notification, the SSD must take such steps as are reasonably practicable to enable it to determine whether the child's welfare is being adequately safeguarded and promoted. It must also consider whether it should exercise any of its functions under the Act (e.g. support functions under Part III). The DH

Children Act Guidance (Volumes 4 and 6) suggests that initial enquiries of the accommodating institution be undertaken within 14 days of notification.

When the child leaves such accommodation, the SSD must be informed. If the child is over 16, he becomes 'a person qualifying for advice and assistance' for the purposes of the aftercare provisions in section 24 of the Act. The accommodating authority or home must accordingly inform the SSD within whose area the child proposes to live.

Refuges for runaways

Section 51 of the Act contains provisions regulating safe houses for runaway children. The section enables the DH to issue a certificate covering a voluntary home, a private children's home or foster carers working for a voluntary organization (or local authority), where it is intended by one of these methods to operate a refuge 'for children who appear to be at risk of harm'. While a certificate is in force, those running the home or the foster carers (as the case may be) are immune from prosecution under various named child abduction and child harbouring statutes.

Section 51 is supplemented by the Refuges (Children's Homes and Foster Placements) Regulations 1991. These prescribe the conditions which must be complied with by organizations which have been granted a certificate. There is also DH guidance contained in Volume 4 of the Children Act series.

The impact of section 51 in the field has been extremely limited. In April 1997 there were only four certificated refuges in the country, a depressingly low figure given the size of the problem.

16

Adoption

The general impact of the Children Act

One of the most welcome features of the Children Act was its all-embracing 'fresh start' approach, whereby all of the basic rules concerning statutory children's procedures were set out in a self-contained package. Unhappily, this approach did not extend to the adoption procedure. On adoption, the Act did not set out the basic rules – these remain as stated in the Adoption Act 1976 – but it proceeded, in Schedule 10, to introduce a number of amendments to these rules. In addition, some parts of the 1976 Act were repealed (by Schedule 15). The result was a rather unintelligible mishmash of provisions. To be fair, this was probably unavoidable. The Children Act was not designed to reform adoption law; after all, comprehensive change had been brought about in 1975 following the review carried out by the Houghton Committee. But amendments to it were inevitable if the custody and care jurisdictions were to be altered, due to the various links between them. Having said this, some of the amendments were inserted, not through necessity, but in order to correct deficiencies in the 1976 Act detected by the Department of Health during the 1980s.

The reform of adoption law

The various amendments to adoption legislation effected by the Children Act were essentially stop-gap measures. While the Act was being passed by Parliament, the Government announced that the whole area of adoption law was to be the subject of a full-scale review. An inter-departmental working party was established to 're-examine adoption law, policy and practice with a view to the formulation of proposals for new legislation which will reflect the developments in practice and changes in related legislation which have taken place since the last review following the Houghton Committee in 1972'. Four discussion papers prepared by the working party were issued during 1991 and 1992 (*The Nature and Effect of Adoption, Agreement and Freeing, The Adoption Process* and *Intercountry Adoption*) and these were followed by a Report to Ministers in October 1992. It had been suggested to the working party that changes to adoption law should not be made until more time had been allowed to consider the effects of the Children Act, but this suggestion was rejected. In the event, however, such a postponement became a reality. Despite the publication of a White Paper in November 1993 (*Adoption: The Future*) and the publication of a draft Adoption Bill in March 1996 (*Adoption – A Service for Children*), the Conservative government appeared unwilling to place firm proposals before Parliament. The incoming Labour Administration was committed to the principle of adoption law reform but no mention of legislation was made in the Queen's Speech of May 1997. This means that when an Adoption Bill is eventually introduced, more than six years will have elapsed since the implementation of the Children Act. The Adoption Act 1976 may well remain in force for the rest of the century. This tortuous road to reform will doubtless seem familiar to those practitioners who remember the history of the Houghton proposals of the 1970s.

The amendments made by Schedule 10

Some of the amendments made by Schedule 10 were purely technical and have had little significance in practice. Those worthy of note are as follows:

- The formal effect of an adoption order is now to vest parental responsibility for the child in the adopters, as opposed to 'the parental rights and duties'. As was seen in Chapter 2, the latter expression has been dropped from children's legislation although rights and duties do, of course, feature in the definition of parental responsibility.
- An adoption order extinguishes the parental responsibility of any person who had it prior to the order. The order also extinguishes any order previously made under the Children Act.
- The normal minimum age limit for married applicants remains at 21. However, where one of the applicants is a birth parent of the child, the limit for that parent is now 18 (section 14(1B) of the Adoption Act).
- The statutory ground for dispensing with parental agreement due to persistent failure to discharge the parental duties now refers to a persistent failure to discharge parental responsibility (section 16(2) of the Adoption Act).
- Under section 18(2) of the Adoption Act, an application to free a child for adoption may be made where the agency is applying for dispensation of the birth parents' agreement and the child 'is in the care of' the agency. Schedule 10 restricts this procedure to local authorities holding a care

order in respect of the child. This type of freeing application is therefore unavailable in cases where the child is being looked after on a voluntary basis. Here we have yet another illustration of the way in which the Children Act confines compulsory State intervention to the care order jurisdiction. It should be noted, however, that if one of the parents consents, a freeing application can be made in respect of an accommodated child.

- A freeing order now vests parental responsibility in the agency instead of 'the parental rights and duties'.
- Section 22 of the Adoption Act requires a minimum of three months notice to be given to the local authority in the case of a non-agency application for adoption. In order to deal with stale cases, Schedule 10 has introduced a maximum period of notice: such an application shall not be made unless the person wishing to make the application has, within the period of two years preceding the making of the application, given notice. This links in with an amendment which has been made to the definition of a 'protected child', for such a status now ceases two years after the giving of a section 22 notice if no adoption application has been made. The significance of this for social services departments is that no further welfare supervision need be undertaken; indeed, the case can be regarded as closed.
- Birth records counselling – mandatory for those adopted before 12 November 1975 – may now be provided by organizations other than those (British-based ones) mentioned in section 51 of the Adoption Act if the applicant is not living in the UK.
- An Adoption Contact Register has been set up by the Registrar General (new section 51A of the Adoption Act). This is a computerized service designed to assist those adopted persons and their birth relatives (i.e. persons who are related by blood – including half-blood – or marriage) who desire to establish contact with each other. The Register is in two parts: Part I for adopted persons and Part II for relatives. Anybody within these categories who is over 18 and possesses a sufficient amount of relevant information can, on payment of a fee, enter himself or herself on the appropriate part. Once an adopted person and a relative of his appear on the Register, the Registrar General transmits the latter's name and address to the former. The address may not be the relative's own address. As the Minister of Health explained in 1989:

> Many relatives will no doubt be happy to give their own address, but care and sensitivity are needed where people are seeking knowledge of each other in these often delicate circumstances. Some people prefer to make a first approach through an intermediary with skill and experience in smoothing the path for both parties.

These arrangements will also allow relatives to explain through a sympathetic intermediary that they prefer to restrict contact to, say, the exchange of information or letters, rather than a meeting.

Actually making contact is left to the two parties. No information about the adopted person will be given to the relative (a feature of the process which may cause immense frustration) but the relative will be told that his or her details have been forwarded if this occurs. The DH has drawn up a leaflet on the Register (reproduced in Volume 9 of the Children Act Guidance) for general public consumption. It draws attention to the fact that advice and counselling services are available from SSDs and other agencies and it gives details of those organizations which have signalled their willingness to act as intermediaries. The papers from the inter-departmental working party of 1989–1992 pointed out that the Adoption Contact Register does not provide for birth parents or other relatives to register a wish that they do *not* wish to be contacted. This omission has been the subject of criticism in some quarters and will be corrected as part of the projected reform of adoption law. Other problems arising out of the operation of the Contact Register since 1991 (e.g. the lack of public awareness, the level of fees and the need for counselling) will also need to be addressed.

- The experimental arrangements for the payment by agencies of adoption allowances have been retained, although the legal framework is different. Instead of the DH having to approve individual agency schemes, countrywide regulations have been made authorizing all agencies to make payments. The Adoption Allowance Regulations 1991 cover such matters as eligibility, assessment, agency procedure and the review, variation and termination of allowances. According to the DH Guidance, 'adoption allowances continue to be the exception rather than the norm. However, like the schemes which they replace, the regulations are intended to give agencies sufficient flexibility to respond to individual needs and circumstances . . . The central principle is still that an adoption allowance may be payable to help secure a suitable adoption where a child cannot be readily adopted because of a financial obstacle'.

The repeals effected by Schedule 15

Schedule 15 to the Children Act removed a number of provisions of the Adoption Act:

- The power of the court, created by section 26 of the 1976 Act, to order a committal to care or local authority supervision on the refusal of an adoption application has been taken away. If an adoption court desires local authority intervention, it must use section 37 of the Children Act to direct an investigation by the authority (see page 163 above). Alternatively, the court can make a family assistance order under section 16 (see page 40).

- The provisions in the 1976 Act which were designed to discourage step-parent adoptions following the birth parents' divorce (sections 14(3) and 15(4)) have been repealed. These were always difficult provisions in the sense that their wording was less than satisfactory, leading different courts to adopt different approaches. The policy behind them was also controversial. Their disappearance, of course, has not meant an end to the controversy. Where a step-parent applies to adopt, although neither custody nor custodianship is available as an alternative – since the Children Act has abolished them – a residence order is available. This is because adoption proceedings are 'family proceedings' for the purposes of the Children Act (see page 258 below). A residence order, like custody, is not as drastic in its legal effect as adoption. In many cases, therefore, social workers and judges still have to make difficult judgments about the respective merits of the two types of order. This is made explicit by the 1991 amendments to the Adoption Rules (see below): as a result of these, social workers who compile 'Schedule 2 reports' are required to state their opinion, if appropriate, on 'the relative merits of adoption and a residence order'. If a parent and step-parent are applying for adoption, the report must record the reasons why they prefer adoption to a residence order. This topic is certain to be reconsidered as part of the projected reform of adoption law.
- The power of the juvenile court to make a place of safety order in respect of a protected child (section 34) has been removed and replaced by the emergency protection powers created by Part V of the Children Act.

The Adoption (Amendment) Rules 1991 and the Family Proceedings Courts (Matrimonial Proceedings etc.) Rules 1991

These rules amended the principal 1984 rules on adoption procedure. They made for the most part technical amendments rendered necessary by the new concepts and terminology introduced by the Children Act. One substantive change concerned adoption applications in the county court: it is now possible to submit an application to any divorce county court, not just the local one.

GALRO panels

Panels of reporting officers and guardians ad litem for adoption proceedings are now subject to the 1991 regulations and guidance referred to in

Chapter 13. The functions of these officers continue to be set out in the 1984 adoption rules of court, not the rules made for Children Act proceedings.

The Children (Allocation of Proceedings) Order 1991

This order, made under Schedule 11 to the Children Act, was described in Chapter 12. Although its main purpose is the regulation of Children Act proceedings, the order should not be overlooked in the adoption context because it contains rules relevant to such cases as well. The effect of the order is as follows:

1 Proceedings under the Adoption Act to extend, vary or discharge an order must be commenced in the court which made the order.
2 Adoption proceedings which may have the effect of varying or discharging an order must be commenced in the court which made the order. This rule applies where an adoption application is made in respect of a child who is presently the subject of a care order or a residence order (such orders, and in fact all other orders under the Children Act, are extinguished by adoption).
3 Adoption proceedings can be transferred after commencement to another court. (In 1993 the Family Division of the High Court issued a practice direction on inter-country adoptions, the effect of which is to oblige county courts to give serious consideration to the advantages of transferring such cases to the High Court.)
4 Where it is intended to commence proceedings in the county court, they are to be commenced in a divorce county court. If the court is notified that an adoption or freeing application will be opposed, it is to transfer the application to a family hearing centre for trial.

Making section 8 orders in adoption proceedings

Because proceedings under the Adoption Act are 'family proceedings' for the purposes of the Children Act (section 8(3) of the 1989 Act) the court is in a position to make one or more section 8 orders in addition to, or instead of, an adoption or freeing order. Such orders can be made upon application or of the court's own motion (section 10(1) of the 1989 Act). Although this gives rise to a large number of possible permutations of orders, in practice, of the four section 8 orders created by the Children Act, the residence order and the contact order are the ones most likely to receive consideration.

Residence orders

The court can decide to refuse an adoption order but make a residence order instead in favour of the applicant or, indeed, some other person (including a birth parent). Reference has already been made to this type of outcome where a step-parent applies to adopt but the option is available generally. It also applies in applications by an adoption agency for a freeing order.

In cases where the court is invited to opt for a residence order rather than an adoption order, the nature and consequences of each order will need to be weighed carefully in the balance. The finality of adoption is often a critical factor in this exercise, as the case of *Re O* (1994) demonstrates. That case was concerned with a child of 10 who had been cared for by the prospective adopters for four years. The birth parents had been off the scene for some considerable time with the result that the prospective adopters had become the child's psychological parents. The birth parents reappeared for the adoption proceedings, however, and put in a claim for the child. The guardian ad litem recommended that the prospective adopters should be refused an adoption order but given a residence order instead, a recommendation regarded by the judge as fundamentally flawed:

> She [the GAL] has, rightly, seen the child's three most important needs: she wants security within the family; she wants no further court proceedings; and she wants an end to social work investigation. There is only one order that can achieve those three requirements and that is an adoption order. The premise that those three goals can be achieved by a residence order is quite unrealistic and demonstrates either naiveté or inexperience of human conduct within the family justice system. Those who sit in this building know how repeatedly, how vainly, how without any seeming justification, how without any seeming change of circumstance parents apply for discharge of care orders. Still readier is the application for the discharge or variation of a residence order.

The case of *Re AB* (1995) shows that there are circumstances in which a court might be prepared to make a residence order to run alongside an adoption order. This case is considered on page 54 above.

Contact orders and open adoption

The court can decide to make a contact order to run alongside an adoption or freeing order. Where this occurs, it will inevitably serve to inject a greater degree of openness into the case. The extent of the increased openness will depend heavily on the type of contact specified by the order, and it should be remembered that Part II of the Children Act gives the court an extremely wide discretion in this matter (see page 29 above). The contact can be of the direct, face-to-face, variety or it can be indirect. It can be frequent or it can be rare. Special conditions and directions can be attached to the contact order under section 11(7) of the Act. Thus in the case of *Re O* (1994), noted above, the judge accepted the child's need for some sort of contact with her Nigerian birth mother but also acknowledged the risks and dangers inherent in such contact due to the particular circumstances of the case. His solution was to make a contact order subject to the condition that the timing and venue of all meetings between mother and child be at the discretion of the local authority, such meetings to be supervised by the authority. This arrangement lacked precision, of course, but it was seen as the most appropriate way of dealing with a complex amalgam of factors which were liable to change in a way that nobody could predict.

The notion of open adoption has attracted extensive interest from practitioners in recent years and it is not difficult to see how the Children Act, with its provisions on the promotion of family links, has been regarded by some as lending support to a greater emphasis on openness. But to repeat a point made earlier, the Children Act was never designed as a vehicle for the reform of adoption law, and the provisions in Part III of the Act on family ties with children being looked after by a local authority were not intended to bring about radical changes in adoption practice; nor were the provisions in Parts IV and V of the Act concerning reasonable contact following the making of a care order or emergency protection order. Some members of the senior judiciary have evidently appreciated these facts because judgments delivered in the period since 1991 have been noticeably cautious on the subject of open adoptions, especially open adoptions marked by the making of a formal contact order. In the case of *Re R* (1993) a county court judge had freed a child for adoption but had also made an order for contact of one and a half hours each month in favour of the mother. On appeal, Lady Justice Butler-Sloss said:

> Despite the optimism of the guardian ad litem, eight months after the freeing order a suitable adoptive family has not been found for this child. It would appear evident that the degree of contact ordered by the judge has been the inhibiting factor and for many of us, monthly contact would seem incompatible with the likely view of most prospective adopters to adoption. We are moving perceptibly into a new and broader perception of adoption, as is shown by the *Review of Adoption Law* (1992). The view, however, of open adoption embraced by the experts does not seem to be shared by many prospective adopters.

In *Re T* (1995) the Court of Appeal set aside a contact order made in the county court. Although the adopters were agreeable to once-a-year contact between the child and her birth mother, they did not wish to be constrained by the terms of an order. They wanted the freedom to respond to changing circumstances by altering the contact arrangements. The Court of Appeal was sympathetic to this argument and, referring to the importance of not fettering adopters 'in the difficult task they have in integrating a child into their family', it indicated that it was generally undesirable to impose contact orders on them against their wishes. The decisions in cases such as these suggest that where openness does feature in the arrangements for an adopted child's upbringing, it is more likely to arise out of non-binding agreements negotiated or re-negotiated between the adopters, the birth relative(s) and the agency, than a formal order of the court.

Applications for section 8 orders following adoption

This matter is discussed in Chapter 4 (see page 57 above). There is a link between this and the section above because the breach of an informal agreement as to post-adoption contact may give rise to an application by the aggrieved party for a contact order. As is pointed out in Chapter 4, the effect of adoption is that a birth parent will have to obtain the leave of the court to proceed with such an application, a requirement which was described by the Court of Appeal in *Re T* (above) as 'a valuable protection, both for the adopters and for the child'.

Children for whom adoption is planned

The Children Act, other Acts relating to child care and their subordinate legislation may be regarded as a sort of jigsaw: there are numerous pieces but they should all fit together. For one particular group of children, however, the jigsaw does not quite fit. These children are the ones being looked after by local authorities who are the subject of adoption plans. Some of the children will be in compulsory care under section 31, others will be accommodated on a voluntary basis under section 20. What is the position when it is decided that 'plans need to be made to find a permanent substitute family' via the adoption process? (The quoted words are taken from the 1991 review regulations described in Chapter 6.)

The important point here is that, although the Adoption Agencies Regulations 1983 will apply in such cases, so will parts of the code of treatment set out in the Children Act and its subordinate regulations. This seems to be the inescapable effect of section 22 of the 1989 Act, which defines the expression 'child who is looked after by a local authority'. Indeed, it would appear that the code of treatment applies to children who have actually been freed for adoption and are awaiting adoption proper. If this is the case, the bizarre result is that the local authority has continuing obligations to the birth parents to promote contact with them and to consult them about decisions. This stands uneasily with the provision in the Adoption Act which requires the birth parents in a freeing case to be given an opportunity of making a declaration that they prefer not to be involved in future questions concerning the child's adoption. It is also difficult to reconcile with the removal of parental responsibility from the parent, which is the hallmark of a freeing order. There is an additional complication in that at one point, the Adoption Act refers to parents of freed children as 'former parents'. Are they therefore non-parents for the purposes of the Children Act code of treatment? The discussion papers issued by the inter-departmental working party in 1991 (in contrast to the DH Children Act Guidance) acknowledged these problems of policy and interpretation but it was not until 1997 that a start was made on sorting out the relationship between the two strands of legislation. The Adoption Agencies and Children (Arrangements for Placement and Reviews) (Miscellaneous Amendments) Regulations 1997 amended the Arrangements for Placement of Children (General) Regulations 1991 and the Review of Children's Cases Regulations 1991 so as to exclude children placed for adoption from the scope of those 1991 regulations. Two overlaps have thereby been eliminated but unfortunately others remain and it is likely that they will be dealt with only when the new Adoption Bill is presented to Parliament.

17

Local authority foster carers

The statutory definition

The Children Act does not contain the expression 'foster carer'. The draftsman chose to employ the more traditional (but increasingly out-dated) term 'foster parent'. Section 23 of the Act defines a 'local authority foster parent' as anyone with whom a child being looked after by a local authority has been placed, unless he or she is a parent of the child, a non-parent with parental responsibility, or, in the case of a child in care, a person who held a residence order prior to the care order being made. It follows from this definition that children in local authority foster care will include:

- children being accommodated on a voluntary basis under section 20
- children in care (i.e. subject to a care order or interim care order)
- children being accommodated under an emergency protection order
- children being accommodated under police protection powers
- children being accommodated under a residence requirement attached to a criminal supervision order
- children on remand
- children being accommodated following their arrest by the police
- children who have been freed for adoption.

Although these are very disparate groups, if their members are being looked after by way of fostering, the Children Act subjects them and their carers to a common code, which consists partly of provisions contained in the Act itself and partly of provisions contained in DH regulations. The code is the subject of extended comment in Volume 3 of the DH Children Act Guidance, which has consequently become a key document for those working in this field. The purpose of the present chapter is to draw the provisions together.

The decision to use fostering

As was stated in Chapter 6, section 23 of the Children Act makes the type of placement for a child a matter for the local authority's discretion. Although fostering is mentioned first in the statutory list of accommodation (and therefore before residential care), there is no legal presumption that it will be employed. The overriding principle, for each child being looked after, is that the local authority must safeguard and promote his welfare. However, as the Guidance states in its opening sentence, 'foster care is frequently the preferred way of providing care and nurture for children who need to be looked after by a local authority'. The regulatory framework acknowledges the status of fostering in public child care arrangements.

If it is proposed to establish a foster placement for a child, the local authority is obliged by the Act to ascertain the wishes and feelings of the child and his parents regarding the matter. It is also obliged to adhere to the other elements of the general code of treatment for looked-after children. This is described in Chapter 6 but it includes rules relating to the child's religious persuasion, racial origin and cultural and linguistic background; the proximity of the accommodation to his home; the accommodation of siblings; provision for disabilities; and the formulation of a plan. These are all matters which the local authority will wish to explore before going ahead with a placement.

The Foster Placement (Children) Regulations 1991

Most of the detailed rules concerning foster care under the Children Act are to be found in these regulations, which superseded the Boarding-out of Children (Foster Placement) Regulations 1988. Their principal features are set out below.

- The regulations apply in principle to any placement of a child by a local authority under section 23(2)(a) of the Act. They do not, however, apply to placements of children in care falling within the scope of the Placement of Children with Parents etc. Regulations 1991, nor to placements of other children with parents or persons with parental responsibility. Furthermore they do not apply to placements for adoption (these are governed by the Adoption Agencies Regulations 1983, although other Children Act rules may apply: see Chapter 16).
- Regulations 3 and 4 prescribe rules relating to the initial approval of foster carers and the review (at intervals of not more than one year) of their suitability and the suitability of their household.
- No child is to be placed with approved foster carers unless they enter into a written agreement covering specified matters. Schedule 2 contains a list of the matters and obligations to be covered in these *foster care agree-*

ments (they are the minimum requirements) and it is interesting to note that the agreement must state that the foster carers will not administer corporal punishment to any child placed with them. This is a development which was strongly fought for during the passage of the Act and it was no surprise that the DH ultimately conceded. A similar rule can be found in the Children's Homes Regulations 1991.

- The SSD is not to place a child with foster carers unless it is satisfied that (a) it is the most suitable way of performing its general welfare duty under the Act and (b) placement with these foster carers is 'the most suitable placement' having regard to all the circumstances. The last words are crucial, recognizing as they do the realities of foster carer availability.
- Except in the case of an emergency or immediate placement (see below for these), the SSD is not to place a child unless the foster carers have entered into a written agreement relating to that child, covering specified matters. Schedule 3 sets out the matters and obligations to be covered in *foster placement agreements* (which are quite distinct from foster care agreements). As one would expect, there is a reference to the arrangements for family contact with the child; these arrangements may have been dictated by the court, either under a section 8 order or under a section 34 order if the child is in compulsory care. The chapter in Volume 3 of the Guidance which deals with contact (Chapter 6) contains a discrete section on the role of the foster carer. The contents of the agreement generally ought to be based on the individual plan for the child formulated under the Arrangements for Placement of Children (General) Regulations 1991.
- Regulation 6 deals with the supervision of placements, including visits by social workers.
- The SSD is not to allow a placement to continue if it appears that the placement is no longer the most suitable way of performing its general welfare duty.
- Special rules apply in the case of an emergency placement (e.g. where the child has been removed under an emergency protection order) and in the case of an immediate placement with a relative or friend of the child. In these circumstances, the usual requirements are relaxed. The DH Guidance seeks to emphasize the exceptional nature of these placements and states that they should be reserved for unforeseen events.
- Special rules also apply to a pre-planned series of short-term placements with the same foster carers. The sensible effect of these rules, which cover the many respite care schemes for children with disabilities, is that the series may be treated as a single placement for the purposes of the regulations. The conditions for a series of short-term placements to be considered as a single one were revised in 1995.
- Placements with foster carers who have been approved by another authority or a voluntary organization are the subject of separate provi-

sions. Their effect is that the approving body must consent to the placement. This, according to the DH Guidance, 'offers scope for co-operation and harmonious working together by the authorities and the foster parent, while introducing safeguards against indiscriminate and ill-considered shared use of foster homes'.

Foster carer recruitment

According to Schedule 2, paragraph 11 to the Act, every local authority shall, in making any arrangements designed to encourage persons to act as local authority foster carers, 'have regard to the different racial groups to which children within their area who are in need belong'. This obligation owes its existence to pressure exerted by the Commission for Racial Equality, which expressed concern about the lack of progress being made by some social services departments in recruiting foster carers from ethnic minority groups. It complements the requirement contained in section 22(5) of the Act under which an authority, in making any decision with respect to a child, is to give due consideration to his religious persuasion, racial origin and cultural and linguistic background.

A careful reading of these provisions shows that they do not require SSDs to follow a strong policy of same-race placements. They were certainly not intended to have this effect. They must, however, have *some* effect in law. At the very least, they are consistent with the view (reiterated in the DH Guidance) that same-race placements have much to offer.

Limit on number of children

Schedule 7 to the Children Act is designed to limit the number of children a foster carer looks after. It covers not just local authority foster carers but also foster carers working for voluntary organizations and private foster carers; indeed, it appears to have been inspired partly by problems of overcrowding in the private sector. Schedule 7 states that a person may not foster more than three children. There is, however, plenty of room for exceptions. In the first place, the limit can be exceeded if the children concerned are all siblings. Secondly, foster carers can be given permission to exceed the limit by the authority in whose area they live. The result is that for local authority foster carers, the three-children limit is more of a guideline than a rule. If the statutory limit is improperly exceeded, the effect in law is that the foster home becomes a private children's home and therefore subject to an entirely separate regulatory regime (referred to in Chapter 15).

Complaints from foster carers

The demanding nature of the fostering task means that there are numerous opportunities for grievances to arise. For those which are directed towards the local authority, the DH has aimed to provide an outlet for foster carers. The statutory complaints procedures which should be available fall into several categories. Under section 26 and its regulations, local authority foster carers can invoke the so-called representations procedure where they wish to make a complaint about the discharge by the authority of its Children Act functions in relation to the child for whom they are caring; and under Schedule 7, foster carers can complain about the way the authority has carried out its functions concerning exemption from the usual fostering limit. Other types of complaint (e.g. complaints about review of approval and general support) should fall within the procedure relating to general social services functions established under the Local Authority Social Services Act 1970.

Allegations against foster carers

The very difficult issue of allegations of abuse made against foster carers is not expressly mentioned in the 1989 Act or the 1991 fostering regulations. It does feature, however, in both the DH Children Act Guidance and *Working Together*. Clearly, where allegations are made the SSD will need to undertake an investigation under section 47 of the Act (see Chapter 7). *Working Together* states that it is important to understand that the department's duty to investigate applies equally to children in foster care and to children living with their own families. As for the Guidance, Volume 3 suggests that a review of the foster carer's approval may be needed in these circumstances. In any event, 'procedures must first and foremost protect the child's welfare but should also take account of the sensitivities and rights of the other parties, including the foster parents'.

The origins of this last reference to the 'rights' of foster carers may lie in a case decided by the High Court in 1988 (*R v Wandsworth London Borough Council, ex parte P*). There, following allegations of sexual abuse, the authority's Director of Social Services had decided that the foster carer's name should be removed from the list of approved carers. The court ruled that if a foster carer's approval was withdrawn for specific misbehaviour or for suspicion of serious abuse or criminal conduct towards a child, he or she was entitled to know what grounds were alleged and to be heard in reply before the decision was taken. Because the foster carer in this case had not been given any opportunity to answer the allegations, the Director had not acted fairly and his decision was set aside. Although the ruling in the case preceded the Children Act, it still has force.

Applications for section 8 orders

The Children Act contains special rules, of a restrictive nature, concerning applications by local authority foster carers for section 8 orders. These rules are described in Chapter 4 (see page 51 above).

Applications for adoption

Although technically outside the scope of this book, it should be noted that local authority foster carers may seek to retain the care of their foster child by submitting an adoption application. This may be done in defiance of the local authority's wishes and plans. Indeed, sections 30 and 31 of the Adoption Act have the effect of requiring the local authority to obtain the leave of the court before removing a child from foster carers who have set adoption proceedings in train. The obtaining of such leave cannot be taken for granted, as the case of *Re C* (1994) demonstrates. In that case, a foster carer notified the local authority of her intention to adopt seven days before the child was due to be moved to other carers. The Court of Appeal decided that the foster carer's adoption application was a genuine one with reasonable prospects of success and the local authority's request for leave to remove the child was rejected. The court noted the apparent anomaly whereby the restrictions in the Children Act covering residence order applications by local authority foster carers have not been carried over into the Adoption Act.

The reality of local authority fostering in the 1990s

In December 1996 the DH published a report compiled by the Social Services Inspectorate entitled *Inspection of Local Authority Fostering 1995–96: National Summary Report*. The report noted that the majority of children looked after by local authorities are placed in foster care. Of the 49 000 children being looked after in England on 31 March 1995, 65 per cent were fostered. (There are, of course, variations in the fostering rate across the country.) Given fostering's central position in the provision of children's placements, it was surprising and disturbing that the inspectors uncovered so many shortcomings in the service. Having concluded an exhaustive investigation in six English SSDs, the inspectors highlighted the excellent work carried out by many individual foster carers and social workers. They also, however, made the following findings:

- The importance of foster care was not always recognized at a strategic level in departmental policies and planning.
- There were a number of ways in which the service did not fully meet the

needs of children requiring a placement. These included the lack of a choice of placements, the shortfall in appropriate placements which met racial and cultural needs, the shortfall in placements for sibling groups and the shortfall in placements near the homes of the children.

• Authorities were failing to comply with statutory requirements. For example, none of the SSDs studied had a system for monitoring the arrangements for statutory reviews.
• The needs of many children had not been adequately assessed.
• Case recording practice was frequently less than satisfactory.

As the accompanying letter from the SSI Chief Inspector made clear, this report provided a challenging agenda for SSD managers. The sense of crisis pervading the fostering service intensified during 1997 in the aftermath of the Roger Saint scandal (in which a man convicted of an indecent assault was permitted to continue to act as a foster carer, with tragic results) and the publication of a report by the Association of Directors of Social Services detailing the recruitment difficulties affecting many local authorities.

18

Financial provision for children

Introduction

The matter of financial support for children is dealt with by a number of provisions of the Children Act. These reflect the various contexts in which the issue of maintenance can arise. Previous chapters of this book have noted the following provisions:

- section 17(6), which enables a local authority to provide financial assistance with a view to safeguarding or promoting the welfare of a child in need
- section 24(7) and (8), which enable a local authority to provide financial assistance to a child as part of its aftercare responsibilities
- Part III of Schedule 2, which enables a local authority to recover from parents contributions towards the maintenance of a child being looked after.

There is, however, a further collection of provisions concerning financial support – indeed, the largest and most complex collection – in Schedule 1 to the Act. These provisions attracted very little comment in 1989 and they were certainly not controversial but a combination of factors, including the enactment in 1991 of the Child Support Act and the delivery of significant court judgments, has served to give Schedule 1 a higher profile than was anticipated. It is the subject of the present chapter.

The background to Schedule 1

Section 15(1) of the Children Act states that Schedule 1 'consists primarily of the re-enactment, with consequential amendments and minor modifications, of provisions of section 6 of the Family Law Reform Act 1969, the Guardianship of Minors Acts 1971 and 1973, the Children Act 1975 and of sections 15 and 16 of the Family Law Reform Act 1987'. This is a highly technical description but it does reveal the main reason why Schedule 1 received so little attention in 1989: it was for the most part a repeat performance of existing law. It will be noted that the existing law being repeated consisted of provisions contained in a number of different statutes, and they were now being drawn together with appropriate changes to terminology. No radical changes were thought necessary. All of the provisions enabled an application to be made to a court for an order relating to the financial support of a child. In other words, they created child maintenance procedures which could be invoked in specified circumstances by specified individuals. However, the procedures that were drawn together in Schedule 1 were not, and are not, the only ones on the statute book. The Matrimonial Causes Act 1973 and the Domestic Proceedings and Magistrates' Courts Act 1978 also contain child maintenance procedures, although these can only be invoked by spouses and they are essentially supplementary ('ancillary') to other procedures, e.g. divorce. Schedule 1 to the Children Act, on the other hand, provides for a free-standing child maintenance procedure.

The effect of the Child Support Act 1991

The provisions of Schedule 1 reflected the traditional view that where parents and other relevant adults could not agree on the most suitable arrangements for a child's maintenance, they should be able to ask a bench of magistrates or a judge to resolve the disagreement. The role of the court was to consider all of the facts and to make an appropriate order, exercising a wide discretion. Such a role had been performed for decades and both the courts and the legal profession were very much accustomed to it. It fitted in comfortably with the role of the court in residence and contact disputes, though that is not to say there were no problems affecting it. This set-up, however, was turned upside-down when the Child Support Act was introduced.

Despite being described by the then Lord Chancellor as 'a natural adjunct' to the Children Act, the Child Support Act is a very different animal:

- It was not preceded by a lengthy research and consultation process led by the Law Commission.
- Its prime purpose was to remove child maintenance from the jurisdiction of the courts and hand it over to an executive agency staffed by civil servants.
- Cases are 'resolved', not by the exercise of a wide judicial discretion but by the mechanical application of a formula.
- The drafting of the Act and its subordinate legislation is complex and generally unhelpful.

It is not proposed to explore here the detailed working of the Child Support Act. Suffice it to say that the Act, and the Child Support Agency it established, have attracted a level of criticism unprecedented in the field of family law. Much of this criticism has been fully deserved and could easily have been avoided by better planning and preparation on the part of those responsible for the legislation. Attempts to remedy some of the defects in the scheme were made in 1995 with the passing of a second Child Support Act but these were only partly successful. Not surprisingly, the incoming Labour Government announced (in June 1997) that a wide-ranging review would be undertaken and so the future is unclear. For many, however, the scheme has lost (or, to put it more accurately, never gained) credibility and needs to be jettisoned.

While the child support scheme is in force, it will have the effect of preventing the courts from exercising many of their powers under the child maintenance procedures referred to earlier, including Schedule 1 to the Children Act. This is made clear by section 8(3) of the Child Support Act which lays down the general rule that where the Child Support Agency would have jurisdiction to make a maintenance assessment with respect to a qualifying child and an absent parent of his, 'no court shall exercise any power which it would otherwise have to make, vary or revive any maintenance order in relation to the child and absent parent concerned'. This is only a general rule, however, and the Act itself provides for exceptions. Furthermore, the courts will not be constrained in cases where the child concerned is not caught by the 1991 Act because, for example, he is not a 'qualifying child' within the meaning of the Act. It should also be noted that the child support scheme is directed only at securing maintenance in the form of periodical payments. It follows that the power of the courts to make orders for lump sums or settlement of property is not affected. This is significant in the present context because Schedule 1 to the Children Act gives the courts power to make capital orders of this type.

By way of summary, we may note that the courts have retained their jurisdiction over child maintenance in relation to the following situations:

- the parties are asking the court to make a maintenance order which is in all material respects in the same terms as a written agreement they have drawn up (section 8(5) of the 1991 Act and the Child Maintenance (Written Agreements) Order 1993)
- the court is asked to make a maintenance order against an absent parent in addition to an assessment already made by the Child Support Agency (section 8(6))
- the court is asked to make a maintenance order solely for the purpose of requiring the absent parent to meet some or all of the expenses incurred in connection with the provision of educational instruction or vocational training for the child (section 8(7))

- the court is asked to make a maintenance order solely for the purpose of requiring the absent parent to meet some or all of any expenses attributable to the child's disability (section 8(8))
- the court is asked to make a maintenance order against the child's absent step-parent (section 3(2))
- the court is asked to make a lump sum order or an order relating to property for the benefit of the child.

Schedule 1 to the Children Act: who can apply?

An application for an order can be made by a parent of the child, a guardian, a step-parent who has treated the child as a child of his family or a person who holds a residence order in respect of the child (paragraphs 1(1) and 16(2)). In special circumstances an application can also be made by an adult against his or her parent (paragraph 2).

Schedule 1: what can the court do?

Paragraph 1(2) sets out the powers of the court. It can make one or more of the following:

(a) an order requiring either or both parents of a child ('parent' for these purposes includes a step-parent who has treated the child as a child of his family) to make specified periodical payments
(b) an order requiring either or both parents to secure periodical payments (this involves setting aside an acceptable form of security as a guarantee of continued payment)
(c) an order requiring either or both parents to pay a specified lump sum
(d) an order requiring a settlement to be made of specified property belonging to either parent
(e) an order requiring either or both parents to transfer specified property belonging to them.

There are supplementary rules covering such matters as:

- the distribution of cases between the courts (the powers of magistrates' courts are less extensive than those of the county courts and the High Court)
- the variation and termination of orders
- the duration of orders for periodical payments
- the matters to which the court is to have regard in deciding whether to make an order (these include the financial resources of the parties, their financial needs and the financial needs of the child)
- interim orders.

Schedule 1: the case law

T v S (1993)

In this case (which arose before the implementation of the Child Support Act) the mother of five children aged between 7 and 15 applied for an order under Schedule 1 against the children's father. The parents had lived together for many years but they were not married and so the father had no support obligations towards the mother. (If the parents had been married, this case would almost certainly have been dealt with under the divorce provisions of the Matrimonial Causes Act 1973.) The trial judge made an order that the father should pay (1) a lump sum of £29 000 to cover school fees for the children and (2) a lump sum of £36 000 to be used to purchase a house for the children (and, necessarily, the mother who was looking after them). Under the terms of the order, the house was not to be sold until the youngest child reached the age of 21 or completed full-time education, whichever was the sooner. Upon this event, the benefit of the property was to pass to the five children in equal shares. On the father's appeal, the High Court stated that the solution of a settlement that had the effect of providing a home for the children was in principle correct. However, it amended the terms of the order by postponing the sale of the property until the youngest child reached the age of 21 or *all* of the children had completed full-time education. Furthermore, because the children should not have any continuing claim upon the father after this event, the interest in the property should at that point revert to the father. In this way, the father's financial obligations to his children as dependent children would be satisfied as far as was practicable. The adverse effect of the revised order upon the unmarried mother was something which the court could not take into account.

Pearson v Franklin (1993)

In this case the unmarried mother of two children had left the family home with the children following the breakdown of her relationship with the father. The home was held by the parents on a joint tenancy granted by a housing association. The mother sought an order excluding the father from the property so that she could move back. The Court of Appeal ruled that in the circumstances (there had been no violence) no exclusion injunction was available. However, it indicated that she did have a remedy: she could make an application under Schedule 1 to the Children Act for an order requiring the father to transfer to her, for the benefit of the children, his interest in the joint tenancy. Such an order would give her, as against the father, an exclusive right to occupy the property. Mr Justice Thorpe said:

The right to apply for the transfer or settlement of the property, including tenancies, is the effective remedy for a parent who has not married and who needs the only available home to enable him or her to care for a child or children after the final separation of the couple.

Phillips v Pearce (1996)

The opening words of the High Court's judgment in this remarkable case were as follows:

> Most people would think that a mother should have no difficulty in obtaining financial support for her child from a father who lives in a house worth £2.6 million and whose standard of living is illustrated by his three motor cars worth respectively £36 000, £54 000 and £100 000. In this case the Child Support Agency thought otherwise.

The Agency had assessed the father's liability under the Child Support Act as zero. This was entirely due to the inability of the child support scheme (as it then stood) to take proper account of absent parents whose financial affairs were conducted in a sophisticated but unorthodox manner (in this case, via a network of companies). Having met with no success under the 1991 Act, the unmarried mother turned to the court which, though unable to make an order for periodical payments, was in a position to exercise its remaining jurisdiction under the Children Act to make capital orders for the child's benefit. The judge ordered the father to make the following provision for the child:

1 To settle upon the child the sum of £90 000 to be used to buy better accommodation. This property would be held by trustees and the child (and the mother) would be entitled to live there until the child completed her education. The mother would be responsible for the repair, upkeep and outgoings on the property.
2 To pay a lump sum of £15 000 to the mother for the purpose of furnishing the new property.
3 To pay a lump sum of £14 300 to cover medical costs in connection with the birth, clothing and baby equipment, and private school registration fees.

In 1996 over 30 per cent of all live births in England and Wales occurred outside marriage. The above-mentioned cases suggest that for unmarried parents, who of course are unable to take advantage of the wide-ranging powers of the divorce court, the procedure established by Schedule 1 to the Children Act may be a useful mechanism when their relationship has foundered. How useful it is will obviously depend on the circumstances. The Law Commission has under review the whole issue of cohabitants' property rights, and further related reforms can therefore be expected at some point in the future.

Appendix A

Volumes of Children Act Guidance

1 Court Orders
2 Family Support, Day Care and Educational Provision for Young Children
3 Family Placements
4 Residential Care
5 Independent Schools
6 Children with Disabilities
7 Guardians ad Litem and other Court Related Issues
8 Private Fostering and Miscellaneous
9 Adoption Issues

Appendix B

The principles of good child care practice (taken from *The Care of Children* (HMSO, 1989))

1 Children and young people and their parents should all be considered as individuals with particular needs and potentialities.
2 Although some basic needs are universal, there can be a variety of ways of meeting them.
3 Children are entitled to protection from neglect, abuse and exploitation.
4 A child's age, sex, health, personality, race, culture and life experiences are all relevant to any consideration of needs and vulnerability and have to be taken into account when planning or providing help.
5 There are unique advantages for children in experiencing normal family life in their own birth family and every effort should be made to preserve the child's home and family links.
6 Parents are individuals with needs of their own.
7 The development of a working partnership with parents is usually the most effective route to providing supplementary or substitute care for their children.
8 Admission to public care by virtue of a compulsory order is itself a risk to be balanced against others. So also is the accommodation of a child by a local authority.
9 If young people cannot remain at home, placement with relatives or friends should be explored before other forms of placement are considered.
10 If young people have to live apart from their family of origin, both they and their parents should be helped to consider alternatives and contribute to the making of an informed choice about the most appropriate form of care.
11 When out-of-home care is necessary, active steps should be taken to ensure speedy return home.

12 Parents should be expected and enabled to retain their responsibilities and to remain as closely involved as is consistent with their child's welfare, even if that child cannot live at home either temporarily or permanently.

13 Siblings should not be separated when in care or when being looked after under voluntary arrangements unless this is part of a well thought out plan based on each child's needs.

14 Family links should be actively maintained through visits and other forms of contact. Both parents are important even if one of them is no longer in the family home and fathers should not be overlooked or marginalised.

15 Wider families matter as well as parents – especially siblings and grandparents.

16 Continuity of relationships is important, and attachments should be respected, sustained and developed.

17 Change of home, caregiver, social worker or school almost always carries some risk to a child's development and welfare.

18 Time is a crucial element in child care and should be reckoned in days and months rather than years.

19 Every young person needs to develop a secure sense of personal identity and all those with parental or caring responsibilities have a duty to offer encouragement and support in this task.

20 All children need to develop self-confidence and a sense of self-worth, so alongside the development of identity, and equally important, is self-esteem.

21 Since discrimination of all kinds is an everyday reality in many children's lives, every effort must be made to ensure that agency services and practices do not reflect or reinforce it.

22 Corporate parenting is not 'good enough' on its own.

23 Young people should not be disadvantaged or stigmatised by action taken on their behalf.

24 Children's long-term welfare must be protected by prompt, positive and pro-active attention to the health and education of those in both short- and long-term care.

25 Young people's wishes must be elicited and taken seriously.

26 As young people grow up, preparation for independence is a necessary and important part of the parental role which child care agencies carry for young people in long-term care.

27 In carrying out the duties and responsibilities laid upon them in legislation and regulations, local authorities should put into practice the principles of good work with children and families [above].

28 The various departments of a local authority should co-operate to provide an integrated service and range of resources.

29 The twin issues of confidentiality and access to records need to be addressed by all local authorities and child care organisations.

30 Caregivers are entitled to have appropriate information about any child or young person placed in their charge and have a duty to keep this confidential.

31 Letters and documents which are sent to parents and young people should be written in language which is fully comprehensible to them.

32 Planning is a crucial responsibility for all agencies providing services to children and their families.

33 Agencies have special, parental responsibilities for the minority of children who are in long-term out-of-home placements.

34 When alternatives are being considered and/or decisions made, certain individuals or groups may need to be involved.

35 A balance must be struck between offering carers support (thus building confidence) and holding them accountable for the child's well-being.

36 Caregivers – whether parents, foster carers or residential staff – need both practical resources and a feeling of being valued if they are to give of their best.

37 Appropriate training should be provided for carers.

38 There should be machinery for resolving differences of view.

39 Agencies have a responsibility to support placements which they have made.

40 Registers and records must be maintained and kept up to date.

41 Co-operation between organisations, departments and individuals is crucial.

42 Foster homes and residential establishments used for the placement of children should be reviewed at regular and suitable intervals.

Index

Child protection investigation (*see also*
  Section 37 investigation)
  access to the child, 116–18, 129
  circumstances giving rise to, 115, 128,
    140, 149
  collaboration, 113, 115, 116
  parental participation in, 118
  purpose of, 115
  section 8 order proceedings, 120–1
  sexual abuse, 119–20
Child protection register, 114, 161–2
Child Support Act, 17, 91, 271–3
Children Act Advisory Committee, 10
Children's home, 84, 152, 236, 250, 251,
  252, 266
Children's rights, 12, 13, 133, 247
Children's services plans, 68
Complaints procedures, 72, 80, 83,
  96–100, 107, 183, 203, 239, 267
Concurrent jurisdiction, 166, 219–20,
  225
Confidentiality, 150, 229, 230, 237, 238
Contact order, *see* Section 8 contact
  order, Section 34 contact order
Corporal punishment, 13, 265
Court welfare officer, 38, 121, 164, 228,
  229, 230
Criminal investigation, 119, 150–1

Day care, 73–4, 152, 250, 251
Default power, 8, 72
Delay, 39, 45, 60, 121, 169–70, 176, 184,
  207, 220, 221, 222, 234, 236
Disabled children, 63, 68, 69, 82, 85, 86,
  265, 273
Discipline, 12, 17
Divorce, 6, 42–4, 162, 163
Doctor, 97

Education, 12, 17, 94
Education supervision order, 209
Emergency protection order
  abduction following, 152–3
  accommodated child, 102
  appeal, 226
  applicants, 127, 150
  child protection investigation,
    causing, 140
  contact under, 131–2
  discharge of, 135
  duration of, 134–5
  effect of, 130–1

entry of premises under, 136, 152
exclusion requirement, 131, 137–40
guardian ad litem, appointment of,
  134, 239
grounds for, 128–9
medical or psychiatric examination,
  132–3
parental responsibility, 20, 131
procedure, 133–4
Emigration, 27, 29, 54, 91–2, 190
Emotional abuse, 69, 162
Evidence, 170–3, 236
Exclusion requirement, 137–40, 205–6
Expert, 121, 171, 172, 173, 230, 242

Family assistance order, 33, 40–2, 60,
  209
Family centre, 70
Family court, 223–4, 243
Financial provision, 61, 270–6
Foster carer, 49, 52, 97, 110, 114, 120,
  152, 194, 250, 252, 263–9
Freeing for adoption, 109, 254, 255,
  261–2

Grandparent, 48, 54
Guardian, 12, 20, 21, 22, 54, 110, 178
Guardian ad litem
  adoption cases, in, 257
  appointment, termination of, 236
  care proceedings, appointment in,
    168
  child protection conference, 240
  complaints, 239
  disclosure of information by, 237–8
  functions of, 196, 233–5, 238
  National Standards, 241
  panels, 238–9
  records, access to, 236–7
  section 37 investigation, 124, 164,
    232
  solicitor, instruction of, 235–6
  specified proceedings, appointment
    in, 89, 134, 144, 231–3
Guidance, 7, 8

Harm, 37, 115, 156
HIV, 222
Hospital, 147, 213, 214, 251

Ill-treatment, 69, 156
Independent visitor, 87–8, 94

Related titles of interest from Wiley...

From Hearing to Healing
Working with the Aftermath of Child Sexual Abuse, 2nd Edition
Anne Bannister
Published in association with the NSPCC
0-471-98298-9   216pp   1998   Paperback

Making Enquiries into Alleged Child Abuse & Neglect: Partnership with Families
Edited by Dendy Platt and David Shemmings
Published in association with the NSPCC
0-471-9722-3   302pp   1996   Paperback

Women Who Sexually Abuse Children
From Research to Clinical Practice
Jacqui Saradjian in association with Helga Hanks
Wiley Series in Child Care & Protection
0-471-96072-1   336pp   1996   Paperback

The Emotionally Abused and Neglected Child
Identification, Assessment and Intervention
Dorota Iwaniec
Wiley Series in Child Care & Protection
0-471-95579-5   222pp   1995   Paperback

Cycles of Child Maltreatment
Facts, Fallacies and Interventions
Ann Buchanan
Wiley Series in Child Care & Protection
0-471-95889-1   328pp   1996   Paperback

 ## Child Abuse Review
ISSN: 0952-9136

 ## Children & Society
Published in association with the National Children's Bureau
ISSN: 0951-0605